PLAIN AND PRECIOUS TRUTHS RESTORED

The Doctrinal and Historical Significance of the Joseph Smith Translation

PLAIN AND PRECIOUS TRUTHS RESTORED

The Doctrinal and Historical Significance
of the Joseph Smith Translation

Papers presented at the BYU Symposium
"As Translated Correctly"
Joseph Smith's Translation of the Bible
January 13 and 14, 1995

EDITED BY

Robert L. Millet & Robert J. Matthews

BOOKCRAFT
Salt Lake City, Utah

Library of Congress Catalog Card Number: 95-77056
ISBN 0-88494-987-7

First Printing, 1995

Printed in the United States of America

Contents

Contents

Preface

Some six hundred years before Christ, Nephi beheld in vision that the book we know as the Bible would come under attack by a great and abominable church. Plain and precious truths, including many covenants of the Lord, would be taken out of the book and kept back from the people. "And all this have they done that they might pervert the right ways of the Lord, that they might blind the eyes and harden the hearts of the children of men." Further, "because of the many plain and precious things which have been taken out of the book, which were plain unto the understanding of the children of men, . . . an exceedingly great many do stumble, yea, insomuch that Satan hath great power over them." (1 Nephi 13:27, 29; see also vv. 26, 28, 32, 34).

But the prophetic picture was not all grim and discouraging. Nephi also witnessed the day of restoration, when God would restore those same plain and precious truths to the earth. First and foremost, the Book of Mormon, Another Testament of Jesus Christ, would be delivered to a world that had been wandering in darkness. In addition, "other books" would come forth by the power of the Lamb. These latter records would "make known the plain and precious things which have been taken away" from the Bible, and "make known to all kindreds, tongues, and people, that the Lamb of God is the Son of the Eternal Father, and the Savior of the world." (1 Nephi 13:35–40.) Those "other books" surely include the Doctrine and Covenants and the Pearl of Great Price, which now comprise a significant portion of our scriptural canon. Included also would undoubtedly be Joseph

Smith's translation of the Bible, one of the great evidences of his prophetic calling.

Prior to June of 1830 the Lord commanded the Choice Seer, Joseph Smith, to begin an inspired translation of the King James Bible. That work proved to be a vital part of the restoration of plain and precious truths, as well as a means whereby the God of heaven could tutor and train his prophet. The labor of translation, which occupied the Prophet for much of his life and ministry, was its own reward, bringing to Brother Joseph and to the Church enlightenment in the form of revelations and prophetic oracles. Joseph Smith himself described this work as a "branch" of his calling. Corrections made by the Prophet to the text of the King James Bible in the form of additions, alterations, and occasional deletions—changes in at least 3,410 verses—have the mark of divine authenticity and bear witness that "Jesus anointed that Prophet and Seer" whom we know as Joseph Smith, Jr.

This book bears testimony of Joseph Smith and, specifically, of the great contribution of his inspired translation of the Bible. The chapters in this volume represent presentations delivered at a symposium held on the Brigham Young University Provo campus on 13–14 January 1995. Each chapter focuses on a different dimension of this prophetic labor—how it was done, how it should be viewed by the Latter-day Saints, some of its doctrinal contributions to our understanding of the Old and New Testaments, its relationship to the other books of scripture, changing attitudes toward it by the LDS and RLDS communities, and its present and eternal relevance. Though the contributors have sought to be in harmony with the scriptural word and the teachings of living prophets, this work is a private endeavor and not an official publication of The Church of Jesus Christ of Latter-day Saints or of Brigham Young University.

The Latter-day Saints are under covenant to live by every word that proceeds forth from the mouth of God (see D&C 84:44); to preach the gospel which we have received, even as we have received it (see D&C 49:1); and, more specifically, to declare the things that have been revealed to Joseph Smith (see D&C 31:4). In speaking of Sidney Rigdon's role as a scribe in the Bible translation, the Lord explained to Sidney: "A commandment I give unto thee—that thou shalt write for him; and *the scriptures shall be given, even as they are in mine own bosom, to the salvation of mine own elect*" (D&C 35:20, emphasis added). Those who love the truth, who cling to the truth, and who strive to live in harmony with that truth seek earnestly to know the mind and will of God as revealed through his servants the prophets. And surely those in our day who honor the name and labors of Joseph Smith and yearn to be true to the Restoration will open themselves to the flood of truth and light that have come to us through his inspired translation of the Bible. To this end this work has been written and compiled. That it might lead men and women to Christ and to a deeper testimony of and appreciation for Christ's pre-eminent prophetic witness in this final dispensation is our prayer.

ROBERT L. MILLET
ROBERT J. MATTHEWS

1

Scripture Reading, Revelation, and Joseph Smith's Translation of the Bible

ELDER DALLIN H. OAKS

I am glad to be with you at this important symposium. I regret that I could not be present to hear all of the scheduled presentations. My interest in this subject is such that I will read all of them as they are made available in written form.

The scriptural text for my remarks is taken from the twenty-eighth chapter of Second Nephi in the Book of Mormon. Speaking of people in the last days, Nephi pronounced wo upon "him that hearkeneth unto the precepts of men, and denieth the power of God, and the gift of the Holy Ghost! Yea, wo be unto him that saith: We have received, and we need no more!" (2 Nephi 28:26–27.) Nephi continues:

> Wo be unto him that shall say: We have received the word of God, and we need no more of the word of God, for we have enough!
>
> For behold, thus saith the Lord God: I will give unto the children of men line upon line, precept upon precept, here a little and there a little; and blessed are those who hearken unto my precepts, and lend an ear unto my counsel, for they shall learn wisdom; for unto him that receiveth I will give more; and from them that shall say, We have enough, from them shall be taken away even that which they have. (2 Nephi 28:29–30.)

My subject is "Scripture Reading, Revelation, and Joseph Smith's Translation of the Bible."

General Principles

At the outset, I wish to review some general principles about scripture reading and revelation. I do this because Joseph Smith's translation of the Bible is the best possible illustration of the true relationship between scripture reading and continuing revelation.

These general principles are taken from my recent article, "Scripture Reading and Revelation," in the January 1995 *Ensign* (pp. 7–9). I will quote about one-fourth of the content of that article as a general introduction, and then make specific application of these general principles to the subject of Joseph Smith's translation of the Bible.

The principal theme of the *Ensign* article is that Latter-day Saints' belief in continuing revelation gives us a different approach to reading and using the holy scriptures. I quote:

"Some Christians accept the Bible as the one true word, completely inspired of God in its entirety. At the opposite extreme, some other Christians consider the Bible as the writings of persons who may or may not have been inspired of God, which writings have little moral authority in our day. The Latter-day Saint belief that the Bible is 'the word of God as far as it is translated correctly' (Article of Faith 1:8) places us between these extremes, but this belief is not what makes us unique in Christianity.

"What makes us different from most other Christians in the way we read and use the Bible and other scriptures is our belief in continuing revelation. For us, the scriptures are not the ultimate source of knowledge, but what precedes the ultimate source. The ultimate knowledge comes by revelation. With Moroni we affirm that he who denieth revelation 'knoweth not the gospel of Christ' (Mormon 9:8).

"The word of the Lord in the scriptures is like a lamp to guide our feet (see Psalm 119:105), and revelation is like a mighty force that increases the lamp's illumination manyfold. We encourage everyone to make careful study of the scriptures and of the prophetic teachings concerning them and to prayerfully seek personal revelation to know their meaning for themselves. . . .

"Nephi attempted to teach his brothers that they could know the meaning of their father's prophetic utterances, 'which were hard to be understood, save a man should inquire of the Lord' (1 Nephi 15:3).

Nephi told them if they did not harden their hearts and would keep the commandments and inquire of the Lord in faith, 'surely these things shall be made known unto you' (1 Nephi 15:11).

"If we harden our hearts, reject continuing revelation, and limit our learning to what we can obtain by study and reason on the precise language of the present canon of scriptures, our understanding will be limited to what Alma called 'the lesser portion of the word' (Alma 12:11). If we seek and accept revelation and inspiration to enlarge our understanding of the scriptures, we will realize a fulfillment of Nephi's inspired promise that those who diligently seek will have 'the mysteries of God . . . unfolded unto them, by the power of the Holy Ghost' (1 Nephi 10:19). . . .

"The Lord promised Nephi: 'Unto him that receiveth I will give more; and from them that shall say, We have enough, from them shall be taken away even that which they have' (2 Nephi 28:30; see also Matthew 13:12). That verse capsulizes the Latter-day Saint belief in the importance of continuing revelation as we read and interpret the scriptures. Even if there were no additional revelations to be added to the published canon, an open canon would still be an essential part of our belief and practice in scripture reading. We believe that the scriptures, which are the revelations of the past, cannot be understood without openness to the revelations of the present. . . .

"Those who believe the scriptural canon is closed typically approach the reading of scriptures by focusing on what was meant at the time the scriptural words were spoken or written. In this approach, a passage of scripture may appear to have a single meaning and the reader typically relies on scholarship and historical methods to determine it.

"The Latter-day Saint approach is different. . . .

"[Professor Hugh Nibley concludes:] 'The question is not whether or not one shall add to the word of the scripture—thousands of volumes of learned commentary have already done that—but whether such addition shall come by the wisdom of men or the revelation of God' (*The World and the Prophets*, *The Collected Works of Hugh Nibley* [Salt Lake City: Deseret Book Co., 1987], 3:206).

"Latter-day Saints know that true doctrine comes by revelation from God, not by scholarship or worldly wisdom (see Moses 5:58).

Similarly, the Apostle Paul wrote that we are not 'sufficient of ourselves to think any thing as of ourselves; but our sufficiency is of God' (2 Corinthians 3:5). Rather than trusting in our own interpretations of written texts, we rely on God and the glorious 'ministration of the spirit' (2 Corinthians 3:8). Here we encounter a new meaning of Paul's familiar teaching that true believers are 'ministers . . . of the spirit: for the letter killeth, but the spirit giveth life' (2 Corinthians 3:6).

"Joseph Smith and Oliver Cowdery set the example for this dispensation. After their baptism, they were filled with the Holy Ghost. Then, as Joseph explained in his personal history, 'Our minds being now enlightened, we began to have the scriptures laid open to our understandings, and the true meaning and intention of their more mysterious passages revealed unto us in a manner which we never could attain to previously, nor ever before had thought of' (Joseph Smith— History 1:74)."

That is the end of quotations from my *Ensign* article on scripture reading and revelation.

To those thoughts I add two additional illustrations. Each is a statement of the Prophet Joseph Smith that confirms the importance of revelation to help us understand the meaning of the written scriptures. While the Prophet was working on his inspired translation of Genesis (the portion we now have in the book of Moses), he referred to the Lord's "giving some more extended information upon the Scriptures" by "reveal[ing] the following doings of olden times, from the prophecy of Enoch" (HC 1:132–33). Later, during the Nauvoo period, the Prophet declared that no man could understand the "secrets" in Second Peter, chapter 1 (the Apostle's great statement on the "more sure word of prophecy" [v. 19]) except by the light of revelation from heaven, since "the things that are written are only hints of things which existed in the prophet's mind."[1]

The principles I have reviewed show the spiritual dangers of ignoring or neglecting the prophetic teachings in what we now call the Joseph Smith Translation (JST). I maintain that these principles dictate a respectful use of the Joseph Smith Translation in our personal scripture study and in our Church teaching and scholarship.

History of Attitudes Toward the
Joseph Smith Translation

Attitudes toward the Joseph Smith Translation have gone through cycles. The initial attitude was enthusiasm, but this gave way to a long period of suspicion or indifference, followed by a transition period of caution, and now a season of selective approval. (The historical review in this section relies to an important degree on the two Matthews books and the earlier Durham dissertation cited hereafter.)

When the Prophet Joseph Smith began his work on an inspired translation of the Bible in 1830, faithful Church members who knew of his work were eager to obtain the increased information they were sure it would provide.

Numerous revelations received by the Prophet make reference to the importance of the translation of the scriptures. The Prophet was told to "hasten to translate my scriptures" (D&C 93:53; also see 73:3–4; 90:13). Church members were commanded to provide means to support his family so he could devote his time to this work (see D&C 43:12–13). The Prophet referred to this translation labor as a "branch of my calling."[2] He made several concerted attempts to obtain economic support to enable him to continue the translation and get it published. As early as October 1831, a committee was organized in Hiram, Ohio, to obtain "means" to continue the translation.[3]

In July 1833 the Prophet stated in a letter to the Brethren in Zion that he had "finished the translating of the Scriptures."[4] From shortly before to several years after that time, the revelations contain repeated references to "the printing of the translation of my scriptures" (D&C 94:10; see also 104:58; 124:89).

During the Nauvoo period the Church made several formal attempts to raise money to publish what was then called "the new translation of the Scriptures,"[5] which, the *Times and Seasons* noted, "has so long been desired by the Saints." In October 1842 the *Times and Seasons* announced the republication of the Book of Mormon and the hymnbook, but observed that the publication of "the new translation of the bible," as well as the Doctrine and Covenants, "are entirely dependent on the liberality of the well-disposed for the cause of our Redeemer."[6]

It is easy to understand the financial strains on a small number of Saints who were trying to gather to Illinois and build up their city of Nauvoo, to conduct missionary work in many lands, and to build a temple. Nevertheless, the Prophet Joseph issued several appeals to the leading quorums of the Church for financial assistance to publish the translation. As a result, the First Presidency issued two and the Quorum of the Twelve issued several epistles during the Nauvoo period requesting that the Saints contribute means to allow the Prophet to complete his work and publish the translation of the Bible.[7] In March 1843 the Quorum of the Twelve issued an epistle to the Saints referring to the need to relieve the Prophet's temporal pressures and requesting financial support to allow him time to devote to the "spiritual interests of the Church," including "the bringing forth of the . . . translation."[8]

Before the necessary support was received, the Prophet was murdered. For the next twenty years all questions of further Church publications had to be subordinated to the Saints' life-and-death struggles to resist armed persecution in Illinois, to survive their exodus to the West, and to establish themselves and commence another temple in the Rocky Mountains. During that time other events involving the Prophet's manuscript and its custodians precluded the Church from carrying out his intent to publish the inspired translation. In the eyes of the leaders and members of The Church of Jesus Christ of Latter-day Saints, these other events put a cloud over the Joseph Smith Translation that was to last for more than a century.

After the Prophet's death, the manuscript containing his inspired corrections to the Bible passed to the possession of his widow, Emma. In 1860, young Joseph Smith III, the son of Joseph and Emma, became the president of the Reorganized Church. At his request Emma gave him the manuscript in 1866. In 1867 the Reorganized Church published the inspired translation under the title *Holy Scriptures*, and began distributing it by means of the missionaries the RLDS sent to England and to the valley of the Great Salt Lake.

In view of these events and of the attitude of antagonism that existed between Brigham Young and Emma Smith and between the two churches, it is not surprising that the leaders of The Church of Jesus

Christ of Latter-day Saints were suspicious of the RLDS publication of the inspired translation. Brigham Young and his associates had no complete, original manuscript to verify the overall accuracy of the volume that came to them as an instrument of the missionary work of the Reorganized Church.

When the members of the Church in the Great Basin showed intense interest in the RLDS publication of the inspired translation and began to buy it in large numbers, Brigham Young voiced doubts about the integrity of the publication and restrained the warm reception the volume was receiving from Orson Pratt and others. President Young set a pattern by refraining from quoting the Joseph Smith Translation in his sermons. The minutes of the School of the Prophets in Salt Lake City in 1868 observed that the translation was "incomplete" at the death of the Prophet and had now been completed by others, who had sent it forth as Joseph's. This influential group counselled the Saints against sending for the book, so it would not get into the hands of their posterity.

This suspicion or hostility toward the RLDS publication of the inspired translation might have been softened during the presidency of John Taylor. In 1878 he sent Elders Orson Pratt and Joseph F. Smith of the Quorum of the Twelve on a mission to the East to obtain additional information about Church history, including the manuscript of the inspired translation. They called at the RLDS headquarters in Plano, Illinois, on their eastbound trip and again on their westbound trip and attempted to see the manuscripts of the translation. Both times they were denied access, a result of the atmosphere of mutual mistrust that characterized LDS and RLDS relationships in that period. A century would pass before an LDS scholar would examine these manuscripts and verify the integrity of the RLDS publication.

In the meantime the Joseph Smith Translation remained under a cloud of doubt and mistrust, but a handful of LDS leaders spoke approvingly of its value and of the importance of this part of the Prophet's work. In general conference in 1878 Elder Orson Pratt illustrated his subject of the content of God's revelations in the book of Moses on the creation of the world by saying: "There are many things in the new translation besides the vision and revelation in regard to the creation, written by Joseph Smith, which are far greater than anything contained in the Bible, or in the Book of Mormon, or in the Doctrine and Covenants."[9]

But these favorable references were the exception. The predominant attitude was to oppose or be indifferent toward the use of the RLDS publication because the Prophet's work was incomplete at the time of his death. President George Q. Cannon reflected the attitude of this period in his influential *Life of Joseph Smith the Prophet*, published in 1888: "We have heard President Brigham Young state that the Prophet before his death had spoken to him about going through the translation of the scriptures again and perfecting it upon points of doctrine which the Lord had restrained him from giving in plainness and fulness at the time of which we write."[10]

Dean Robert J. Matthews has reminded us that the time referred to here was 1833, and that "during the eleven years of his life after that time, the Prophet apparently did much of what he desired to do with the JST."[11]

In his 1965 doctoral dissertation, "The History of the Joseph Smith Revision of the Bible," Reed C. Durham, Jr., illustrates the theme of incompleteness. He cites numerous examples to demonstrate the undoubted fact that the Prophet had not completed a thorough and final review of the entire Bible. He had not even incorporated into this manuscript all of the inspired explanations of Bible passages received by him in connection with his sermons, his work on the Book of Mormon, and the revelations received and published in the Doctrine and Covenants after 1833. For example, the Prophet corrected a passage in 2 Chronicles (18:20–22), but omitted to correct the parallel passage in 1 Kings (22:21–23). He modified many passages stating that "the Lord repented" for some action (e.g., JST, Exodus 32:14), but he left another such reference uncorrected (JST, Deuteronomy 32:36).

In his definitive book, *"A Plainer Translation," Joseph Smith's Translation of the Bible*, Robert J. Matthews records a long list of evidences of the incomplete status of the Joseph Smith Translation.[12] In his later book, *A Bible! A Bible!* Dean Matthews puts these evidences in perspective by pointing out that the Prophet continued to make manuscript corrections during the eleven years that followed his declared "completion" of the work. "That the work was not perfected is clear," Dean Matthews observes. "But it is equally clear that it was nearer the stage necessary for publication than casual observers have realized."

On this subject, I concur with Dean Matthews's conclusion: "The major reason for failure to publish appears to have been [not what some have implied to be the "grossly unfinished" state of the manuscript, but] an inadequate response from the Saints in providing temporal assistance. The basic conclusion seems to be that the *work* of translation was acceptable as far as the Lord required it of the Prophet at that time, but the *manuscript* was not fully prepared for the press."[13]

The incompleteness of the inspired translation was stressed by President J. Reuben Clark in a notable address to Church education teachers at Brigham Young University on 7 July 1954. He said: "The Prophet Joseph began a revelatory revision of the Bible, but it was not finished, for which reason the Church has never adopted it as a whole. The parts we accept will be found in the Pearl of Great Price in the Book of Moses and the revision of the twenty-third (last verse) and the twenty-fourth chapters of Matthew."

The incompleteness President Clark cited surely explains the oft-stated position of the Church that the inspired translation does not replace the King James Version as "the English-language Bible used by The Church of Jesus Christ of Latter-day Saints" (letter of the First Presidency to General Authorities and local leaders in English-speaking units, 22 May 1992). But this does not contradict the value to be placed on the Bible corrections Joseph Smith did make, especially in view of the fact that he announced his work on the inspired translation as "complete" and repeatedly tried to obtain the resources to publish it in his lifetime.

When President J. Reuben Clark detailed "the parts we accept" and referred only to those embodied in the standard works, he should not be understood as ruling out the use of other corrections the Prophet Joseph Smith made during his work on the inspired translation. Indeed, in the immediately succeeding sentences of his talk to the Church educators, President Clark described the principle that even requires our selective use of corrections noted in the inspired translation. He described our reliance on the Savior's teachings in

3 Nephi in the Book of Mormon as scripture that "may be fully relied upon because it is the product of an actual revelation." He also included the book of Abraham, referring to it as "a revelatory translation [of the writings of Abraham] upon which we may rely."[14] The same should be said of the Prophet Joseph Smith's writings in what we call the Joseph Smith Translation of the Bible.

When President Clark outlined the principle of relying on "revelatory translation[s]," neither he nor most of his listeners were willing to apply that principle to Joseph Smith's inspired translation of the Bible because they lacked the assurance that the words published by the Reorganized Church in 1867 and succeeding editions were the words the Prophet Joseph Smith had written on the manuscripts as he sought to prepare his work for publication. Two decades later, these doubts were resolved by Professor Robert J. Matthews, who ended the century of unfortunate noncommunication between the LDS and RLDS leadership on this question by obtaining access to the RLDS manuscripts. When he shared his findings with the LDS community in his 1975 book, the last logical obstacle to the use of the Prophet's work on the inspired translation was removed. Professor Matthews concluded: "Comparison of the printed Inspired Version with the original manuscripts of the translation shows that the printed editions are accurate and faithful to the manuscript in almost every particular. Recent editions are more accurate than the first edition of 1867."[15]

Now that the integrity of the Joseph Smith Translation has been established, we have no reason to refrain from using this valuable resource in our teaching and scholarship.

The Current Standing of the Joseph Smith Translation

How one feels about the Joseph Smith Translation depends on what one expects of it. If we expect the kind of completeness that would make it a candidate to be published by The Church of Jesus Christ of Latter-day Saints as a replacement for our officially recognized King James translation, then the Joseph Smith Translation surely falls short. But if the issue is whether the Joseph Smith

Translation contains inspired revisions to Bible passages that further our knowledge of the scriptures in the same way as the revisions in some portions of the Doctrine and Covenants and the Pearl of Great Price, then the Joseph Smith Translation surely fulfills our expectations. It contains important truths—heaven-sent revelations of the mind and will of God—not based on scholarly analysis and not available from any other publication.

In an important editorial in the *Church News* in December 1974, readers were told: "The Inspired Version does not supplant the King James Version as the official church version of the Bible, but the explanations and changes made by the Prophet Joseph Smith provide enlightenment and useful commentary on many biblical passages."[16]

The Church's most authoritative pronouncement on the standing of the Joseph Smith Translation is contained in actions, not words. After prolonged and prayerful deliberation, the First Presidency and Quorum of the Twelve included over six hundred quotations from the Joseph Smith Translation in the Church's monumental new edition of the King James Bible published in 1979 and in every printing since that time. As you know, most of these quotations are in explanatory footnotes to the language of the King James Version, Old Testament and New Testament.

As the First Presidency noted in their 1992 letter, "The LDS edition of the Bible (1979) contains the King James Version supplemented and clarified by footnotes, study aids, and cross-references." The most substantive of these footnotes and study aids are the footnote quotations from the Joseph Smith Translation. In addition, we must not overlook the significance of the fact that scores of Joseph Smith Translation excerpts too lengthy for inclusion in footnotes are included in their entire text following the Bible Dictionary. These passages, from Genesis 9 through Revelation 12, comprise sixteen and one-half pages in the 1979 edition. That is approximately the same amount of text as the combined books of James, 1 Peter, and 2 Peter in the New Testament.

Elder Bruce R. McConkie described the significance of these Joseph Smith Translation inclusions when he said: "I think much of the prejudice of the past was based on a lack of understanding and has faded away since we have published our new Church edition of the

King James Version with its repeated references to the Joseph Smith Translation." Elder McConkie referred to the Joseph Smith Translation as a "restoration" of the Bible "by revelation." His answer to the question "Why we should use the Joseph Smith Translation" was typically direct:

> Of course the revealed changes made by Joseph Smith are true—as much so as anything in the Book of Mormon or the Doctrine and Covenants.
>
> Of course we have adequate and authentic original sources showing the changes—as much so as are the sources for the Book of Mormon or the revelations.
>
> Of course we should use the Joseph Smith Translation in our study and teaching. Since when do any of us have the right to place bounds on the Almighty and say we will believe these revelations but not those?[17]

In that same vein, Dean Matthews described the fundamental principle that should govern our attitude towards the Joseph Smith Translation when he said: "There is no difference, in terms of their nature and source, between the revelations in the Joseph Smith Translation and those in the Doctrine and Covenants and the Pearl of Great Price."[18]

Yet some remain reluctant to use the Joseph Smith Translation. As Dean Matthews observed: "We seem to be too timid, perhaps a little too reluctant, maybe even a little embarrassed when we confront the academic world with a Bible based on revelation from God through a prophet and not certified by a manuscript already accepted by the world."[19]

An attitude that would reject a text based on revelation not verifiable from an available manuscript would, of course, reject the Book of Mormon and the seventh section of the Doctrine and Covenants. An attitude that would reject the revision of existing texts such as the Bible on the basis of revelation rather than scholarship would, of course, reject the book of Moses in the Pearl of Great Price.

Here we should recall the words of the Book of Mormon with which I began my remarks: "Wo be unto him that shall say: We have received the word of God, and we need no more of the word of God, for we have enough! For behold, thus saith the Lord God: I will give unto the children of men line upon line, precept upon precept, here a little and there a little; and blessed are those who hearken unto my precepts, and lend an ear unto my counsel, for they shall learn wisdom; for unto him that receiveth I will give more; and from them that shall say, We have enough, from them shall be taken away even that which they have." (2 Nephi 28:29–30.)

Those who will not rely on revelation and who insist on a manuscript so they can concentrate on the original meaning and intent of the words spoken by the author can be expected to ignore the Joseph Smith Translation. In contrast, those who understand that the importance of the scriptures is what the Lord would have us understand today are anxious for revelatory insight into the current significance of scriptural texts and concepts. They understand that some things we have already received are hard to understand without the Lord's help (see 1 Nephi 15:1, 3, 8, 11), and that we can never receive enough of the word of God. Persons with this attitude are anxious to have every source of revelation to help us to know what the Lord would have us understand from the scriptures today. Such persons will welcome the revelatory insights—even additions—by the prophets of this dispensation.

I believe that Professor Robert L. Millet had it right ten years ago when he said: "There is so much beauty and depth of doctrine and insight to be had within the Joseph Smith Translation of the Bible that it is foolish to study and teach without it; to do so is tantamount to being choosy about what we will receive from the Lord and what we will not."[20]

In summary, there should be no doubt about the current status of the Joseph Smith Translation of the Bible. It is a member of the royal family of scripture. While the Joseph Smith Translation does not enjoy the sovereign status of canonized scripture (except those chapters included in the Pearl of Great Price), as a member of the royal family of scripture it should be noticed and honored on any occasion when it is present.

Suppose a person quotes the King James Version and not the Joseph Smith Translation in a circumstance where the Joseph Smith Translation makes a substantive change? We do it all the time. This is the same as quoting one of the four gospels without quoting a parallel but different phraseology in another gospel, or quoting one of the four gospels and not quoting a significant clarification the Savior gave when he spoke to the Nephites in 3 Nephi. The thrust of what I have said is to encourage and endorse the use of the Joseph Smith Translation, not to condemn any individual circumstance where someone neglects to use it. As always, if we neglect to use the best sources, we diminish our personal understanding and the quality of our message to others.

Belief in and receptivity to continuing revelation is an inherent part of our Latter-day Saint approach to the reading of the scriptures. We must never be guilty of saying "We have received, and we need no more!" (2 Nephi 28:27.) I pray that we will always be open and receptive to the revelations God will give us "line upon line." I witness of Jesus Christ, who is the author of that revelation, the light and life of the world. In the name of Jesus Christ, amen.

Notes

1. *History of the Church* 5:401–2; hereafter cited as HC.
2. HC 1:238.
3. HC 1:219.
4. HC 1:368.
5. HC 4:164, 187.
6. *Times and Seasons* 3:958.
7. HC 4:137, 164, 187.
8. HC 5:293.
9. *Journal of Discourses* 20:73.
10. George Q. Cannon, *Life of Joseph Smith the Prophet* (Salt Lake City: Deseret Book Co., 1986), p. 148.
11. Robert J. Matthews, *A Bible! A Bible!* (Salt Lake City: Bookcraft, 1990), p. 142; hereafter cited as *Bible*.
12. Robert J. Matthews, *"A Plainer Translation," Joseph Smith's*

Translation of the Bible (Provo: Brigham Young University Press, 1975), pp. 210–14; hereafter cited as *Plainer Translation*.

13. *Bible*, p. 142, published earlier in *Ensign*, January 1983, p. 64.

14. Manuscript, p. 5; see also *Church News*, 31 July 1954, p. 9.

15. *Plainer Translation*, p. xxviii; see also *Bible*, p. 90, which refers to the RLDS editions as "correct and careful representations of the Prophet's work."

16. *Church News*, week ending December 7, 1974, p. 16.

17. "The Doctrinal Restoration," in *The Joseph Smith Translation*, Monte S. Nyman and Robert L. Millet, eds. (Provo: BYU Religious Studies Center, 1985), pp. 12, 14.

18. *Bible*, p. 147.

19. *Bible*, p. 154.

20. "Joseph Smith's Translation of the Bible: A Historical Overview," in *The Joseph Smith Translation*, p. 46.

2

Restoring Plain and Precious Truths

JOSEPH FIELDING MCCONKIE

Ours is a story of intrigue. One in which precious jewels are taken from the crown of salvation and worthless stones left in their stead. It is one of betrayal, fraud, deceit, and murder. It is one in which the words of scripture are changed, and entire books disappear; it is one in which spurious writings become almost as common as the false prophets and teachers who author them. In lieu of truths "plain" to the understanding we now have incomprehensible mysteries; in place of the "precious" we are left with the vulgar; and in the stead of sacred "covenants," meaningless ritual. The plot is an international one and spans ages. No one who loves truth has been left unaffected by it. Because of it, Nephi told us, "an exceedingly great number do stumble, yea, insomuch that Satan hath great power over them" (1 Nephi 13:29). Even among those who are "the humble followers of Christ," Nephi tells us, "they are led, that in many instances they do err because they are taught by the precepts of men" (2 Nephi 28:14).

History of the Bible Foretold

In a prophetic description of Bible history Nephi tells us that the writings of its original authors contained "the covenants of the Lord" which he had made with the house of Israel, along with many other prophecies. He likened its contents to the brass plates, though he said the plates were more extensive (see 1 Nephi 13:23). This makes the Book of Mormon promise of the restoration of the brass plates, and the announcement that their content will yet go to all the nations of the earth, all the more significant (see 1 Nephi 5:16–18; Alma 37:3–4). Nephi further indicated that the Bible, meaning the library of sacred writings of which it is composed, as originally written "contained the fulness of the gospel of the Lord," but that after these books had gone forth from the hand of the Twelve Apostles the great and abominable church took from them many of their plain and precious parts "and also many covenants of the Lord" (1 Nephi 13:24, 26). This was done to blind the eyes and harden the hearts of the children of men.

I emphasize that this happened before the Bible went forth to the nations of the earth! It means—and this is not generally understood by Latter-day Saints—that our greatest concern with Bible accuracy and reliability is not one of translation but one of transmission. At BYU we have people with sufficient understanding of ancient languages to protect the Church against difficulties in translation. The greater issue is transmission. What language skills don't allow us to do is restore missing manuscripts or other original sources. By way of analogy, suppose someone went through the general conference reports and took out all the great doctrine, and then someone else came and made a correct translation of what was left. That is essentially what has happened to the Bible. What we have is marvelous, but it is not nearly as good as it originally was. Because of what was taken, Nephi tells us "an exceedingly great many" people stumble and Satan has obtained great power over the hearts of men (see 1 Nephi 13:29).

Nevertheless the promise was also given that "after the Gentiles do stumble exceedingly, because of the most plain and precious parts of the gospel of the Lamb which have been kept back by that abominable church, which is the mother of harlots, saith the Lamb—I will be merciful unto the Gentiles in that day, insomuch that I will bring forth unto them, in mine own power, much of my gospel, which shall be plain and precious, saith the Lamb" (1 Nephi 13:34).

A significant collaborating text for Nephi's prophetic description of Bible history is found in a revelation given to Joseph Smith. It is the explanation of the parable of the wheat and tares found in Doctrine and Covenants 86. It will be recalled that in this parable the servants of the householder sowed in the Master's fields the seed that had been given them, but that while they slept an enemy came and sowed tares among the wheat. When the blade sprang up, so did the tares. The servants asked their Master if they had been given good seed. He assured them they had, explaining that the tares were the work of an enemy. The servants then asked if they should weed the fields, but were told that by so doing they would root up the wheat also. Thus they were instructed to let both wheat and tares grow together until the time of harvest, when the reapers could gather the tares and bind them in bundles to be burned and then gather the wheat into the barn. (See Matthew 13:24–30.)

The seeds in this parable can be seen to represent Israel in its scattered condition. The teachings of the Apostles find a natural place in their hearts, but the enemy of eternal truth also seeks to sow doctrinal tares in those heaven-sent teachings. There is no neutrality here. The doctrinal tares seek to choke the tender blades, meaning the plain and precious. Explaining the parable, the Lord said that after the death of the Apostles "the great persecutor of the church, the apostate, the whore, even Babylon, that maketh all nations to drink of her cup, in whose hearts the enemy, even Satan, sitteth to reign—behold he soweth the tares [meaning he brought into the Church those who were offended with the doctrines taught by the Apostles, those who sought to liberate the Church from the "narrow-mindedness" of the Apostles]; wherefore, the tares choke the wheat and drive the church into the wilderness." This, of course, represented the great apostasy. The Church would remain in the wilderness until the last days, "even now" when the Lord would "bring forth the word" once again. (See D&C 86:1–7.)

This is a multi-dispensation parable. It applies to the meridian dispensation and then anew to our own. Commenting on it Joseph Smith said:

> As the servants of God go forth warning the nations, both priests and people, and as they harden their hearts and reject the light of truth, these first being delivered over to the buffeting of Satan, and the law and

the testimony being closed up, as it was in the case of the Jews, they are left in darkness, and delivered over unto the day of burning; thus being bound up by their creeds, and their bands being made strong by their priests, are prepared for the fulfillment of the saying of the Savior—"The Son of Man shall send forth His angels, and gather out of His Kingdom all things that offend, and them which do iniquity, and shall cast them into a furnace of fire, there shall be wailing and gnashing of teeth."[1]

This is the same story that Nephi is telling. The plain and precious teachings planted by the Apostles were choked by doctrinal tares spread by the enemy of all righteousness. This re-seeding was so extensive that we have been told that truth will appear strange, being made to appear as error, and that Satan will stir men up to anger against it. (See 2 Nephi 28:16–20.) Thus when the tender blade of truth comes forth again many both reject and fight against it. As part of that replanting, Nephi said, "other books" would also come forth "by the power of the Lamb" to convince scattered Israel of the truth of the Bible. The angel of the Lord told Nephi: "These last records, which thou hast seen among the Gentiles, shall establish the truth of the first, which are of the twelve apostles of the Lamb, and shall make known the plain and precious things which have been taken away from them; and shall make known to all kindreds, tongues, and people, that the Lamb of God is the Son of the Eternal Father, and the Savior of the world; and that all men must come unto him, or they cannot be saved" (1 Nephi 13:40).

Source of the Plain and Precious

Those "other books" include the Doctrine and Covenants, the Pearl of Great Price, and the Joseph Smith Translation of the Bible. In some future day other records will be added to these, including the sealed portion of the Book of Mormon, the brass plates, the book of Enoch (D&C 107:57), the writings of John the Baptist (D&C 93:18), other writings of the meridian Twelve (D&C 63:21–22), and the writings of those visited by the Savior after his visit to the Nephites (2 Nephi 29:13–14).

Bible Clues

A careful reading of the Gospels indicates that many of the prophecies known to those of Jesus' day are lost to us. For instance, the Gospel of John begins with a story in which a delegation of priests and Levites from the temple go down to Jordan to interrogate the Baptist, who was preaching and baptizing there. Having found John, they asked him a series of questions from which, if we pay careful attention, we can learn a good deal about the theological expectations of the day. It may also be significant to note that though John gave forthright answers to their questions he made no effort to teach them. He gave them no additional information. First, they asked if he was the Christ. He assured them that he was not. They asked if he was Elijah, for they knew that Elijah would be among those who would come to prepare the way for Christ. Again, his answer was, "I am not." They then asked if he was "that prophet," apparently referring to some prophet who was to play a key role in the preparations for the Messiah, and who was sufficiently well known that a reference vague to us had very identifiable meaning to them. John told them he was not "that" prophet. Who, then they asked, did he profess to be? "I am," he said, "the voice of one crying in the wilderness, Make straight the way of the Lord," as said the prophet Isaiah. (John 1:19–23.)

The questions that were being asked illustrate that those associated with the temple, or the spiritual leadership of the nation, anticipated not only the coming of a messiah but also the return of ancient prophets. Other Gospel texts too suggest this, and also the rising up of a prophet who would stand at the head of this heaven-sent restoration.[2] The coming of the Messiah and those who were to prepare the way before him appears to have posed a threat to those in authority in the temple. The fact that John did not attempt to teach them suggests that he viewed them as opponents.

It would have been natural for them to anticipate that these events could precipitate in their losing their position of authority. The inter-testamental book of Maccabees suggests this to be the case. After Judas's great victory over the Greeks in the second century before Christ, in which the Jews' temple had been restored to them, the Maccabean or Hasmonean family was awarded the hereditary priestly office because of their valiant leadership. This was done, however, with the understanding that theirs was a temporary stewardship, to be surrendered with the coming of a prophet who it was understood would establish the true and proper order of things.[3] This has something to do with the Qumran community, from whom we got the Dead Sea Scrolls; they thought themselves to be the rightful heirs of those offices and awaited a future time when they would gain possession of the temple. It also relates to a legend, then popular among the Jews, of a great prophet who was to come on the scene just prior to the return of Elijah and the coming of the Messiah to restore Israel to her ancient greatness, including the restoration of the ten tribes and the restoration of true temple worship. This prophet of restoration was to be a descendant of Joseph who was sold into Egypt and thus was known as Messiah ben Joseph.[4] All of which is to say that there was a lot going on here.

The next series of questions asked by this temple delegation also adds to our understanding of their expectations. "Why baptizest thou then, if thou be not that Christ, nor Elias, neither that prophet?" (John 1:25.) In my judgment this is a remarkably significant question. Consider what it is telling us. Not only did they anticipate the coming of a messiah but also they knew that one of the identifying characteristics of his ministry would be baptism! "Why baptizest thou then," if you are not the Christ? Similarly, they knew that when Elijah and the prophet of restoration came their ministries too would be associated with the ordinance of baptism.

We ought not miss the significance of what is taking place here. These people expect a restoration of the ancient order of things and they expect it to take place at the hands of prophets, both ancient and those raised up among their own number. Further—and this is something lost to both the Old Testament and the New—they anticipated that the coming of these anointed ones will be associated with the baptismal covenant. What we are being told here is that new dispensations require a new baptism, and that anciently baptism was the covenant of salvation. Is there any wonder, then, that the leaders in the temple would be both interested and concerned when some strange preacher comes out of the wilderness baptizing according to a prophetic pattern apparently well known to them though lost to us?

This delegation from the temple had every reason to be interested in what was taking place at Bethabara (House of the ford) near Jordan, where John was baptizing. They were familiar with the words of Malachi, who referred to the Messiah as "the messenger of the covenant" and foretold another who would come to prepare the way before him. (Malachi 3:1.) Surely there were those who remembered the events associated with the birth of the child of miracle to Zacharias and Elisabeth. On the day of his circumcision and naming an angel of God ordained him "to overthrow the kingdom of the Jews, and to make straight the way of the Lord before the face of his people, to prepare them for the coming of the Lord, in whose hand is given all power" (D&C 84:26–28). Of that day Luke records that "fear came on all that dwelt round about them: and all these sayings were noised abroad throughout all the hill country of Judea. And all they that heard them laid them up in their hearts, saying, What manner of child shall this be!" (Luke 1:65–66.)

There is something else of considerable interest taking place here. It centers in the Book of Mormon. The two major themes that bind that book together are its testimony of Christ and its promises relative to the restoration of Israel. Add to this the fact that in the first of its fifteen books it gives a prophetic description of the coming forth of the Bible. In doing so it repeatedly announces that "plain and precious things" will be taken from it along with "many covenants of the Lord" (see 1 Nephi 13:26, 28, 29, 32, 34, 35, 40). When Joseph Smith brought forth the Book of Mormon he could not have brought forth a book that fit more perfectly the anticipation of the Jews of Jesus' time, as illustrated by the delegation of priests and Levites that came to question John.

Precious Truths Restored

It is significant that the restoration anticipated by those of Jesus' day has taken place in our own. As prophesied, Elijah and many of the other ancient prophets have returned to restore their keys and authorities[5] and, also as anticipated, a great prophet has come forth from the midst of his brethren to stand at the head of this the dispensation of the fulness of all gospel dispensations. Indeed, we learn that Joseph of

Egypt identified the great prophet of the last days not only as his descendant but as bearing his name and as being the source of salvation for his descendants (see JST, Genesis 50:33; 2 Nephi 3:15). The knowledge that the gospel would be taken from the Jews in the meridian of time and given to the Gentiles and then taken from the Gentiles to be restored to another people in the last days is among the plain truths taught by the Savior to his meridian disciples. Such knowledge is restored to us in the Joseph Smith Translation (See JST, Matthew 21:51–56).

Comments frequently made to Mormon missionaries follow this pattern: "We don't need the Book of Mormon—we have the Bible." "We don't need living prophets—we have the words of the ancient prophets." And "The last thing this world needs is another church." There is a common element in such statements. It is the idea of sufficiency. The same people who would be embarrassed to be confined to the standard of living known to their parents are, in the realm of religious things, quick to tell our missionaries that what was good enough for their parents is good enough for them.

The doctrine of sufficiency is not new. In an interesting JST text we find Christ instructing the newly called Twelve to tell those they are teaching to "ask God" about the truthfulness of their message. The response of the Twelve indicates that they had already been inviting people to pray about their message and knew what their response would be: "We have the law for our salvation, and that is sufficient for us."

This appears to be the classic line for use in rejecting the living voice. To the Twelve, Christ then gave a chain of thought to illustrate that communication between a father and his children was never to cease. "What man among you, having a son, and he shall be standing out, and shall say, Father, open thy house that I may come in and sup with thee, will not say, Come in, my son; for mine is thine, and thine is mine?" (JST, Matthew 7:12–17). The response is perfect. A loving father, God being the perfect example, would never turn away a son or daughter who came seeking sustenance. A loving parent just doesn't say, "Well, I fed you before and that is sufficient"; or "I fed your older brother when he was hungry, you have a written account of that, go read it." The idea that a loving Father would ever quit speaking to his children is simply ludicrous.

It is significant that this warning against the doctrine of sufficiency is among the plain and precious things no longer to be found in
the Bible text. Equally significant is its restoration in the Book of
Mormon. It is Nephi who pens the words, but obviously the Spirit
that dictates them: "Wo be unto him that shall say: We have received
the word of God, and we need no more of the word of God, for we
have enough! For behold, thus saith the Lord God: I will give unto
the children of men line upon line, precept upon precept, here a little
and there a little; and blessed are those who hearken unto my precepts, and lend an ear unto my counsel, for they shall learn wisdom;
for unto him that receiveth I will give more; and from them that shall
say, We have enough, from them shall be taken away even that which
they have." (2 Nephi 28:29–30.)

Of this we can be certain: the greater the doctrine the more it will
be opposed, and the sooner it will disappear in the night of apostate
darkness. Apostasy will always involve the closing of the heavens and
silencing of living oracles. This will be accomplished in the guise of
loyalty to dead prophets, whose words will be declared complete and
final on all matters of faith. The pattern is always the same. First
comes the silencing of the prophetic voice; second, the taking from
and adding to what the prophets said. After the prophets have been
silenced, and after what they have said has been tampered with, the
remaining words can then be reverenced as inerrant and infallible.
And finally comes the reinterpreting of the words of the prophets in
such a manner as to give them a meaning entirely different from the
original.

Edwin Hatch captures this historical pattern in his outstanding
work *The Influence of Greek Ideas on Christianity*. He observes that the
great battle of the second century was over the issue of whether the
canon was to remain open to continuous revelation or be closed. The
victory, he says, went to the closed canon. The great battle of the
third century, he says, was whether the closed canon was to be interpreted literally or figuratively. The victory, he says, went to the figura-
tive.[6] If it is false prophets and false Christs a person wants, this is perfect. The meaning of scripture is at the mercy of its interpretation.

Thus we can have the assurance that any book seeking to restore
the "ask God" doctrine is going to draw the wrath of hell. That doc-

trine, of course, is the heart of the Book of Mormon message. Nephi taught the principle with eloquence. Inspired by the visionary experience of his father, he sought to experience the same things. "I was desirous," he said, to "see, and hear, and know of these things, by the power of the Holy Ghost, which is the gift of God unto all those who diligently seek him, as well in times of old as in the time that he should manifest himself unto the children of men. For he is the same yesterday, to-day, and forever; and the way is prepared for all men from the foundation of the world, if it so be that they repent and come unto him. For he that diligently seeketh shall find; and the mysteries of God shall be unfolded unto them, by the power of the Holy Ghost, as well in these times as in times of old, and as well in times of old as in times to come; wherefore, the course of the Lord is one eternal round." (1 Nephi 10:17–19.)

This right of all mankind to communicate with the heavens on equal terms is one of the major threads that binds all scripture together. Alma teaches the doctrine succinctly as he reasons with his son Corianton. "Is it not as easy at this time for the Lord to send his angel to declare these glad tidings unto us as unto our children, or as after the time of his coming?" (Alma 39:19.) Similarly, Moroni directs himself to those who deny the necessity of continuous revelation or any of the gifts and powers of God:

> I speak unto you who deny the revelations of God, and say that they are done away, that there are no revelations, nor prophecies, nor gifts, nor healing, nor speaking with tongues, and the interpretations of tongues;
>
> Behold I say unto you, he that denieth these things knoweth not the gospel of Christ; yea, he has not read the scriptures; if so, he does not understand them.
>
> For do we not read that God is the same yesterday, today, and forever, and in him there is no variableness neither shadow of changing?
>
> And now, if ye have imagined up unto yourselves a god who doth vary, and in whom there is shadow of changing, then have ye imagined up unto yourselves a god who is not a God of miracles.
>
> But behold, I will show unto you a God of miracles, even the God of Abraham, and the God of Isaac, and the God of Jacob; and it is that same God who created the heavens and the earth, and all things that in them are. (Mormon 9:7–11.)

The Nature of God and Men

As already noted, in times of apostasy the greatest truths are always the first to be lost. The greatest truths are those that deal with the nature of God, his Son Jesus Christ, and the Holy Ghost. It is natural to assume that these will also be the first truths to be restored when we are invited once again to stand in the light of heaven. The book of Moses, which is an extract from JST Genesis, is a classic illustration. Whereas the creeds of men declare God to be incorporeal, and sectarian commentators tell us that when scripture says we are in the image and likeness of God it is only to be understood figuratively, the book of Moses declares: "In the image of his own body, male and female, created he them, and blessed them" (Moses 6:9). Thus the knowledge that God is a corporeal being, which Joseph Smith would have assumed from the First Vision, was affirmed for him in 1830. He was further told that in the language of Adam, God was known as "Man of Holiness" and Christ as "the Son of Man" (Moses 6:57). As genealogies are traced, Adam is identified as the "firstborn" (Abraham 1:3) of the inhabitants of this earth and as "the son of God" (Moses 6:22). We are further told that "a book of remembrance was kept . . . of the children of God." This, of course, would include all descendants of Adam (Moses 6:5–8). Thus we find Enoch saying to God, "thou hast made me, and given unto me a right to thy throne" (Moses 7:59). It doesn't take any stretch of the imagination to see why such statements would have been taken from the scriptures. They are all very plain and very precious.

The Revelation of God and Christ

The opening of the heavens brings the same kind of transformation to the New Testament. For instance, the text in the first chapter of John that reads "No man hath seen God at any time" was corrected by the Prophet to read: "No man hath seen God at any time, except he hath borne record of the Son; for except it is through him no man can be saved" (John 1:18; JST, John 1:19). We have an equally confusing text in the tenth chapter of John, where Christ is recorded as saying, "All that ever came before me are thieves and robbers." This statement, which would have to include the Old Testament prophets, reads in the JST, "All that ever came before me who testified not of me are thieves and robbers." (John 10:8; JST, John 10:8.) The implications are profound, because it means that all Old Testament prophets knew of Christ and testified of him.

One would be hard pressed to prove this with the Old Testament as it presently stands, yet the book of Moses and the Book of Mormon spell it out as plainly as language permits. Starting with father Adam we learn that an angel of the Lord explained the nature of the sacrifices he had been commanded to offer since he left Eden as "a similitude of the sacrifice of the Only Begotten of the Father." And further, that he was to do all that he did in the name of the Son of God and to "repent and call upon God in the name of the Son forevermore" (Moses 5:7–8). Thus we are told that God himself spoke to Adam saying: "I am God; I made the world, and men before they were in the flesh, and he also said unto him: If thou wilt turn unto me, and hearken unto my voice, and believe, and repent of all thy transgressions, and be baptized, even in water, in the name of mine Only Begotten Son, who is full of grace and truth, which is Jesus Christ, the only name which shall be given under heaven, whereby salvation shall come unto the children of men, ye shall receive the gift of the Holy Ghost, asking all things in his name, and whatsoever ye shall ask, it shall be given you" (Moses 6:52).

The Book of Mormon is a powerful confirmation that the ancients knew of Christ and his gospel from the very beginning. More than five hundred years before the birth of Christ, Jacob recorded this testimony:

> For, for this intent have we written these things, that they may know that we knew of Christ, and we had a hope of his glory many hundred years before his coming; and not only we ourselves had a hope of his glory, but also all the holy prophets which were before us. Behold, they believed in Christ and worshiped the Father in his name, and also we worship the Father in his name. And for this intent we keep the law of Moses, it pointing our souls to him; and for this cause it is sanctified unto us for righteousness, even as it was accounted unto Abraham in the wilderness to be obedient unto the commands of God in offering up his son Isaac, which is a similitude of God and his Only Begotten Son. (Jacob 4:4–5.)

Contrast this statement with the following, which comes from a symposium on messianic expectations in earliest Judaism and Christianity recently held at the Princeton Theological Seminary. Both Jewish and Christian scholars were involved. James H. Charlesworth, the editor for the symposium, observed: "No member of the Princeton Symposium on the Messiah holds that a critical historian can refer to a common Jewish messianic hope during the time of Jesus or in the sayings of Jesus. It may not even be easy to demonstrate a common messianic hope among his earliest followers."[7]

Critics of modern revelation have rejected it on the grounds that it is too Christ-centered. Their argument is that people in Old Testament times did not know who Christ was. The argument is based on the fact that he is not mentioned in extant texts. As Latter-day Saints we are trying to tell them that their texts were tampered with and that from revealed sources we know that that knowledge was once a part of the text. Since the real issue here is what the revelation originally said, we invite them to test our claim by seeking the spirit of revelation. That is the spirit by which the revelation was originally given. Moroni stated it perfectly: "When you shall receive these things, I would exhort you that ye would ask God, the Eternal Father, in the name of Christ, if these things are not true; and if ye shall ask with a sincere heart, with real intent, having faith in Christ, he will manifest the truth of it unto you, by the power of the Holy Ghost. And by the power of the Holy Ghost ye may know the truth of all things." (Moroni 10:4–5.) For the most part that invitation is rejected under the guise of loyalty to the doctrine of sufficiency.

Chief among the truths restored are those dealing with the nature of the Father, the Son, and the Holy Ghost. These are matters over which there have been centuries of debate and conflict resulting in historical Christianity's adoption of an incomprehensible God. As his nature was reinterpreted by the wisdom of men he became increasingly abstract and transcendental. Thus we find him today languishing in the outer reaches of space without body, parts, passions, speech, and of course without gender. Is it any wonder that he is too embarrassed to reveal himself to prophets as he did anciently? "Now, what do we hear in the gospel which we have received? A voice of gladness!" The testimony that God reigns and the promise that "As the dews of

Carmel, so shall the knowledge of God descend upon" us. (D&C 128:19.)

Whereas the Bible can be searched in vain for a definition of resurrection, for example, the Book of Mormon speaks with marvelous plainness. Amulek gives it thus: "This mortal body [is to be] raised to an immortal body, that is from death, even from the first death unto life, that they can die no more; their spirits uniting with their bodies, never to be divided; thus the whole becoming spiritual and immortal, that they can no more see corruption" (Alma 11:45). Alma explains it this way: "The soul shall be restored to the body, and body to the soul; yea, and every limb and joint shall be restored to its body; yea, even a hair of the head shall not be lost; but all things shall be restored to their proper and perfect frame" (Alma 40:23). By announcing that we may reclaim our physical bodies in the eternal worlds, the Book of Mormon makes heaven a tangible and corporeal existence. And if God's children have bodies then, what of him in whose image and likeness they were created?

Restoring the Covenants of the Lord

As to sacred covenants of the Lord, it was while translating the Book of Mormon that Joseph Smith and Oliver Cowdery learned of the importance of the ordinance of baptism. As they inquired of the Lord to know how they were to conform with this sacred ritual they set in order a sequence of events that resulted in the restoration of priesthood keys, powers, and authority. The knowledge of other sacred covenants followed in rapid succession.

Chief among the keys restored was that authority known to us as the sealing power. This is the authority by which the union of the man and woman as husband and wife is bound both on earth and in heaven. In turn their children are eternally sealed to them, so that salvation becomes a family affair. Now be reminded that all the ordinances of the temple are predicated on the nature of the resurrection. If we didn't get our bodies back, if there were no distinction as to gender in the resurrection, if men were no longer men and women no longer women, then there would be no purpose for marriage or families. Everything in the temple centers around the eternal nature of the family; not just families for this world but families for the endless duration of the eternities. As already noted, it was in the restoration of a Genesis text that we learn that in the language of Adam, God was known by the name "Man of Holiness" and the promised Messiah as "the Son of Man" (Moses 6:57; JST, Genesis 6:60). "If the veil were rent today," Joseph Smith explained, "and the great God who holds this world in its orbit, and who upholds all worlds and all things by his power, was to make himself visible,—I say, if you were to see him today, you would see him like a man in form—like yourselves in all the person, image, and very form as man."[8]

Again the contrast is remarkable. Historical Christianity has been about the matter of body snatching for centuries. When Plato made it unfashionable for God to have a body, reasoning that such would confine him to time and place, both Judaism and Christianity followed suit. This notion gave birth to the idea that the body was simply a prison in which the soul had been confined as a punishment for the fall of Adam. In the early centuries of Christianity asceticism became the rage, with the attendant idea that sins were to be atoned for by mortification of the flesh.

One extreme gave birth to another, and so we had the flight to the desert where men lived in circumstances more austere than those of animals and with fewer pleasures. Martyrdom, at least for a period, became the rage as an acceptable way to free oneself from the bodily prison. Celibacy became the way for men to avoid any pleasure that might be derived by association with women. For the fairer gender the response became lifelong virginity and nunneries. Children, it was determined, were born in sin, which in turn created the necessity of infant baptism. Mary, who in addition to her firstborn had given birth to at least four other sons and some daughters (see Matthew 13:55), was declared to be the perpetual virgin. Joseph was declared to be impotent, and of course Jesus was consigned, contrary to all acceptable social practices of the day, to bachelorhood. The commandment that a man was to leave his father and mother and cleave unto his wife and they in turn were to multiply and replenish the earth now became a practice relegated to those without the spiritual strength to avoid such soul-demeaning alliances.

It is remarkable how quickly the sword of truth can slay the dark dragon of error and falsehood. Consider the significance of the revelation of Lehi and Nephi that Mary was the "mother of the Son of God, after the manner of the flesh" (1 Nephi 11:18). Our prophets have not been backward in interpreting this statement. Ezra Taft Benson explained: "The Church of Jesus Christ of Latter-day Saints proclaims that Jesus Christ is the Son of God in the most literal sense. The body in which He performed His mission in the flesh was sired by that same Holy Being we worship as God, our Eternal Father. Jesus was not the son of Joseph, nor was He begotten by the Holy Ghost. He is the son of the Eternal Father!"[9]

Such a doctrine strikes a fatal blow to the idea of immaculate conception and its train of attendant doctrines. What a remarkable contrast we have when words are permitted to mean what they say, when *father* means "father," *mother* means "mother," *son* means "son," and *begotten* means "begotten." Contrast this with the decision of Nicea, where it was determined that the Son was his own Father, they being of the same substance, which substance consisted of immaterial or non-existent matter. In the first instance, God is a personal Being, a loving Father who desires to manifest himself to all his children; in the second, he is an incomprehensible mystery.

When Were They Taken?

At what point in history were these plain and precious truths deliberately taken from the library of scriptural texts? The answer is whenever the adversary could get away with it, and scriptural history attests that was quite frequently. Nephi indicated that the brass plates, that is, scripture written in Old Testament times, were more complete than the Bible record (see 1 Nephi 13:23). From the Book of Mormon we know that the writings of Zenos, Zenock, Neum, and Ezias did not survive as part of the Old Testament record. There can be little question that other records were also taken from the library of sacred writings. Our Bible Dictionary, under the heading "Lost Books," lists a dozen Old Testament books now lost to us. These are books that were obviously regarded as scripture by Old Testament writers.[10] There are yet other allusions to writings in the Old Testament in which it is difficult to determine whether they are lost books or extant books by other titles. Tampered-with remnants of these books may have survived in the ever-expanding library of pseudepigraphic and apocryphal works. From what Nephi said, we must conclude that these changes took place shortly after the death of the Apostles and before the formation of any church known to our modern day. Significantly, authorities tell us that "the worst corruptions to which the New Testament has ever been subjected, originated within a hundred years after it was composed."[11]

How Were the Plain and Precious Parts Taken from the Bible?

In response to the question, How were the plain and precious parts taken from the Bible? we know enough to say, quite deliberately. It is not scribal error that we are talking about, nor is it faulty translation. Both are matters of some importance but they are not the major concerns that taking out verses, chapters, and whole books are. Two classic quotations from the Prophet Joseph Smith illustrate the matter. The first is found in the preface to D&C 76. It reads as follows: "From sundry revelations which had been received, it was apparent that many important points touching the salvation of man had been taken from the Bible, or lost before it was compiled."[12] The second is the revelation given in response to the Prophet's question as to whether the Apocrypha should be a part of his labor known to us as the Joseph Smith Translation of the Bible. "There are," the Lord said, "many things contained therein that are true, and it is mostly translated correctly; there many things contained therein that are not true, which are interpolations by the hands of men" (D&C 91:1–2). An "interpolation" is an insertion.[13]

What we have, then, is evidence of both the taking from and the adding to texts that in their origin were inspired. Again, this is not scribal error. It is deliberate, premeditated mischief. It is the kind of thing that has gone on virtually from the beginning of time and over which there was no control until the invention of the printing press about 1450. Prior to the printing press, no two books would ever have been entirely the same. As to scripture, no autographs (meaning original copies) exist for any book of the Bible. There is no absolute or sure checkpoint. The great changes that were made in the biblical text were made early, and those making them were careful to cover their tracks. The era in which this took place, as far as the New Testament is concerned, is known to us as a historical dark hole. Records of what was happening simply did not survive.

Without Records How Do We Know What Happened?

Those seeking to change the doctrines of the Church did so from within. They did it early, and when they took the enemy camp they left no survivors. How then do we know what happened? The restoration of the gospel is the most perfect evidence. To restore is to bring back; it is not to create anew. It is an everlasting gospel of which we speak, meaning that it is everlastingly the same. Thus that which has been given to us is of necessity what was given to our counterparts in ages past.

Should Latter-day Saints Have Their Own Bible?

In a revelation given to Joseph Smith the Lord said, "Behold, I do not bring it [having reference to the Book of Mormon] to destroy that which they have received [meaning the Bible], but to build it up" (D&C 10:52). "Yea, and I will also bring to light my gospel which was ministered unto them, and, behold, they shall not deny that which you have received, but they shall build it up, and shall bring to light the true points of my doctrine, yea, and the only doctrine which is in me" (D&C 10:62). That is to say, one purpose of the Book of Mormon is to sustain the Bible as mankind presently has it. In the prophecy cited earlier about the latter-day prophet who was to bear the name of Joseph of Egypt we read:

But a seer will I raise up out of the fruit of thy loins; and unto him will I give power to bring forth my word unto the seed of thy loins—and not to the bringing forth my word only, saith the Lord, but to the convincing them of my word, which shall have already gone forth among them.

Wherefore, the fruit of thy loins shall write; and the fruit of the loins of Judah shall write; and that which shall be written by the fruit of thy loins, and also that which shall be written by the fruit of the loins of Judah, shall grow together, unto the confounding of false doctrines and laying down of contentions, and establishing peace among the fruit of thy loins, and bringing them to the knowledge of their fathers in latter days, and also to the knowledge of my covenants, saith the Lord. (2 Nephi 3:11–12.)

Conclusions

Jesus accused the scribes of his day of taking "away the key of knowledge," or "the fulness of the scriptures" (JST, Luke 11:53). Nephi assures us that they would not be alone in such nefarious labors, for after the death of the Apostles Christian scribes would tamper with the New Testament scripture in a like manner. The host of truths restored to us through the Prophet Joseph Smith, truths that are singularly ours as Latter-day Saints, constitute the illustration of what was taken. Ours is a restored gospel. We profess no doctrines new to the faithful of ages past but a host of doctrines unknown to those of the religious world today. Chief among these doctrines are those dealing with the nature of the Godhead and the ordinances of salvation. Perhaps the most obvious of the plain and precious things taken was the office and call of the Twelve Apostles. In Joseph Smith—Matthew we learn that Christ warned the meridian Twelve that they would be martyred and that their deaths would come at the hands of those espousing doctrines of false Christs (see Joseph Smith—Matthew 1:5–7). Thus it appears that the death of the Apostles, contrary to Christian tradition, was an inside job.

Perhaps the most important lesson to grow out of this brief review of doctrinal history is that those truths that are to us most plain and precious are always in danger of perversion, and that perversion can only come from within our own ranks. The warning is obvious—

beware of those who would have us mingle our doctrine with the philosophies of men.

The priesthood and its quorums have been restored. The greater priesthood has been charged with the responsibility to administer the gospel, with the First Presidency and the Quorum of the Twelve holding all the keys of the kingdom. Of any who would seek to advocate either a course or a doctrine contrary to that given us by those who hold the keys of the kingdom, again we would say, beware! Theirs has already been proven a course of darkness, one which results in the loss of what is plain and precious.

Notes

1. Joseph Smith, *Teachings of the Prophet Joseph Smith*, sel. Joseph Fielding Smith (Salt Lake City: Deseret Book Co., 1938), p. 101; hereafter cited as TPJS.

2. After the Apostles had been out proselyting, Christ called them together and asked, "Whom do men say that I the Son of man am?" Their answers included John the Baptist, who by this time was dead, and his death was known to the people. This suggests that they expected him to be among those who would return from beyond the veil. They also named Elijah, and Jeremiah, and others who would "rise again." (See Matthew 16:13–14; Luke 9:19.) As to the matter of "that prophet," or the prophet of the restoration, there seemed to be an ongoing debate as to whether Jesus of Nazareth was the prophet of the restoration or the Messiah (see John 7:40–41).

3. 1 Maccabees 14:42.

4. Joseph Fielding McConkie, *His Name Shall Be Joseph: Ancient Prophecies of the Latter-day Joseph* (Salt Lake City: Hawkes Publishing Co., 1980), pp. 153–84.

5. See, for instance, Matthew 16:14 and Luke 9:8, which suggest that those of Jesus' day expected that John the Baptist, Elijah, Jeremiah, and others of the ancient prophets would return.

6. Edwin Hatch, *The Influence of Greek Ideas on Christianity* (Gloucester, Massachusetts: Peter Smith, 1970), pp. 324–25.

7. James H. Charlesworth, ed. *The Messiah—Developments in Earliest Judaism and Christianity* (Minneapolis: Fortress Press, 1992), p. 5.

8. TPJS, p. 345.

9. Ezra Taft Benson, *Come unto Christ* (Salt Lake City: Deseret Book Co., 1983), p. 4.

10. LDS Bible Dictionary, pp. 725–26.

11. Frederick Henry Ambrose Scrivener, *A Plain Introduction to the Criticism of the New Testament*, 3d ed. (Cambridge: Deighton, Bell and Col, 1883), p. 511.

12. HC 1:245–52.

13. John Ayto, *Dictionary of Word Origins* (New York: Arcade Publishing, 1990), p. 302.

3

The Role of the Joseph Smith Translation in the Restoration

ROBERT J. MATTHEWS

The purpose of this symposium is to present the major principles, facts, doctrines, and historical events that are associated with the Joseph Smith Translation (hereafter JST) and to do it in such a way that everyone who learns of these things will rejoice and praise the Lord for his servant Joseph Smith and the scriptures that were brought forth by his hand.

The Prophet Joseph's work with the Bible is one of the great evidences of his divine calling, and is a mainstream accomplishment of his ministry. For various reasons the work of Joseph Smith with the Bible has been somewhat misunderstood, often neglected, and in some instances even criticized. We hope that anyone who attends these sessions or who reads the written report of this conference will have a new birth of appreciation, testimony, and gratitude to the Lord for this great work that was done by the choice Seer Joseph Smith.

The Dispensation of the Fulness of Times

Many have supposed that the translation of the Bible was only a sideline, a matter of personal but passing interest to the Prophet Joseph. But that is a mistaken notion. We hope to demonstrate in this

conference, by historical fact, by scriptural evidence, by sound reasoning, and by personal testimony, that Joseph Smith was commanded of
the Lord to do this great work; that it was central to the Restoration,
to the establishment of the dispensation of the fulness of times; and
that to neglect or ignore the role of the JST is to miss a major dimension of the work of God in this dispensation. I personally believe that
anyone who becomes acquainted with the discussion of this conference and who asks the Lord if what is said here is both true and important, will receive a similar testimony. A knowledge of the Joseph
Smith Translation will enlarge your perception of Church history, of
the Doctrine and Covenants, of the Pearl of Great Price, of the nature
of scripture, of the nature of revelation, and of the value of reading
scripture to obtain revelation from God.

Our good friend Joseph F. McConkie has explained how the
Apostasy occurred in the church of New Testament times, and how
that apostasy resulted in the alteration and changing of the holy scriptures. He has demonstrated what is meant by the eighth article of
faith, and the thirteenth chapter of 1 Nephi, both of which give us
ample warning that the Bible has not come to us through the centuries in its original purity and completeness. Because many plain and
precious truths, and even whole books, and many covenants of the
Lord have been taken from the Bible, and since there are no known
original manuscripts available today, and because the Apostasy was
complete and worldwide, it became necessary that there be a restoration so that the same priesthood authority, the same doctrines, the
same covenants, the same scriptures, and the same faith would be
available to the Latter-day Saints that were available to the early-day
Saints of all ages that are past.

We are talking about revelation from God. The dispensation of
the fulness of times is a dispensation of restoration. If it were not a
restoration, it could not be the fulness of times, meaning a dispensation
culminating in the doctrines and scriptures and purposes of God of all
former dispensations. It is the time of the "restitution of all things"
spoken of by Peter (Acts 3:21). Since the Bible is the collection that
has survived covering the time from the Creation on down through
the centuries to the time of Jesus and the Apostles, it became a major
instrument in the hands of the Lord to bring about the doctrinal

restoration for the last days through the ministry of Joseph Smith. The Book of Mormon is part of that restoration, the book of Abraham is part of that restoration, the ancient record of the ten tribes of Israel will be part of that restoration, as will be the sealed plates containing the vision of the brother of Jared.

Joseph Smith was a restorer of knowledge and of scripture that originally existed in olden times. As a seer, he could talk about the past as easily as about the future. It is customary to think of a prophet as foretelling the future. That is one of the prophetic gifts. But Joseph Smith has revealed to us a great deal about the past because he is the prophet of the Restoration, and so much of the past has become clouded, blurred, and lost to us because many of the plain parts have been taken from the Bible. The Lord declared that he had given Joseph Smith "the keys of the mystery of those things which have been sealed" (D&C 35:18). Thus the Lord inspired Joseph Smith to use the marvelous though inadequate Bible to be a sacred working document in bringing to pass the necessary restoration.

Statements by the Prophet Joseph Smith About the Bible

The Prophet Joseph Smith freely discussed his work of translation and the reasons why a new translation was needed. Among his statements are the following:

> Much conjecture and conversation frequently occurred among the Saints, concerning the books mentioned, and referred to, in various places in the Old and New Testaments, which were now nowhere to be found. The common remark was, "They are *lost books*;" but it seems the Apostolic Church had some of these writings, as Jude mentions or quotes the Prophecy of Enoch, the seventh from Adam. To the joy of the little flock . . . did the Lord reveal the following doings of olden times, from the prophecy of Enoch [now Moses, chapter 7].[1]

> Upon my return from Amherst Conference, I resumed the translation of the Scriptures. From sundry revelations which had been received, it was apparent that many important points touching the salvation of men, had been taken from the Bible, or lost before it was compiled.[2]

We believe the Bible to be the word of God as far as it is translated correctly (Articles of Faith 1:8).

I am now going to take exceptions to the present translation of the Bible in relation to these matters [the books of Daniel and Revelation]. Our latitude and longitude can be determined in the original Hebrew with far greater accuracy than in the English version. There is a grand distinction between the actual meaning of the prophets and the present translation.[3]

There are many things in the Bible which do not, as they now stand, accord with the revelations of the Holy Ghost to me.[4]

I believe the Bible as it read when it came from the pen of the original writers. Ignorant translators, careless transcribers, or designing and corrupt priests have committed many errors.[5]

The Prophet Joseph Smith was a believer in the original inspiration of the Bible, and he knew firsthand of its spiritual value. However, he also knew, from his own experience as well as from the testimony of the Book of Mormon (1 Nephi 13:20–42), that many plain and precious truths had been deleted or obscured. President Gordon B. Hinckley has clearly stated the situation: "One of the projects undertaken by Joseph Smith before his removal to Ohio was a revision of the English Bible. He did not discredit the King James translation, but he knew, as has since been more generally recognized, that certain errors and omissions in that record had led to numerous difficulties among the sects of Christendom."[6]

Making the JST

By divine command, Joseph Smith proceeded to make a new translation of the Bible. He would read the King James Version, and by revelation through the Holy Spirit and by vision a fuller meaning would be made known to him. Sometimes this restoration consisted of clarification of a passage, sometimes it consisted of producing material entirely new to our time but which once was known in ancient days and had been lost either by accident or by deliberate removal from the Bible record.

Many of the specific doctrines and revelations will be dealt with in detail by other speakers in this conference, but I think it would not infringe on anyone if I gave a quick overview. As Joseph Smith began the translation, he naturally started with Genesis. He first received a revelation which we call the "visions of Moses," which is printed in the Pearl of Great Price as Moses chapter 1. This is a record of a series of visions that Moses received *before* he composed the book of Genesis. It seems fitting that as Joseph Smith began his work as a *restorer* of Genesis he should receive some of the same information that Moses had received before he wrote the book of Genesis. Let us remember that Joseph Smith was no less of a prophet and seer than was Moses.

As the Prophet Joseph worked through Genesis he received information about the creation of the world, Adam and Eve, the origin of Satan, the fall of man, the revelation of the gospel to Adam, the introduction of the law of sacrifice, the doctrine of the atonement by the Only Begotten, and so forth. Soon he received a revelation about Enoch and the city of Enoch, which was called Zion. The King James Bible says nothing about Enoch's city. But while Joseph Smith was translating the book of Genesis the Lord revealed to him that Enoch had a city called Zion, and the people of that city were of "one heart and one mind" and had "no poor among them" (see Moses 7:18–19). Eventually they were taken to heaven, with the promise that they would return to earth in the last days and be joined to the New Jerusalem. All of this is now contained in Genesis 7 of the JST and in Moses 7 of the Pearl of Great Price.

Immediately after this Enoch material was received through the translation, the Lord directed the Prophet to move the Church out of New York to Ohio, from which it would later move to Missouri. There the Latter-day Saints received the same laws of consecration that Enoch had known. The translation of Genesis made known the Enoch material, which laid the foundation for the law of consecration to be revealed, as recorded in the Doctrine and Covenants beginning with section 42 and continuing for several other sections.

Other doctrines, such as the law of celestial marriage, the age of accountability at eight years, the degrees of glory, possibly the duties of the various quorums and councils of the priesthood, and much about the second coming of the Lord Jesus, were made known to Joseph Smith in the process of the translation. The translation was a learning experience for the Prophet.

We have been in the habit of thinking of the JST as only a work with the Bible, with the goal of making a better Bible. Well, it is at least that. It is the best Bible on the face of the earth today, but it is much more than that. When we see the JST in its wider mission we realize that the JST is just as much at home in a symposium of Church history, or of the Doctrine and Covenants, or of the Pearl of Great Price, or a symposium on revelation, or on doctrine, as it is in a symposium on the Bible.

Appearance and Conditions of the
Original JST Manuscript

The manuscripts of the JST that were prepared by the Prophet Joseph Smith and his scribes consist of the following:

1. A large pulpit-style leather-bound edition of the King James Version (9″ x 11″ x 2 1/2″) published by H. and E. Phinney Company of Cooperstown, New York. On the flyleaf, in what appears to be the handwriting of Oliver Cowdery, is the following inscription:

> The book of the Jews and the property of
> Joseph Smith Junior and Oliver Cowdery
> Bought October the 8th 1829 at Egbert B. Grandins
> Book Store Palmyra Wayne County New York
> Price $3.75.
> Holiness to the Lord

This Bible contains the Old and New Testaments and the Old Testament Apocrypha. The margins of the Bible are filled with printed references and notes, allowing little room for words to be written. The value of this Bible is that it contains markings of various kinds—sometimes in pencil, sometimes in ink—indicating passages or words that are in need of correction. Old Testament markings begin at Genesis 25:7. New Testament markings begin at John 6:12. Most of the Old Testament markings are in pencil. Most of the New Testament markings are in ink. There are no markings in the Apocrypha.

The primary purpose of this King James Version seems to be to provide a text for the Prophet to read from in dictating corrections to a scribe. It also serves as a guide to indicate some of the passages needing attention.

This Bible is now in the custody of the Reorganized Church of Jesus Christ of Latter Day Saints in Independence, Missouri. I have carefully examined it on several occasions.

2. The handwritten manuscripts are in a good state of preservation, although the paper has yellowed slightly; and the ink, once black, has oxidized to an attractive rich brown. The edges are sometimes ragged. The pages are 17″ x 14″ folded to make four sides 8½″ x 14″. Writing is on both sides. At the beginning of the translation every chapter was written out, even whole chapters that contained no corrections. The translation began with Genesis 1 and was written completely through Genesis 24. Then attention was given to the New Testament, beginning with Matthew chapter 1. From Matthew 1:1 to John 6:11 the text is written in full. A shorter method was then devised, only the corrections being written. This shorter method necessitated the markings in the Bible to show where the briefer notations should be inserted. Thus in the printing of the JST the marked Bible had to be used in conjunction with the shorter method. The marked Bible was not essential to the printer for places where the text was written in full.

In all, there are 464 pages of manuscript.

Geographic Locations and Persons Involved in the Translation

The translation was begun at Harmony, Pennsylvania, in June 1830, at the small home of Joseph Smith. The materials we now call Moses 1–5 were received at that place between June and August 1830, Oliver Cowdery acting as scribe. The Prophet then moved to Fayette, New York, and lived in the home of Peter Whitmer, Sr., where the translation was continued through Moses 6 with John Whitmer as scribe, Oliver Cowdery having been called to Missouri on missionary service. Brother Whitmer was scribe from 21 October 1830 until early December that year. The Whitmer home was the same residence in which some of the Book of Mormon had been translated and in which the Church had been officially organized.

Sidney Rigdon arrived from Ohio in early December 1830, and was called to be the scribe (D&C 35:20). He began to write at what is now the beginning of Moses 7, and was the principal scribe of the JST for the remaining two and one-half years.

An important feature of the original JST manuscripts is that they reflect the dates, places, and scribes as the translation progressed. This makes it possible to tie it in with sections of the Doctrine and Covenants. The manuscripts also show that there were preliminary drafts and also more extensive drafts containing additional corrections, punctuation, and versification. A correct knowledge of the nature of the manuscripts is an important factor, as will be seen later in this address.

The translation continued to progress in Kirtland, and in Hiram, Ohio. The manuscript shows that the Brethren had gone entirely through the Bible by 2 July 1833. However, in the eleven years remaining in the Prophet's life he continued to edit and refine the documents.

The marked Bible and the voluminous manuscripts are in the archives of the RLDS church in Independence, and I am personally indebted to the personnel of the RLDS Historical Department for allowing me the privilege and experience of working with these sacred documents. (A more complete description and discussion of the manuscripts and the publication process is contained in R. J. Matthews, "A *Plainer Translation," Joseph Smith's Translation of the Bible* [BYU Press, 1975].)

The JST Is a Restoration of Some of the Bible's Plain and Precious Parts

To illustrate what the Prophet Joseph Smith has done for the Bible, I will compare it to what has recently been done to the famous Michelangelo paintings in the Sistine Chapel in the Vatican. Years of grime, smoke, dust, and "doctoring" by inexperienced and incompetent artisans had obscured the work of Michelangelo in the past four hundred years, until viewers could no longer discern how clear and colorful the originals had been. Some even thought that the artist hadn't liked bright colors, and had painted with darker paint. However, during the past fifteen years these paintings have been cleaned, and now they show the original brightness and clarity. The *National Geographic* magazine issues of December 1989 and May 1994 contain remarkable photos of the restorative process that has taken place with these famous art works. Several years ago I purchased an album of the Sistine paintings. I have enjoyed the masterwork of Michelangelo. However, now that I realized the album shows the paintings before the cleaning I am no longer satisfied with it and I want a new restored edition. In like manner we will no longer be content with other Bibles after we have seen the beauty of the JST.

I refer to these *National Geographic* photos because they illustrate the type of thing the Prophet Joseph Smith has done with the Bible. There are several parallels between what has happened to the Sistine paintings and what has happened to the Bible. Many people today think that the Bibles now in common use in the world are just the way the ancient prophets originally wrote. It is not so. Through centuries of copying and translation, and worst of all through wilful changes and omissions by dishonest persons, the Bible has lost much of its original sparkle and clarity. Thanks be to God, who through Joseph Smith has revealed much, but not yet all, of the original meaning. How could we be content any longer without the greater light the Lord has given us through the Prophet Joseph Smith? Millions of tourists will flock to the Vatican to see the marvelous restoration of those Michelangelo masterpieces. Someday even more millions of Saints will praise the even greater work of restoration and meaning of the Bible wrought by the hand of Joseph Smith.

How Is the JST a Restoration of the Original Text?

The JST seems to consist of several kinds of information. Some of it surely is a restoration of lost material. Other parts may be a clarification for our understanding. If the JST were a literal restoration, it would be in Hebrew, Aramaic, and Greek, instead of in English. I believe that the JST is tantamount to an English translation of what the original authors wrote in their language.

But whether or not the JST is a technical restoration of the original biblical text is not as important as whether or not it is a restoration of original *meaning*. This distinction can be illustrated by the following true story.

For several years my wife and I lived in Soda Springs, Idaho, while I was teaching seminary in the winter and attending BYU in the summer. About the middle of July 1958 we received a letter in Provo from a couple in Soda Springs whom we knew well, and who planned to be in Salt Lake City on 24 July. The letter contained an invitation for us to spend the day with them socially in Salt Lake City. The woman who wrote the letter was the junior high English teacher and very proper in writing and speaking. One sentence of the letter specifically read: "I don't know whether we will watch it on the street, or on television, but when it is over, why don't you meet us at our hotel?"

I remember reading the letter and thinking that she didn't identify what "it" had reference to. She knew what she meant, and we knew what she meant, but the letter did not specify. Readers who did not know of the customs and the events that occur in Salt Lake City on 24 July would not know the full intent or meaning of that sentence. Now the question: If that sentence were to be rendered into any other language, what would be a correct translation? And what would be the aim of such a translation? Would it not be to render in the other language the author's intent and meaning? To correctly do so would require that the words *the parade* be inserted as the translation or interpretation of the word *it*. Yet to do so would add something not in the original text. Although it would add to the text, it would not add to the author's meaning. Some would call this type of action "inspired commentary." But whatever you wish to call it, such is essential to the meaning.

The same type of circumstance applies to many passages of the JST. Perhaps the JST does sometimes go beyond the actual words of the original in order to convey the intent of the author. However, common sense and practical understanding should convince us that words are only expressions of ideas. It is the author's ideas we seek to discern and preserve. The JST, being a product of revelation from the same divine source that inspired the biblical authors, is able to give (or restore) that meaning. The JST can do this better than other translations now do, or ever can do, because translators who are not prophets are limited to the particular wording of an inadequate manu-script. Ancient biblical texts are often inadequate due to ambiguous wording or to alterations of the text. Since no originals of any part of the Bible are available today, only a prophet or seer could now cor-rectly give the original author's intended meaning. Because prophets speak by the Spirit, a translation must have the same spirit to correctly render the thoughts in another language. A seer can restore the proper meaning whether the passage is vague or incorrectly stated, or even if the text is entirely lost. I have noticed that often other Bibles tell *what* occurred anciently, but the JST adds *why*.

Textual Evidence of a Restoration

It is one thing to discuss theory and principle. It is another to find hard textual evidence. A legitimate question could be asked: Does the JST offer any substantial evidence that would indicate a restoration of original material? Indeed it does! It is found in the literary style of the JST. It is significant to notice not only *what* is said in the JST, but *how* it is said, and *where* it is said. For example, much of the new material in the books of Matthew and Luke is in the form of direct dialogue, first-person conversation between Jesus and the Twelve or between Jesus and the Jewish rulers. It is the kind of information that would normally be in quotation marks if the Bible used such marks. A sizable amount of this dialogue is of subject matter not found in any other Bible or any source known to exist today. If Joseph Smith were only commenting on the Bible, or even giving inspired commentary, it would seem strange to put it in the form of direct conversation, unless such conversation actually did occur at some ancient time. When we remember that the Bible is sacred scripture, it is unlikely that the Prophet would invent imaginary and fictitious conversation and place it as coming out of the mouth of Jesus.

Another dimension of the literary style is that every writer has his own style and format. Students of the New Testament soon notice that the flow, the rhythm, the subject matter, and the vocabulary of Matthew is different from that of Luke, or of John, or of Paul. As a reader becomes more familiar with the scriptures, this individuality becomes increasingly evident. I have found that the JST not only preserves the natural style of each book but also in some instances even enhances it. This is evident in those cases where the JST has lengthy additions so that style and substance can be compared. For example:

One of the principal objectives of the book of Matthew is to demonstrate to Jewish readers that Jesus Christ is the promised Messiah spoken of in the Old Testament. As a consequence, Matthew contains more references to the Old Testament prophets than either Mark, Luke, or John. Frequently Matthew introduces these Old Testament quotations with an attitude of proof such as, "Now all this was done, that it might be fulfilled that was written by the prophets . . ." This pattern is visible in every version of the Bible available today. Does it seem significant that the JST not only preserves all of the passages of this type that are found in the King James Version, but adds nine others besides? (See JST, Matthew 1:4; 2:1; 3:4, 5, 6, 34; 4:18; 23:39; 27:12). Thus the JST not only preserves Matthew's intent but also magnifies its effectiveness over what is found in the King James Version. I think this fact is a reflection that JST Matthew presents a clearer, brighter, more complete restoration of the original than any other Bible. But the clincher, the confirming witness in this case, is that the JST does not develop this particular trait in any of the other books to the same extent that it does in Matthew. There is a little of it in the others, but not to the same extent. If the Prophet Joseph Smith were simply going through the Bible to update it on doctrinal matters, then an item might as well occur in one place as another. But a restoration would follow the individual pattern of the original author, as we have seen.

Other such literary evidences exist, but they are too numerous to mention here. They occur in both the Old and New Testaments, but are most easily discovered in the books of Matthew, Mark, Luke, and John because of the subject matter. I will mention briefly one aspect of JST Luke. The subject matter and vocabulary of the book of Luke shows a universality as to the mission of Jesus. He is not only the Messiah of Israel but also the Savior of the Gentiles. The King James Version and all other versions of Luke contain this trait. Well, as you might expect, the JST offers several additional statements in Luke that are favorable to the Gentiles. And as you might further expect, such JST references about the Gentiles occur primarily in Luke and not in the other books.

Furthermore, scholars have noted an affinity between the vocabulary and subject matter of Luke's writings and the writings of Paul. This affinity is even greater in the JST. For example, there are three well-known phrases that in other Bibles occur in Paul's writings but not in the book of Luke. The phrases are "the fulness of times" (Ephesians 1:10); "a thief in the night" (1 Thessalonians 5:2; 2 Peter 3:10); and "muzzle the ox" (1 Timothy 5:18). Not only does the JST contain all of the other similarities between Luke's and Paul's writings, but these three passages are also included in the JST rendition of Luke. But they are not included in Matthew, Mark, or John.

Now, what do we make of this? We all know that spiritual truth cannot be proven by secular means. Circumstantial evidence may be assembled, but ultimately spiritual conviction comes only by the Holy Spirit and by testimony. It seems to me that these literary items bespeak a restorative nature in the JST. To think otherwise is to suggest that Joseph Smith was a literary genius. He would have to be an ultra-literary genius to create a different literary style consistent with each book. Either Joseph Smith is a prophet of God or he is not. Since we know that he is a prophet, what have we against believing that he was inspired to give us at least a partial restoration of the original?

It might be asked if there is any precedent for lost scripture being restored, such as Joseph Smith was doing with the JST. The answer is "Yes," and it can be found in Jeremiah 36:1–32. Jeremiah the prophet used a scribe named Baruch to record the word of the Lord concerning the king and the house of Judah. The people wanted verification or authentication for the words, "and they asked Baruch, saying, Tell us now, How didst thou write all these words at his mouth? Then Baruch answered them, He pronounced all the words unto me with his mouth, and I wrote them with ink in the book" (Jeremiah 36:17–18). The king, Jehoiakim, did not like what Jeremiah had caused to be written, so he took a knife, cut the document in pieces, and destroyed it in the fire. When Jeremiah learned what had been done, he was undaunted. The word of the Lord came and he was commanded to take "another roll, and write in it all the former words that were in the first roll" (vv. 27, 28). Jeremiah did as he was instructed, dictated to Baruch, who "wrote therein from the mouth of Jeremiah all the words of the book which Jehoiakim king of Judah had burned in the fire: and there were added besides unto them many like words" (v. 32).

If the Lord can do this kind of work in 600 B.C. with Jeremiah, can he not do it in A.D. 1830 with Joseph Smith also? Joseph Smith was no less of a prophet than Jeremiah.

To bring this discussion about restoration to a close, I would cite the fact that the JST changes the titles of each of the books of Matthew, Mark, Luke, and John from "the gospel according to," to "the testimony of," so that the title reads, "The Testimony of St. Matthew," and so on. Matthew in KJV has 1,050 verses. Joseph Smith added 55 verses and substantially altered over five hundred others. For Joseph Smith to alter over 50 percent of the book of Matthew, increase its volume by 10 percent, and call the new version the "Testimony of Matthew" emphasizes original authorship and seems to say that the Prophet Joseph Smith regarded his work as a divinely revealed restoration of what Matthew and the others originally wrote. I know by the Spirit that he was a chosen and faithful prophet and was called of God to make the Bible translation. Some are hesitant to receive the JST as a restoration because it is not supported by the available Greek and Hebrew manuscripts, none of which are originals. We might ask ourselves why any of these secondary documents can command greater respect and acceptance with us than the work of Joseph Smith the Seer? If known biblical manuscripts had this material the JST would not have been so sorely needed.

Use of the JST in the Church in the 1830s, the 1840s, and Since

Let us now shift to another theme, the early use of the JST. The early brethren made good use of the JST, even though it was not published as a separate book. Excerpts from JST Genesis, Romans, and Hebrews are used in the *Lectures on Faith*, which were published as part of the Doctrine and Covenants from 1835 to 1921. These can be found in *Lectures* at the following references: 1:8; 2:5–11, 21–24; and 3:1.

Excerpts from the JST were also printed in the early Church magazines: *The Evening and the Morning Star*, 1832–33; *Times and Seasons*, 1843; and *Millennial Star*, 1851. A one-page tract consisting of Matthew 24 was also published and distributed in Kirtland about 1835.

Several years ago, a group of BYU students searched through the general conference addresses to see how often the Brethren quoted from the Pearl of Great Price, and what specific passages were used. These students learned that one of the most frequently cited scriptures was, "For behold, this is my work and my glory—to bring to pass the immortality and eternal life of man" (Moses 1:39). That inspired utterance is one of the hallmarks of the gospel in these latter days. But all of you realize, of course, that what we call the book of Moses is none other than an excerpt from the Joseph Smith Translation of Genesis. We are quoting the JST when we quote any part of the book of Moses. The JST has had a significant impact on the doctrine and the literature of this Church, yet we have so far realized but the tip of the iceberg.

How Did the Notion Arise That the RLDS Altered the Joseph Smith Translation?

A question which has often arisen is: "Did the RLDS church alter the Joseph Smith Translation in their printing of it?" This has been a very common misunderstanding and an oft-repeated accusation.

I think I can explain how that mistaken notion got started. When we work our way through it, we need no longer be hampered by it. Remember that the manuscripts of the Joseph Smith Translation consist of preliminary drafts and later drafts. These represent different stages of the revision. Earlier manuscripts have fewer revisions than the later ones. The earlier manuscripts naturally do not reflect the later corrections.

In the early days of the Church, excerpts from the Joseph Smith Translation were published in *The Evening and the Morning Star* and the *Times and Seasons*, and in the *Lectures on Faith*. Also, short excerpts were copied for personal use by various individuals, such as John Whitmer, Edward Partridge, Newel K. Whitney, and others. These were all done using early, preliminary drafts as the source. After Joseph Smith's death, the entire manuscript was retained by Emma Smith, and eventually it was given to the RLDS church in 1866. It was not available to the LDS church in Utah.

In 1851, when the Moses and Matthew material in the Pearl of Great Price was first published by Elder Franklin D. Richards in Liverpool, England, the source documents were the early printings from the Church newspapers, which were based on the preliminary documents representing the early stages of the translation. When the RLDS church printed the Joseph Smith Translation in 1867, it used the later manuscripts containing the final revisions and corrections made by the Prophet Joseph Smith. Hence, when LDS people—using *The Evening and the Morning Star, Times and Seasons, Lectures on Faith,* and the Pearl of Great Price as their standard—compared their text with the RLDS printed text, they naturally concluded that the RLDS church had made many alterations. The mistaken notion came about because of a lack of understanding about the nature and condition of the original manuscripts. Since the RLDS church would not allow LDS persons to see the JST manuscripts, the suspicion increased. Had the Bernhisel copy of 1845 been more widely known, it could have been of service, because, though incomplete, it reflects the later JST text and thus certifies the progressive nature of the manuscripts and the authenticity of the later changes.

It would be well if we could free ourselves of the idea that the RLDS changed the text. We could then put our energies into studying the material, being thereby lifted spiritually. I should add that the Pearl of Great Price and the *Lectures on Faith* have since been updated. They now reflect the later revision and agree with the published Joseph Smith Translation. This update was done by Elder Orson Pratt in 1878. I have diligently compared the manuscripts of the JST with the RLDS printed editions of the Bible, and I conclude that those editions were conscientiously prepared and accurately portray the manuscripts.

The Mortar Effect

To close this discussion I will tell of an experience in which I learned about the use of mortar—the stuff that holds the bricks or blocks together in a wall or a house. Without mortar the blocks would soon slip and separate and the structure would be rendered ineffective, if not unusable.

A few years ago I saw a wall in north Orem that was made of cement blocks, but no mortar. This was on the road to my home in Lindon, so I passed it almost every day. The wall looked nice, and for a few weeks everything seemed all right. Then I noticed that some of the blocks were developing wide spaces between them. The wall began to look uneven, not as smooth at first. Later, some blocks had fallen to the ground. The rumble of big trucks, the force of the wind, the effect of people leaning on the wall—all this took its toll. Eventually the wall had to be redone—with mortar. Today it still stands as solid as the day when it was reconstructed. I see a lesson here with regard to the Bible.

I have noticed that many items in the King James Bible seem to be unconnected and unrelated, even though they may be in the same chapter or book. In the King James Version and other versions there is no evidence that Adam knew Enoch, or that Enoch knew of the ministry of Adam or the future work of Noah. There is not any hint that any of these prophets knew of each other or of the work that each would do, or that they had the gospel, or the priesthood, and so forth. The lack of these huge, substantial "blocks" of information in KJV Genesis leaves it with neither continuity nor unity of purpose. There is no mortar.

One of the contributions of the JST is that it tells us all of these great patriarchs were witnesses for Jesus Christ, they each had the same priesthood, they all had the same gospel ordinances, they knew of each other; and there is continuity. This close relationship was contained in Genesis when the book was first written. But the effect of taking out the precious parts was the same as removing the mortar from between the blocks. The continuity, relationship, and purpose were all but lost.

Similar situations exist in the New Testament. One of the most striking is found in Matthew 9:14–17, and another in Luke 16:13–19. In each of these passages several events follow in sequence, with no apparent connection or meaningful relationship in the King James Version. But in the JST there are connecting links and inserts so that the narrative is made clear and is easily understood.

One of the greatest contributions of the JST is the enhancement of Jesus' personality. The Savior is wonderful in any Bible, but in the JST he is magnificently greater. If you have not discovered the superiority of the JST in its witness of Jesus Christ, then be assured that you have yet a great experience awaiting you.

Testimony

I close with a testimony of the worth of the JST. As in all scripture, the JST is a witness for the Lord Jesus Christ. It is not a perfect record, but it is much better than anything else we have in a Bible. Many years ago, when I was a teenage boy, the Lord touched my heart regarding the JST, and I learned then, and have never lost sight, that Joseph Smith received direct revelation from God in making the corrections in the Bible.

Notes

1. HC 1:132–33 (December 1830).
2. TPJS, pp. 9–10 (16 February 1832).
3. TPJS, pp. 290–91 (8 April 1843).
4. TPJS, p. 310 (11 June 1843).
5. TPJS, p. 327 (15 October 1843).
6. Gordon B. Hinckley, *Truth Restored* (Salt Lake City: The Church of Jesus Christ of Latter-day Saints, 1979), p. 39.

4

The Joseph Smith Translation's Doctrinal Contributions to the Old Testament

MONTE S. NYMAN

*J*oseph Smith's translation of the Bible was a great contribution to the understanding of correct doctrine in the newly restored Church. The Old Testament had a unique role in this project. Many of the changes made in the Joseph Smith Translation of the Old Testament have indirect doctrinal implication, but in this analysis I will consider only those changes that directly state doctrine. Also, because of the wide variety of doctrinal changes, I will group them into significant categories. Although the final category will be a miscellaneous grouping, I will not attempt to include every one of the Prophet's doctrinal changes, nor changes that reflect only historical or textual accuracies and clarifications.

Another exclusion is the book of Moses as published in the Pearl of Great Price. Many members of the Church probably are not cognizant that the book of Moses is the final product of Joseph's work on the first six chapters of Genesis (Genesis 1:1–6:13 as translated became Moses 2:1–8:30 in the Pearl of Great Price). The spiritual and physical creations, the Grand Council in heaven, and Satan's rebellion are clarified in the book of Moses; also that there were children born to Adam and Eve before Cain and Abel, that Cain organized secret combinations, that the gospel of Jesus Christ was preached by Adam, Enoch, and Noah. These and the marvelous prophecies of

Enoch and his people being translated are among the great doctrines of the book of Moses. These chapters from the JST contain some of the most significant doctrines of the Restoration.

Genesis 6:13–19:11

The Prophet did extensive work on the translation between Genesis 6:13 and Genesis 19:11, perhaps more than on any other section of the Old Testament. There are four major doctrinal contributions in these chapters. The first one may be termed a word of wisdom given to Noah and his people; it also further confirms the Lord's stand on capital punishment. A comparison of the KJV text and the JST text is beneficial.

KJV Genesis 9:4–7	JST Genesis 9:10–14
But flesh with the life thereof, which is the blood thereof, shall ye not eat.	But, the blood of all flesh which I have given you for meat, shall be shed upon the ground, which taketh life thereof, and the blood ye shall not eat.
And surely your blood of your lives will I require; at the hand of every beast will I require it, and at the hand of man; at the hand of every man's brother will I require the life of man.	And surely, blood shall not be shed, only for meat, to save your lives; and the blood of every beast will I require at your hands.
Whoso sheddeth man's blood, by man shall his blood be shed: for in the image of God made he man.	And whoso sheddeth man's blood, by man shall his blood be shed; for man shall not shed the blood of man.
And you, be ye fruitful, and multiply; bring forth abundantly in the earth, and multiply therein.	For a commandment I give, that every man's brother shall preserve the life of man, for in mine own image have I made man.
	And a commandment I give unto you, Be ye fruitful and multiply; bring forth abundantly on the earth, and multiply therein.

The sacredness of the life of both man and beast in the eyes of the Lord and man's accountability for both is sustained in these JST restorations.

A second major contribution of this section is the covenant of the Lord, extended to Noah "even as I have sworn unto thy father Enoch, that of thy posterity shall come all nations" (JST, Genesis 8:23; see Genesis 6:18 and LDS Bible footnote). The three sons of Noah and their posterity became the fathers of all nations following the Flood. These nations are designated in Genesis chapter 10, which is some-times called the table of nations. The Lord affirms this continuation of the covenant through Noah and his seed three more times in Genesis chapter 9 (v. 9, JST Genesis 9:15 LDS Bible footnote; v. 11, JST Genesis 9:17 LDS Bible footnote; and v. 15, JST Genesis 9:20 LDS Bible footnote). The covenant of Enoch was also extended to Abraham, a descendant of Noah through Shem (JST, Genesis 13:14; see Genesis 13:13 and LDS Bible footnote).

An extension of the covenant made with Enoch was to be fulfilled in the latter days, the return to the earth of the translated city of Enoch and the general assembly of the church of the Firstborn. Again a comparison of the KJV text and the JST text illustrates the impor-tance of this restoration.

KJV Genesis 9:16–17	JST Genesis 9:21–25
And the bow shall be in the cloud; and I will look upon it, that I may remember the everlasting covenant between God and every living creature of all flesh that is upon the earth.	And the bow shall be in the cloud; and I will look upon it, that I may remember the everlasting covenant, which I made unto thy father Enoch; that, when men should keep all my command-ments, Zion should again come on the earth, the city of Enoch which I have caught up unto myself.
And God said unto Noah, This is the token of the covenant, which I have established between me and all flesh that is upon the earth.	And this is mine everlasting covenant, that when thy posterity shall embrace the truth, and look upward, then shall Zion look down-ward, and all the heavens shall shake with gladness, and the earth shall tremble with joy.

> And the general assembly of the church of the first-born shall come down out of heaven, and possess the earth, and shall have place until the end come. And this is mine everlasting covenant, which I made with thy father Enoch.
>
> And the bow shall be in the cloud, and I will establish my covenant unto thee, which I have made between me and thee, for every living creature of all flesh that shall be upon the earth.

The people of Enoch and the members of the general assembly of the church of the Firstborn, now resurrected beings (D&C 76:54–55), will establish residence "or have place until the end come," or until the end of the Millennium. Their functions and the time they will spend on earth will be known or revealed at a future time. The Prophet Joseph Smith made further comment regarding the covenant of Enoch and the bow in the cloud. The bow shall be in the cloud "for a sign that while it shall be seen, seed time and harvest, summer and winter shall not fail; but when it shall disappear, woe to that generation, for behold the end cometh quickly."[1] The rainbow as a sign of production crops for that year is of extreme doctrinal significance.

The third major contribution of this section is about Melchizedek, a person of little-known background in the Bible (see Hebrews 7). The JST wording may be suggesting that a form of the sacrament was administered by Melchizedek to Abraham. He "break bread and blest it; and he blest the wine, he being the priest of the most high God" (JST, Genesis 14:17). Sixteen verses about Melchizedek are added to the end of KJV Genesis chapter 14. Since these verses are included in the Joseph Smith Translation appendix of the LDS Bible, they will not be included here. These verses illustrate the greatness of Melchizedek. Doctrinally, they substantiate what we learn about him and the order of the priesthood in Alma 13:14–19; they clarify the things said about him in Hebrews chapter 7; and they confirm

Doctrine and Covenants 107:1–4, which tells why the priesthood was called after his name. They also teach us about the doctrine of translation, a blessing enjoyed by some of Melchizedek's people.

The fourth major contribution of the extensive JST Genesis chapters 6–19 concerns the apostasy in the days of Abraham. These apostates trusted in the blood of Abel rather than the atoning blood of Christ, and instituted the practice of baptizing little children. The JST shows that the law of circumcision at the age of eight days was initiated with Abraham as a covenant with God to remind parents that children are not accountable before him until they are eight years old (JST, Genesis 17:3–12). Since these verses are in the appendix of the LDS Bible, they will not be quoted here.

There are other historical and textual corrections in the above section of Genesis, such as Abraham rejoicing, instead of laughing, over the Lord's promise of a son (JST, Genesis 17:23) and the account of Lot and his daughters in Sodom (JST, Genesis 19), but those discussed above are the most important doctrinal restorations of these chapters of Genesis.

Genesis 48 and 50

Eight of the first ten verses (all but vv. 3 and 8) of Genesis 48 have additional or corrective verses added, making the text more accurate. Two of those verses more firmly establish Ephraim and Manasseh as two of the twelve tribes of Israel.[2]

KJV Genesis 48:5–6	JST Genesis 48:5–6
And now thy two sons, Ephraim and Manasseh, which were born unto thee in the land of Egypt before I came unto thee into Egypt, are mine; as Reuben and Simeon, they shall be mine.	And now, of thy two sons, Ephraim and Manasseh, which were born unto thee in the land of Egypt, before I came unto thee into Egypt; behold, they are mine, and the God of my fathers shall bless them; even as Reuben and Simeon
And thy issue, which thou	

begettest after them, shall be thine, and shall be called after the name of their brethren in their inheritance.

they shall be blessed, for they are mine; wherefore they shall be called after my name. (Therefore they were called Israel.)

And thy issue which thou begettest after them, shall be thine, and shall be called after the name of their brethren in their inheritance, in the tribes; therefore they were called the tribes of Manasseh and of Ephraim.

The JST adds another five verses following verse 6. The basic doctrine in this addition is the role of Joseph and his seed in bringing salvation to the rest of the children of Israel (see JST, Genesis 48:7–11 in the JST appendix, page 799, LDS Bible).

In the JST, the last three verses of Genesis 50 (24–26) are expanded into fifteen verses (24–38). These fifteen verses are essentially the same as 2 Nephi 3:5–21, although with some important differences. Lehi apparently quoted from the plates of brass, but either he paraphrased some of the verses or else Joseph Smith clarified their meaning in his translation. The prophecy of Joseph of Egypt establishes the concept of Moses leading the children of Israel out of Egypt and Joseph Smith bringing forth the Book of Mormon and the restoration of the gospel in the latter days. The complete JST textual addition is included in the LDS Bible appendix, pages 799 and 800.

Jesus Christ—Jehovah of the Old Testament

When the Lord God appeared to Moses, he identified himself as Jehovah who had earlier appeared to Abraham, Isaac, and Jacob. The JST clarifies a confusing verse in this introduction and establishes the doctrine of Jehovah (Jesus Christ) being the God of the Old Testament house of Israel.

KJV Exodus 6:3–4	JST Exodus 6:3–4
And I appeared unto Abraham, unto Isaac, and unto Jacob, by the name of God Almighty, but by my name JEHOVAH was I not known to them. And I have also established my covenant with them, to give them the land of Canaan, the land of their pilgrimage, wherein they were strangers.	And I appeared unto Abraham, unto Isaac, and unto Jacob. I am the Lord God Almighty; the Lord JEHOVAH. And was not my name known unto them? Yea, and I have also established my covenant with them, which I made with them, to give them the land of Canaan, the land of their pilgrimage, wherein they were strangers.

In a later appearance to Moses, the Lord teaches the doctrine of how mortals are able to behold His face and live.

KJV Exodus 33:20–23	JST Exodus 33:20–23
And he said, Thou canst not see my face: for there shall no man see me, and live. And the Lord said, Behold, there is a place by me, and thou shalt stand upon a rock: And it shall come to pass, while my glory passeth by, that I will put thee in a clift of the rock, and will cover thee with my hand while I pass by: And I will take away mine hand, and thou shalt see my back parts: but my face shall not be seen.	And he said unto Moses, Thou canst not see my face at this time, lest mine anger be kindled against thee also, and I destroy thee, and thy people; for there shall no man among them see me at this time, and live, for they are exceeding sinful. And no sinful man hath at any time, neither shall there be any sinful man at any time, that shall see my face and live. And the Lord said, Behold, thou shalt stand upon a rock, and I will prepare a place by me for thee. And it shall come to pass, while my glory passeth by, that I will put thee in a cleft of a rock, and cover thee with my hand, while I pass by.

> And I will take away mine hand, and thou shalt see my back parts, but my face shall not be seen, as at other times; for I am angry with my people Israel.

The doctrine taught above is also confirmed in other latter-day revelation (D&C 67:10–12).

Jehovah Is an Unchanging God

Many verses in the KJV depict the Lord repenting and changing his decrees. The JST changes almost all of these verses to establish that Jehovah or Jesus Christ is the same yesterday, today, and forever, as taught in the New Testament (Hebrews 13:8). The account of Moses speaking with the Lord concerning his threat to destroy the children of Israel, who were worshipping the golden calf, illustrates the mercy of the Lord replacing the law of justice upon the condition of the people repenting.

KJV Exodus 32:14	JST Exodus 32:14
And the Lord repented of the evil which he thought to do unto his people.	And the Lord said unto Moses, If they will repent of the evil which they have done, I will spare them, and turn away my fierce wrath; but, behold, thou shalt execute judgment upon all that will not repent of this evil this day. Therefore, see thou do this thing that I have commanded thee, or I will execute all that which I had thought to do unto my people.

From the many other similar changes,[3] it seems that Joseph went through the Old Testament text to rectify most verses concerning the Lord repenting that had been incorrectly translated.

Another doctrine of the attributes of Jehovah prevalent in the book of Exodus relates to the Lord's causing the heart of Pharaoh to be hardened. While the KJV text makes the Lord responsible for Pharaoh's actions, the JST shows that it was the Pharaoh's choice to harden his heart. However, as taught by Brigham Young and Willard Richards, "He [the Lord] manifested Himself in so many glorious and mighty ways, that Pharaoh could not resist the truth without becoming harder."[4] There are many such references[5] but one will suffice as an example.

KJV Exodus 4:21	JST Exodus 4:21
And the Lord said unto Moses, When thou goest to return into Egypt, see that thou do all those wonders before Pharaoh, which I have put in thine hand: but I will harden his heart, that he shall not let the people go.	And the Lord said unto Moses, When thou goest to return into Egypt, see that thou do all those wonders before Pharaoh, which I have put in thine hand, and I will prosper thee; but Pharaoh will harden his heart, and he will not let the people go.

The omniscience of Jehovah is further confirmed in the JST. In Amos 3:6 we read:

KJV Amos 3:6	JST Amos 3:6
Shall a trumpet be blown in the city, and the people not be afraid? shall there be evil in a city, and the Lord hath not done it?	Shall a trumpet be blown in the city, and the people not be afraid? shall there be evil in a city, and the Lord hath not known it?

Not only does this change verify the omniscience of Jehovah, but it also corrects the notion that evil comes from the Lord, a contradiction to the Book of Mormon statement "that which is evil cometh of the devil" (Moroni 7:12).

The Melchizedek Priesthood Covenant

The KJV text implies that when Moses came off the mountain and broke the tables upon which God had written the law with his finger, God's writing on the second tables Moses subsequently made was the same as that on the first tables. The JST shows that this was not so; the second set of tables did not contain the doctrine of the oath and covenant of the Melchizedek Priesthood.

KJV Deuteronomy 10:1–2	JST Deuteronomy 10:1–2
At that time the Lord said unto me, Hew thee two tables of stone like unto the first, and come up unto me into the mount, and make thee an ark of wood.	At that time the Lord said unto me, Hew thee two other tables of stone like unto the first, and come up unto me upon the mount, and make thee an ark of wood.
And I will write on the tables the words that were in the first tables which thou brakest, and thou shalt put them in the ark.	And I will write on the tables the words that were on the first tables, which thou breakest, save the words of the everlasting covenant of the holy priesthood, and thou shalt put them in the ark.

Doctrine and Covenants 84:33–42 and also the Prophet Joseph Smith, as recorded in *Teachings of the Prophet Joseph Smith*, page 323, confirm the JST correction.

Spirits Not of the Lord

An important JST doctrinal correction in the Old Testament is the distinction between the spirits from the Lord and those of Satan. When David was anointed king of Israel the Spirit of the Lord came upon him and departed from Saul, whom David had replaced by divine decree. Following this action, the KJV records four times that an evil spirit from the Lord troubled Saul or came upon him (1 Samuel 16:14–16, 23). The JST changed those verses to read, "an evil spirit which was not of the Lord" troubled him.

Another incident about Saul illustrates the operation of evil spirits among the Old Testament people. They were known as familiar
spirits and were a part of the practice of witchcraft. According to the
KJV, Saul went to the witch of Endor and requested to speak with
Samuel, whom the witch then endeavored to call forth out of his
grave in the earth. Saul had previously decreed that all of those who
practiced witchcraft or dealt with familiar spirits should be put to
death, so the woman denied that she dealt with familiar spirits.[6] After
Saul had assured the woman that he would not disclose her, she
agreed to bring up Samuel. Upon doing so she recognized Saul and
was again assured of her safety by him. Samuel then spoke to Saul.
However, from the JST account it appears to be a false spirit representing Samuel, although the message is not false.

KJV 1 Samuel 28:11–15

Then said the woman, Whom
shall I bring up unto thee? And he
said, Bring me up Samuel.

And when the woman saw
Samuel, she cried with a loud voice:
and the woman spake to Saul, saying, Why hast thou deceived me?
for thou art Saul.

And the king said unto her, Be
not afraid: for what sawest thou?
And the woman said unto Saul, I
saw gods ascending out of the earth.

And he said unto her, What
form is he of? And she said, An old
man cometh up; and he is covered
with a mantle. And Saul perceived
that it was Samuel, and he stooped
with his face to the ground, and
bowed himself.

And Samuel said to Saul, Why
hast thou disquieted me, to bring
me up? And Saul answered, I am
sore distressed; for the Philistines

JST 1 Samuel 28:11–15

Then said the woman, The
word of whom shall I bring up unto
thee? And he said, Bring me up the
word of Samuel.

And when the woman saw the
words of Samuel, she cried with a
loud voice; and the woman spake to
Saul, saying, Why hast thou deceived me? for thou art Saul.

And the king said unto her, Be
not afraid; for what sawest thou?
And the woman said unto Saul, I
saw the words of Samuel ascending
out of the earth. And she said, I saw
Samuel also.

And he said unto her, What
form is he of? And she said, I saw an
old man coming up, covered with a
mantle. And Saul perceived that it
was Samuel, and he stooped, his face
to the ground, and bowed himself.

And these are the words of
Samuel unto Saul, Why hast thou

make war against me, and God is departed from me, and answereth me no more, neither by prophets, nor by dreams: therefore I have called thee, that thou mayest make known unto me what I shall do.

disquieted me, to bring me up? And Saul answered, I am sore distressed; for the Philistines make war against me, and God is departed from me, and answereth me no more, neither by prophets, nor by dreams; therefore I have called thee, that thou mayest make known unto me what I shall do.

The Lord does not give messages through false mediums, but the devil might give true messages in order to deceive. Because the JST says it is the "words of Samuel" instead of Samuel himself, it suggests that there was probably deception.

There is another incident concerning false spirits that Joseph Smith clarified in the translation. Standing before King Ahab of Israel and King Jehoshaphat of Judah, the prophet Micaiah prophesied and told of a heavenly vision he had seen in which, according to the KJV, "there came out a spirit, and stood before the Lord" (2 Chronicles 18:20). Joseph Smith corrected this to read, "there came out a *lying* spirit, and stood before *them*."[7] The following verse speaks of that spirit volunteering to be a lying spirit in the mouth of all the Lord's prophets, and the JST adds the Lord saying, "all these have sinned against me" (JST, 2 Chronicles 18:21). The next verse also has a significant correction. The KJV has Micaiah say to the two kings, "The Lord hath put a lying spirit in the mouth of these thy prophets" (2 Chronicles 18:22). The JST corrects the sentence to read, "The Lord hath found a lying spirit in the mouth of these thy prophets." Thus the prophets spoken of are false ones, and the Lord is not responsible for their lies.

Servants Sent to the Gentiles

Part of the mission of Christ was to "bring forth judgment to the Gentiles" (Isaiah 42:1). Later in the chapter, those who are deaf and blind are invited to hear and to look that they may see (42:18). The text that follows in the KJV is confusing without Joseph's translation.

KJV Isaiah 42:19–22	JST Isaiah 42:19–23
Who is blind, but my servant? or deaf, as my messenger that I sent? who is blind as he that is perfect, and blind as the Lord's servant?	For I will send my servant unto you who are blind; yea, a messenger to open the eyes of the blind, and unstop the ears of the deaf;
Seeing many things, but thou observest not; opening the ears, but he heareth not.	And they shall be made perfect notwithstanding their blindness, if they will hearken unto the messenger, the Lord's servant.
The Lord is well pleased for his righteousness' sake; he will magnify the law, and make it honourable.	Thou art a people, seeing many things, but thou observest not; opening the ears to hear, but thou hearest not.
But this is a people robbed and spoiled; they are all of them snared in holes, and they are hid in prison houses; they are for a prey, and none delivereth; for a spoil, and none saith, Restore.	The Lord is not well pleased with such a people, but for his righteousness' sake he will magnify the law and make it honorable.
	Thou art a people robbed and spoiled; thine enemies, all of them, have snared thee in holes, and they have hid thee in prison houses; they have taken thee for a prey, and none delivereth; for a spoil, and none saith, Restore.

From Joseph Smith's translation we learn that the servants (Israel) will be sent to the Gentiles who are spiritually blind and deaf and will thereby be given an opportunity to receive the blessings of Israel.

In a later chapter of Isaiah the same concept of the Gentiles being given an opportunity to have the gospel or the blessings of Israel is qualified in the JST.

KJV Isaiah 65:1–2	JST Isaiah 65:1–2
I am sought of them that asked not for me; I am found of them that sought me not: I said, Behold me,	I am found of them who seek after me, I give unto all them that ask of me; I am not found of them

behold me, unto a nation that was not called by my name.

I have spread out my hands all the day unto a rebellious people, which walketh in a way that was not good, after their own thoughts;

that sought me not, or that inquireth not after me.

I said unto my servant, Behold me, look upon me; I will send you unto a nation that is not called after my name, for I have spread out my hands all the day to a people who walketh not in my ways, and their works are evil and not good, and they walk after their own thoughts.

Paul's quoting to the Romans this passage of Isaiah supports the JST text (see Romans 10:20–21). The Gentiles' opportunity to receive the gospel is a major doctrine of the JST.

Miscellaneous

A few other important doctrines will be considered.

The KJV states that of those who are in the book of the Lord, none will want her mate. The JST shows this to be the names of those who have had their calling and election made sure and therefore will have their mates sealed to them and will not yearn for them because they will be together.

KJV Isaiah 34:16

Seek ye out of the book of the Lord, and read: no one of these shall fail, none shall want her mate: for my mouth it hath commanded, and his spirit it hath gathered them.

JST Isaiah 34:16

Seek ye out of the book of the Lord, and read the names written therein; no one of these shall fail; none shall want their mate; for my mouth it hath commanded, and my Spirit it hath gathered them.

The following verse (17) also changes the pronoun "he" to "I" and indicates that the Lord has given the (celestial) earth to the righteous (those who are sealed and endure in faith to the end).

The middle chapters of Isaiah that are taken from the book of Kings (Isaiah 36–39, 2 Kings 18:13–20:19) speak of a remnant going out of Jerusalem. The JST revisions of these verses seem to be a prophecy about the Mulekites, who are spoken of in the Book of Mormon (Mosiah 25:2; Helaman 6:10; 8:21). This is also the interpretation by Elder Orson Pratt.[8]

KJV Isaiah 37:32–33	JST Isaiah 37:32–33
For out of Jerusalem shall go forth a remnant, and they that escape out of mount Zion: the zeal of the Lord of hosts shall do this.	For out of Jerusalem shall go forth a remnant; and they that escape out of Jerusalem shall come up upon mount Zion; the zeal of the Lord of hosts shall do this.
Therefore thus saith the Lord concerning the king of Assyria, He shall not come into this city, nor shoot an arrow there, nor come before it with shields, nor cast a bank against it.	Therefore thus saith the Lord concerning the king of Assyria, He shall not come into this city, nor shoot an arrow there, nor come before it with shields nor cast a bank against it.

Isaiah 52:15 speaks of the sprinkling of many nations. The JST changes the word *sprinkle* to *gather*, which fits the context of the verse much better and agrees with the teachings of the Savior to the Nephites—that when the prophecies of Isaiah are fulfilled, then will the covenants with the house of Israel also be fulfilled (3 Nephi 20:11–12). Joseph Smith also changed Zechariah 8 verses 7 and 13 from the Lord will "save" his people to the Lord will "gather" his people. Although the word *save* might imply a gathering, a people may be gathered and some of them not saved. The word *gather* is therefore a better translation.

A verse in the book of Amos well known among the Latter-day Saints is "Surely the Lord God will do nothing, but he revealeth his secret unto his servants the prophets" (Amos 3:7). Although Joseph Smith made just one slight change in this verse, it is important doctrinally. He changed the word *but* to *until*. The Lord works through his prophets. As stated in Doctrine and Covenants 1:38, the Lord's word "shall all be fulfilled, whether by mine own voice or by the voice of my servants, it is the same." The doctrine of the Lord working through his servants was further emphasized in JST, Zechariah 3:9 and 4:10, where Joseph interpreted a vision given to Zechariah of a stone having seven eyes as seven servants of the Lord; and in a later vision to Zechariah he interpreted "four spirits of the heavens" (Zechariah 6:5) to be "four servants of the heavens." The Lord does work through his servants the prophets.

Joseph Smith made many corrections to the book of Psalms. The fourteenth and fifty-third psalm are essentially the same in the KJV. Joseph Smith corrected both of these Psalms but did not make the same corrections in each. Those corrections in the fourteenth psalm were the most extensive and seem to have relevance to Joseph Smith's first vision, while the corrections of the fifty-third Psalm retained the general concept that those who deny the things of God are fools.

Many of the corrections in the Psalms are "tense" changes reflecting a latter-day fulfillment rather than merely a musical rendition by David (for example see Psalms 10 through 12). The ending of the twenty-fourth Psalm makes its fulfillment millennial, as preceded by the second coming of Christ. The corrections in the Psalms make them more applicable to the latter days and the members of the Church than is the case with the KJV.

Doctrinal changes in the JST Old Testament are significant and extremely beneficial for an understanding of the gospel of Jesus Christ in a biblical setting. We should study the changes and correlate them with modern scripture in order to gain the greatest benefit.

Notes

1. TPJS, p. 305.
2. Levi was appointed as the priesthood administrator among all the other tribes, therefore Manasseh (Numbers 8:4–16) replaced Levi as one of the twelve tribes and Ephraim carried on in place of his father, Joseph.

3. See Judges 2:18; 1 Samuel 15:11, 35; 2 Samuel 24:16; Jeremiah 18:8; 26:3, 13, 19; Hosea 11:8; Amos 7:3, 6; Joel 2:13–14; Jonah 3:9–10; Psalm 90:13.

4. HC 4:264.

5. See Exodus 7:3, 13; 9:12; 10:1, 20, 27; 11:10; 14:4, 8, 17; Joshua 11:20.

6. The witch's denial that she dealt with familiar spirits is added in JST, 1 Samuel 28:9.

7. This JST change was not footnoted in the LDS Bible, although other verse changes in this chapter were included.

8. *Orson Pratt's Works*, pp. 280–81.

5

Doctrinal Contributions of the Joseph Smith Translation of the New Testament

ANDREW C. SKINNER

*I*t is not only appropriate but imperative that we discuss at this symposium the doctrinal contributions of the Joseph Smith Translation of the New Testament; for *the* thing that makes the JST better than any Bible in the whole world is doctrine—doctrine received by revelation and passed on to us in purity and clarity. I have divided my remarks into three categories: 1) General doctrinal contributions of the Joseph Smith Translation of the New Testament; 2) Contributions to our understanding of the life, ministry, and personality of Jesus; and 3) Contributions of the JST New Testament in explaining and augmenting specific doctrines of the plan of salvation.

General Doctrinal Contributions

In December 1830, as the Prophet was engaged almost daily in making his translation of the Bible, the Lord spoke the following words to Sidney Rigdon: "And a commandment I give unto thee— that thou shalt write for him; and the scriptures shall be given, even as they are in mine own bosom, to the salvation of mine own elect" (D&C 35:20).

By the Lord's own declaration, the Joseph Smith Translation of the Bible contains "the scriptures as they are in [his] own bosom." The JST scriptures reflect truth as it exists in God himself. The doctrine of the JST is pure as God is pure.

Contribution 1: *Unlike other versions of the New Testament, the JST teaches first-century Church doctrine in its purest form, unfiltered, and uncorrupted.* The JST New Testament is unadulterated and unfiltered. The JST did not pass through several recensions or editings at the hands of unordained editors and translators, as all other versions of the Bible have. The words of the Joseph Smith Translation constitute something of the "autograph" editions of biblical books, those long-lost original texts as they first appeared from their actual authors in pristine form, and which some scholars claim can never be recovered. In truth, the JST of the New Testament is better than any autograph edition because it presents the words of scripture which come directly from the source of all light and truth. The words of the JST New Testament contain the scriptures as they exist in the Lord's "own bosom." No other version of the Bible can make that claim.

Contribution 2: *The JST New Testament was given for the elect.* As Doctrine and Covenants 35:20 makes plain, the JST was given *through* the Lord's special prophet; it was given *for* the Lord's elect, for their salvation. There is glorious doctrine which the elect can possess that others do not have. The elect of the Lord have this special gift—the JST New Testament—to enhance their knowledge. The elect of the Lord are those who will use the JST New Testament and cherish it, for as the Lord said, "the elect hear my voice and harden not their hearts" (D&C 29:7). The voice of the Lord is found in the JST New Testament.

The translation of the New Testament occupied so much of the Prophet's time and was such a major part of his ministry that for us to ignore the JST New Testament, or slight it in any way, is to discount the Lord's word. I just don't think the elect would do that. When we refuse to learn and teach from the JST New Testament we are turning our backs on what the Lord said to his prophet. And the elect would not do that. Joseph Smith "said that God had often sealed up the heavens . . . and except the Church receive the fulness of the Scriptures that they would yet fall."[1] The Prophet's own attitude toward his translation of the New Testament is perhaps best summarized in a statement he made in a letter to W. W. Phelps. "We have finished the translation of the New Testament," he said, "great and glorious things are revealed."[2]

Contribution 3: *The JST New Testament helps us to better understand the nature of Joseph Smith's prophetic duties and the magnitude of his calling.* The work of the JST New Testament was commissioned by the Lord directly. The new translation of the Bible was an important part of Joseph Smith's calling. It was not an "aside" nor was it simply an activity the Prophet drummed up to fill in his spare time. The Prophet himself described his work on the Bible as a "branch of my calling."[3] In 1833, after the Book of Mormon had already come forth, the Lord said to Joseph Smith: "And, verily I say unto you, that it is my will that you should hasten to translate my scriptures . . . and all this for the salvation of Zion" (D&C 93:53).

Joseph Smith and his scribe recognized that the translation of the New Testament was more than spiritual busy-work. The entry at the top of page 1 of the manuscript of the Gospel of Matthew reads: "A Translation of the New Testament translated by the power of God."[4]

Contribution 4: *The translation of the New Testament was a major means of educating the Prophet—so that more doctrine could be restored.* The JST New Testament was a major tool the Lord used to teach Joseph Smith line upon line, the same way the Savior learned in mortality (as we discover in D&C 93:12–14). This is what the Lord said to Joseph Smith in March 1831: "And now, behold, I say unto you, it shall not be given unto you to know any further concerning this chapter, until the New Testament be translated, and in it all these things shall be made known; wherefore I give unto you that ye may now translate it, that ye may be prepared for the things to come. For verily I say unto you, that great things await you." (D&C 45:60–62.)

This helps us to understand that God does not reveal everything all at once; not to us, nor to Joseph Smith, nor even to his Only Begotten Son. He teaches us little by little, and thus prepares us for the future. The JST New Testament is a pattern for the way revelation comes to all of us, and who knows but what "great things" await all of us as we use the Joseph Smith Translation!

Perhaps an illustration from the JST New Testament itself can show how this "line upon line" principle operated in the education of the Prophet. The King James Version (KJV) of Revelation 1:6 reads: "And [Jesus Christ] hath made us kings and priests unto God and his Father; to him be glory and dominion forever and ever. Amen."

The wording of this passage seems to give significant scriptural support for the doctrine of the plurality of Gods, as the text says "God [or Heavenly Father] and his Father." However, in 1832, when Joseph Smith was working on the new translation, he changed this verse by omitting the *and* after *God* and inserting a comma. The words then read: ". . . and hath made us kings and priests unto God, his Father." In Nauvoo twelve years later, on June 16, 1844, just eleven days before his death, the Prophet gave a sermon in the grove, east of the temple. He took for his text Revelation 1:6, which he read from the King James Version, without any changes. He then made these comments:

> It [the verse] is altogether correct in the translation. . . .
>
> I will preach on the plurality of Gods. I have selected this text for that express purpose. . . .
>
> Our text says, "And hath made us kings and priests unto God and His Father." The Apostles have discovered that there were Gods above. . . .
>
> Paul says there are Gods many and Lords many. . . . But if Joseph Smith says there are Gods many and Lords many, they cry, "Away with him! Crucify him! Crucify him!"
>
> Mankind verily say that the Scriptures are with them. Search the Scriptures, for they testify of things that these apostates would gravely pronounce blasphemy. Paul, if Joseph Smith is a blasphemer, you are. I say there are Gods many and Lords many, but to us only one.[5]

Why the change in Joseph Smith's understanding of Revelation 1:6? Why did he change the King James Version in 1832 but state in 1844 that the KJV is altogether *correct* in its wording? I think it is because the Prophet had learned much over twelve years; he had learned that his translation of 1832 was doctrinally correct, but it didn't, at that time, reflect the fulness of doctrine. The JST New Testament was given to prepare him and the Saints for greater knowledge to be revealed in the future. By 1844 the Prophet had been carefully tutored, and the fulness of the doctrine of God had been revealed. The 1832 translation was still correct, but by 1844 much more information had been added by the Lord. Unfortunately, in 1844 Joseph paid for the fulness of this doctrine with his life because some rebelled against the fulness. (Had he taught the fulness of the doctrine of God in 1832, would he have been killed that much earlier?) In fact, in 1841 he made an interesting statement about rejecting revealed truth: "The moment we revolt at anything which comes from God, the devil takes power."[6]

Contribution 5: *The Joseph Smith Translation of the Bible was a catalyst for, and the seed-bed of, other major revelations and doctrines.* Other revelation came as a direct result of Joseph Smith's translating the New Testament. Professor Dahl will have more to say about this, so I will simply pose this hypothetical question: If the Joseph Smith Translation of the New Testament had never been undertaken, and all the sections of the Doctrine and Covenants which came as a direct result of the Prophet's translation of the New Testament were omitted, which sections would be missing from our current Doctrine and Covenants?

Answer: Sections 74, 76, 77, and 86. (In addition there are other major sections of the Doctrine and Covenants which were greatly influenced by the JST New Testament, including sections 84 and 88.) One of the most impressive is section 76. Of this section the Prophet wrote:

> Upon my return from Amherst conference, I resumed the translation of the Scriptures. From sundry revelations which had been received, it was apparent that many important points touching the salvation of man had been taken from the Bible, or lost before it was compiled. It appeared self-evident from what truths were left, that if God rewarded every one according to the deeds done in the body, the term "Heaven," as intended for the Saints' eternal home, must include more kingdoms than one. Accordingly, while translating St. John's Gospel, myself and Elder Rigdon saw the following vision.[7]

It was after the Prophet had translated John 5:29 that section 76 was given. The profound concepts and doctrines it elucidates are these:

The Lord is God; Mysteries of the kingdom will be revealed to all the faithful; All shall come forth in the resurrection of the just or the unjust; Inhabitants of many worlds are begotten sons and daughters unto God through the atonement of Jesus Christ; An angel of God fell and became the devil; Sons of perdition suffer eternal damnation; all others gain some degree of salvation; The glory and reward of exalted beings in the celestial kingdom; Those who shall inherit the terrestrial kingdom; Status of those in the telestial, terrestrial, and celestial glories; All the faithful may see the vision of the degrees of glory.[8]

I confess I am partial to section 76 because it contains some of my favorite verses in all of scripture:

And now, after the many testimonies which have been given of him, this is the testimony, last of all, which we give of him: That he lives!

For we saw him, even on the right hand of God; and we heard the voice bearing record that he is the Only Begotten of the Father—

That by him, and through him, and of him, the worlds are and were created, and the inhabitants thereof are begotten sons and daughters unto God. (D&C 76:22–24.)

It is striking to realize that this doctrine came out of Joseph Smith's translation of the New Testament.

Contribution 6: *The JST New Testament shows us how intimately Joseph Smith knew the Savior and knew what the Savior wanted the New Testament to teach its readers.* It is my conviction that from the time of Adam to our present day there has been no patriarch, prophet, priest, or preacher who has known more about the life of Jesus than Joseph Smith. I believe that no individual has ever lived who knew as much about the New Testament (how it is given or for what purpose) and what the original Apostles and witnesses thought and wrote, than Joseph Smith—except our Lord, on whom the New Testament centers. No other person on this earth has known as clearly as Joseph Smith what words and *meanings* God intended the New Testament to teach its readers.

There are 7,913 verses in the King James Version of the New

Testament. Through inspiration Joseph Smith changed 2,096 verses in the JST New Testament. By far the overwhelming number of those changes are in the four Gospels or "Testimonies," as he called them.

	No. of Verses in KJV	Number Changed in JST[9]
Luke	1,151	563
Matthew	1,071	483
Mark	678	349
John	879	159
Romans	433	118
Revelation	404	75
1 Corinthians	437	68
Hebrews	303	47
Acts	963	42
2 Corinthians	257	24
1 Peter	105	24
2 Peter	61	20

Many of these changes are details that reflect an intricate knowledge of the biblical text. And yet they are also too consistent with details found in other volumes of scripture to be labelled guess-work or frivolous. Joseph knew the Savior intimately, and he knew intimately the texts which testify of the Savior. He knew what concepts the Savior wanted us to know concerning Deity in these latter days.

The 1948 edition of the LDS hymnbook contained a song entitled "The Seer, Joseph, the Seer." The lyrics were written by John Taylor (a man not unfamiliar with revelation or Deity). The first verse speaks volumes about President Taylor's regard for Joseph Smith's intimate association with the heavens:

> The Seer, the Seer, Joseph, the Seer! . . .
> His equal now cannot be found
> By searching the wide world around.
> With Gods he soared in the realms of day,
> And men he taught the heavenly way. . . .
> The earthly Seer! the heavenly Seer!
> I love to dwell on his memory dear.

I too love to dwell on his memory, what he taught and what he knew about the Savior. Much of that very personal knowledge is found in the JST New Testament. Of Joseph Smith, Wilford Woodruff said: "His mind was opened by the visions of the Almighty, and the Lord taught him many things by vision and revelation that were never taught publicly in his days; for the people could not bear the flood of intelligence which God poured into his mind."[10]

Contribution 7: *The JST New Testament "preserves the scriptures in safety" in an age of doctrinal calamity and theological chaos.* In the preface to the Doctrine and Covenants we read these sobering words: "Wherefore, I the Lord, knowing the calamity which should come upon the inhabitants of the earth, called upon my servant Joseph Smith, Jun., and spake unto him from heaven, and gave him commandments. . . . That mine everlasting covenant might be established; that the fulness of my gospel might be proclaimed. . . . And inasmuch as [my servants] sought wisdom they might be instructed. . . . And inasmuch as they were humble they might be made strong, and blessed from on high, and receive knowledge from time to time." (D&C 1:17, 22–23, 26, 28.)

I am convinced that here the Lord is speaking, in part, of the Joseph Smith Translation of the New Testament. Doctrinally and theologically we are living in a time of tremendous calamity and chaos. The authority and reliability of the sacred texts or testimonies found in the four Gospels are coming under sophisticated attack. Notorious in this regard is the recent work of the Jesus Seminar, whose seventy-seven members met twice a year for eight years *to vote* on which words of Jesus in the four standard Gospels, plus the apocryphal Gospel of Thomas, are original and which ones are later fabrications. Said one prominent member of the group, the aim of the Seminar is to "rescue Jesus from the spin doctors" who wrote the Gospels.[11]

As a result of their deliberations the seminar published a new version of the Gospels (with commentary) which maintains that 82 percent of the words ascribed to Jesus in the Gospels were not spoken by him. They claim that virtually all of the Gospel of John presents an unauthentic picture of what Jesus really said and did. Several other passages in the synoptic Gospels (Matthew, Mark, and Luke)[12] are also regarded as later interpolations.[13] In particular, all passages which depict Jesus ascribing to himself exalted status (Messiah, Son of God, light of the world, bread of life, and so on), all passages which speak of Jesus dying for the sins of the world, and all passages which speak of Jesus' second coming are counted as embellishment—the work of Christian apologists, theologians, and propagandists writing *years* after the death of Christ.[14]

The Jesus Seminar exemplifies one of two contrasting trends. Scholars who are not prophets want to reduce, take away, decrease, and diminish. On the other hand, the tendency of prophets is to add to, increase, restore, and give us more.

The grounds on which certain matters are rejected by the Jesus Seminar are described as rational. The Jesus of history and the Christ of faith are described as two different beings. Prominent advocates of this approach say that one being is rooted in the real or natural world, the other in the mythic or supernatural world, which, as observation demonstrates, is not the way the world operates. "The distinction between the two figures is the difference between a historical person who lived in a particular time and place and was subject to the limitations of a finite existence, and a figure who has been *assigned* a mythical role, in which he descends from heaven to rescue humanity and, of course, eventually returns there. The church appears to smother the historical Jesus by superimposing this heavenly figure on him."[15]

These modern ideas are most significant when considered in light of the Lord's declaration of February 1831. At that time Joseph Smith was deeply involved in the work of translating the Bible. Of that enterprise the Lord said to the Prophet: "Thou shalt ask, and my scriptures shall be given as I have appointed, and they shall be preserved in safety" (D&C 42:56).

Thus an important, indeed a vital, contribution of the JST New Testament is its preservation of the Lord's scriptures in safety against those in this age of chaos who would do violent damage to the eyewitness testimonies of our Lord's life and ministry. In fact, you will note that one of the major doctrinal contributions of the JST New Testament is its retitling of the Gospels. Yes, they proclaim "good news" (the etymology of *Gospel*), but they are "Testimonies"—"The *Testimony* of Matthew," "The *Testimony* of Mark," and so on. When we read the JST New Testament we do not have to wonder if we're reading authentic, uncorrupted text. We know the four Testimonies are reliable; they are the words of the Lord. We can then get on with the business of implementing the doctrines of the New Testament into our lives.

To plumb the depths of the JST New Testament is to learn the truth. To then teach from the JST New Testament is to fortify ourselves and the Church against the onslaught of the so-called New Testament experts who would have us believe that the New Testament Gospels are corrupted beyond recognition; that Jesus never really said or did much of what is reported; and that the New Testament only reflects the propaganda of the later Christian community.

Contributions to Our Understanding of the Life, Ministry, and Personality of Jesus

No other version of the New Testament, indeed no other record, contributes so much to an in-depth understanding of the earthly ministry of Christ as does the Joseph Smith Translation. The Book of Mormon contains profound truths about Christ and his disciples, but the JST New Testament has more. The personalities of Jesus and his associates are more fully portrayed in the JST than elsewhere. In his chastisements the Savior is more blunt and stern with religious leaders who knew the truth but did not live it. However, in his approbation he is also more tender, and more compassionate with the honest in heart. The JST interprets parables and miracles of Jesus and provides a more complete picture of the life and times of Jesus the Messiah than any other single volume of scripture we possess.

Contribution 8: *The JST New Testament provides us with details about essential attributes and character traits of the major figures associated with the Savior's life.* A good example is King Herod. We learn plainly in the JST that Herod knew the testimonies of the prophets regarding the coming of the Messiah. When the wise men came to him announcing their knowledge of the advent of Christ, it was no great surprise. As the JST clearly indicates, Herod called the chief priests and scribes of the Jews, but not to ask them about some startling news regarding the coming of a Messiah. Rather, he demanded to know where the birthplace of the Messiah was located, "*that is written of by the prophets.*" And then this telling insight is presented: *"For he greatly feared, yet he believed not the prophets"* (JST, Matthew 3:4–6). Herod was not ignorantly sinful. He had been educated. He *chose* to reject the prophets.

We also learn from JST, Matthew 3 that the wise men knew they were seeking not just the King of the Jews but, indeed, the Messiah (JST, Matthew 3:2). And thanks to the JST, we even know that the Jewish chief priests and scribes themselves knew of the birthplace of the Messiah from an inspired reading of Micah 5:2. They recited to Herod: *"The word of the Lord came unto us saying, And thou, Bethlehem, which lieth in the land of Judea, in thee shall be born a prince, which art not the least among the princes of Judea; for out of thee shall come the Messiah, who shall save my people Israel"* (JST, Matthew 3:6). This is a significant point, one for which we actually get some of the Old Testament text restored to us by the JST New Testament! Of course, this also means that the chief priests (Sadducees) and the scribes (many of whom were Pharisees) did not ignorantly reject Jesus, either.

Contribution 9: *The JST New Testament tells us more about John the Baptist than any other version of the Bible, or any other single book of scripture.* The JST makes it clear that John understood the grand sweep of the gospel and the Savior's role in it. In the JST, John tells his listeners that he will know and bear record of the Messiah. He also emphasizes the need for repentance *before* baptism (JST, Matthew 3:38–39). The JST reveals that John testified that both he and Jesus were Eliases; he was the Elias of preparation and Jesus was the Elias of restoration (JST, John 1:20–28). The JST emphasizes that John both saw the heavens opened and heard the voice of the Father testifying of his Only Begotten Son. The JST restores the words the Father spoke, commanding John, *"Hear ye him."* (JST, Matthew 3:45–46.)

In a major addition to the biblical record the JST plainly teaches that John understood and testified of the differences between the Lord's first and second comings. The JST also points out that John knew Christ's preaching to the Jews was a preparatory step for the gospel to go to the Gentiles.

For behold, and lo, he shall come, as it is written in the book of the prophets, to take away the sins of the world, and to bring salvation unto the heathen nations, to gather together those who are lost, who are of the sheepfold of Israel:

Yea, even the dispersed and afflicted; and also to prepare the way, and make possible the preaching of the gospel unto the Gentiles;

And to be a light unto all who sit in darkness, unto the uttermost parts of the earth; to bring to pass the resurrection from the dead, and to ascend up on high, to dwell on the right hand of the Father.

Until the fulness of time, and the law and the testimony shall be sealed, and the keys of the kingdom shall be delivered up again unto the Father;

To administer justice unto all; to come down in judgment upon all, and to convince all the ungodly of their ungodly deeds, which they have committed; and all this in the day that he shall come. (JST, Luke 3:5–9.)

The JST also declares that Jesus knew when John was cast into prison, and he specifically sent angels to minister to his cousin (JST, Matthew 4:11). Many other things are taught in the JST about John the Baptist, making it the most informative source on the life, ministry, and understanding of John the Baptist, the last legal administrator of the Aaronic order.

Contribution 10: In the JST we learn more authoritative information about the childhood of Jesus than anywhere else, except modern prophets. In the JST we learn that Jesus grew up with brothers. This implies the normal give-and-take relationships of family life. We learn that he worked under the tutelage of his stepfather, Joseph, and grew strong over the years. The JST confirms that the great difference between Jesus and other individuals was that he knew early on of his special ministry and quickly outstripped all other mortals in terms of knowledge and spirituality. He "waited upon the Lord for the time of ministry to come. . . . for he needed not that any man should teach him." (JST, Matthew 3:24–26.)

This striking addition to our knowledge of Jesus' youth is corroborated by the JST account of his experience in the temple during Passover at twelve years of age. The JST makes a significant change in Luke 2:46–47. In the KJV, Jesus is sitting in the midst of the doctors of the law, hearing them and asking them questions. In the JST, however, Jesus is portrayed as the God he truly is. He is teaching the doctors of the law, and they are asking him questions. Supplementing the information in the JST, Joseph Smith further taught: "When still a boy

[Jesus] had all the intelligence necessary to enable Him to rule and govern the kingdom of the Jews, and could reason with the wisest and most profound doctors of law and divinity, and make their theories and practice to appear like folly compared with the wisdom He possessed; but He was a boy only, and lacked physical strength even to defend His own person; and was subject to cold, to hunger and to death."[16]

With the additions and insights supplied by JST, Matthew 3; JST, Luke 2; and the statements of the Prophet Joseph Smith, no one has as much accurate and helpful information about the early life of Jesus as the Latter-day Saints.

Contribution 11: *The JST New Testament presents the most complete authoritative picture of Palestinian Judaism during Jesus' day of any original sources available to the layman.* The JST makes plain that the Jewish leaders of Jesus' day possessed an overpowering belief in the efficacy of the law to save. The law was their mediator and savior; nothing else could possibly be needed. Though other JST passages teach the same thing, an example from JST Matthew, material added to the Sermon on the Mount in the JST, will suffice: "*And then said his disciples unto him, they [the Jews] will say unto us, We ourselves are righteous, and need not that any man should teach us. God, we know, heard Moses and some of the prophets; but us he will not hear. And they will say, We have the law for our salvation, and that is sufficient for us.*" (JST, Matthew 7:14–15.)

Here we see that Jewish attitudes were so deep-rooted that the disciples knew Jewish leaders would not automatically accept their initial preaching about Jesus as Messiah. But what is more astounding is that the Jews themselves were sure the heavens were closed, that revelation had long since ceased. "God, we know, heard Moses and some of the prophets; but us he will not hear," they said. (Notice they didn't even believe God had heard all of the prophets.) This exclusive and explicit insight of the JST tells us of the tragic state of affairs in Judaism during the Savior's lifetime.

Another prevalent Jewish concept consistently emphasized by the JST is that the Jews maintained they were scrupulously keeping the whole law. But Jesus constantly reminded them that they did not keep the law of Moses as found in the scriptures. They had rejected the words of the prophets, as JST, Mark 7:10 makes plain. Had they been more intense in their study of the *real* law as found in holy writ, and not commentary *on* the law known as the "tradition of the elders" or the "tradition of men" (see Mark 7:5–10), they would have recognized Jesus as the Messiah because he fit all the qualifications and prescriptions which made up the central message of the law of Moses. The whole point of the law of Moses was to direct Israel to the true Messiah, as the following makes clear: "*Then certain of them came to him, saying, Good Master, we have Moses and the prophets, and whosoever shall live by them, shall he not have life? And Jesus answered, saying, Ye know not Moses, neither the prophets; for if ye had known them, ye would have believed on me; for to this intent they were written. For I am sent that ye might have life. Therefore I will liken it unto salt which is good; but if the salt has lost its savor, wherewith shall it be seasoned?*" (JST, Luke 14: 35–37.)

We learn from the JST many other things about Judaism that are too numerous to discuss in detail, but you will want to look for them. For example, the JST confirms that the Jews of Jesus' day performed baptisms (JST, Matthew 9:18); they thought of themselves in Judea as a great invincible kingdom (JST, Matthew 21:48); and they had a welfare system which was funded by excess money in the temple treasury (JST, Luke 3:19–20). In summary, however, I think the most telling and chilling description of the Judaism of Jesus' day is provided by the Joseph Smith Translation of Luke 16:16–23 (almost all of which is not found in the KJV). This passage in and of itself constitutes a major contribution to our study of the New Testament:

> *And they said unto him, We have the law, and the prophets; but as for this man we will not receive him to be our ruler; for he maketh himself to be a judge over us.*
>
> *Then said Jesus unto them, The law and the prophets testify of me; yea, and all the prophets who have written, even until John, have foretold of these days.*
>
> Since that time, the kingdom of God is preached, and every man who seeketh truth presseth into it.
>
> And it is easier for heaven and earth to pass, than for one tittle of the law to fail.
>
> *And why teach ye the law, and deny that which is written; and condemn him whom the Father hath sent to fulfill the law, that ye might all be redeemed?*

> *O fools! for you have said in your hearts, There is no God. And you pervert the right way; and the kingdom of heaven suffereth violence of you; and you persecute the meek; and in your violence you seek to destroy the kingdom; and ye take the children of the kingdom by force. Woe unto you, ye adulterers!*
>
> *And they reviled him again, being angry for the saying, that they were adulterers.*
>
> *But he continued, saying,* Whosoever putteth away his wife, and marrieth another, committeth adultery; and whosoever marrieth her who is put away from her husband, committeth adultery. *Verily I say unto you, I will liken you unto the rich man.* (JST, Luke 16:16–23.)

This may well be the most startling revelation about Palestinian Judaism provided in the JST New Testament: namely, that a main reason for the decrepit spiritual condition of the Jewish nation was the sexual misconduct of the Pharisees and doctors of the law. The Jewish leaders were adulterers! Now all the references to adultery and adulterers in the New Testament begin to make sense. When Jesus says to certain Jewish leaders (i.e., scribes and Pharisees) on different occasions, "An evil and adulterous generation seeketh after a sign" (Matthew 12:39), he is using the word *adulterous* as a specific adjective to describe their actual lifestyle. This is not some abstract metaphor or symbolism. The Savior isn't saying that the mentality which causes people to seek for spiritual proofs is also the mentality which puts people in danger of committing adultery. He is saying that sexual immorality has ruined the spiritual sensitivity of the Pharisaic leaders. They can't see that Jesus is the Messiah because they are engaged in this specific sin, which has led to other sins. This historical circumstance is illuminated by the JST.

Contribution 12: *The JST New Testament reveals the thoughts and feelings of the earthly Jesus as no other version of the New Testament can.* No other version of the Bible reveals the thinking of Jesus the person as completely as does the JST New Testament. In the King James Version of Luke 12:9 Jesus says: "But he that denieth me before men shall be denied before the angels of God." Now note what the JST adds at this point:

> *Now his disciples knew that he said this, because they had spoken evil against him before the people; for they were afraid to confess him before men.*

And they reasoned among themselves, saying, He knoweth our hearts, and he speaketh to our condemnation, and we shall not be forgiven. But he answered them, and said unto them.

Whosoever shall speak a word against the Son of Man, *and repenteth,* it shall be forgiven him; but unto him *who* blasphemeth against the Holy Ghost, it shall not be forgiven him. (JST, Luke 12:10–12.)

What do we learn from the JST? We now understand why Jesus emphasized the seriousness of blasphemy against the Holy Ghost—because his disciples had spoken against him without possessing the sure knowledge brought by the Holy Ghost. We see that Jesus knew the minds and hearts of his disciples. And we see the Savior's compassion. He knew they had made a mistake, so he told them that they could be forgiven of their denial of him, *if they repented* (an important addition in the JST). We also see the inner thoughts of the disciples in a new light, and this takes us to the next contribution.

Contribution 13: *The JST New Testament uncovers the innermost feelings, motives, and intents of the heart of Jesus' disciples.* No other version of the New Testament reveals the authentic thoughts and intents of the original disciples as plainly as does the JST New Testament. The JST "gets into the minds" of Jesus' followers. This is a major contribution of the JST New Testament. Let me provide a significant illustration.

The King James Version of the Gospel of Mark tells us that after Jesus and his disciples had sung a hymn, they went forth from the upper room into the Mount of Olives:

And they came to a place which was named Gethsemane: and he saith to his disciples, Sit ye here, while I shall pray.

And he taketh with him Peter and James and John, and began to be sore amazed, and to be very heavy;

And saith unto them, My soul is exceeding sorrowful unto death: tarry ye here, and watch. (Mark 14:32–34.)

Note the corresponding section of the Joseph Smith Translation:

And they came to a place which was named Gethsemane, *which was a garden; and the disciples began to be sore amazed, and to be very heavy, and to complain in their hearts, wondering if this be the Messiah.*

> *And Jesus knowing their hearts, said* to his disciples, Sit ye here, while I shall pray.
>
> And he taketh with him, Peter, and James, and John, *and rebuked them*, and said unto them, My soul is exceeding sorrowful, *even* unto death; tarry ye here and watch. (JST, Mark 14:36–38.)

What do we learn from the JST that the KJV does not tells us? First, we learn that Mark originally referred to Gethsemane as a garden. None of the synoptic Gospels (i.e., Matthew, Mark, and Luke) of the King James Version include that information.

Second, we learn what was in the minds of the Apostles; it was the Apostles who began to be "sore amazed" and "very heavy" . . . "and to complain." This is new information, a new insight, since the KJV indicates that it was Jesus who was sore amazed and heavy. Now, Jesus himself very well may have been amazed at the intensity of the experience in Gethsemane. (He was, after all, perfect; and up to that point had not experienced firsthand what sin felt like physically.) But the Lord's intention in JST Mark seems to be to explain to us what was in the minds of the Apostles, and why.

Third, we learn that the amazement, the heaviness, and the complaining of the Apostles was a function of their doubt or lack of faith; the Apostles began to wonder whether Jesus really *was* the Messiah. This helps us to appreciate how difficult that horrible Thursday night actually was for the Savior. Jesus' closest friends didn't just abandon him physically by falling asleep. They abandoned him spiritually and emotionally.

Fourth, we learn that Jesus knew what was in their hearts, and he rebuked them for their doubt. This is important because we now understand why the Savior continued to be so concerned about their falling asleep and entering into temptation (see Matthew 26:40–41; Mark 14:38; Luke 22:46). Doubt had already opened the door to apostasy. Jesus' rebuke for unbelief was really a way of protecting the disciples against further spiritual problems. Doubt can lead to full-fledged unbelief; unbelief leads to rebellion against the things of God. Again the Prophet's statement is applicable: "The moment we revolt at anything which comes from God, the devil takes power."[17] There is no question that Satan was afoot in Gethsemane that Thursday night.

The picture painted in this JST Mark passage is not just complete. It is truly profound. It tells us what was in the minds of the disciples as well as that of the Savior during the events of the Atonement. It is also consistent with what we know about the spiritual difficulties of the disciples as portrayed throughout the New Testament. They had doubts about the Savior's messiahship throughout his ministry, and they continued to have doubts about him right up to the end. This kind of doubt always brought a rebuke from the Savior. In fact, even after the Crucifixion the despondency felt by the disciples on the road to Emmaus seems to have been rooted in doubt about whether Jesus really was the Messiah. He rebuked them as well: "O fools, and slow of heart to believe all that the prophets have spoken" (Luke 24:25).

But there is a significant lesson to be learned as we examine these great men who, like us, were disciples of the Master and yet had doubts at times. They did not turn their backs and harden their hearts because they had been rebuked. Rather, they were humble enough to accept those rebukes and work to *change* their hearts, so that, like the two specific disciples on the road to Emmaus, they all came to know with a testimony more sure than sight that Jesus was the Messiah. "Did not our heart burn within us?" (Luke 24:32) was the question that became their foundation.

Contribution 14: *The JST New Testament plainly teaches that opposition to Jesus began early in his ministry, it never decreased, it even came from his disciples, and it was intense.* Numerous passages in the JST indicate that Jesus encountered opposition from every quarter, even from his own disciples right up to the bitter end. This opposition began immediately after the inaugural Passover of his ministry and quickly became so intense that the Pharisees sought to kill him even before he began his Galilean tour. Thus Jesus had to face the threat of death throughout the entire three years of his ministry. Here is an example from JST, John 4:1–4: "When therefore the Pharisees had heard that Jesus made and baptized more disciples than John, *they sought more diligently some means that they might put him to death; for many received John as a prophet, but they believed not on Jesus. Now the Lord knew this,* though he himself baptized not *so many as* his disciples; *for he suffered them for an example, preferring one another.*"

Of course this passage is significant because it not only teaches about the early and intense opposition Jesus encountered but also clarifies an important point of doctrine, namely, that Jesus himself performed the ordinance of baptism, showing his disciples how it should be done.

Contribution 15: *The JST provides new insight on the specific focus and theme of the Sermon on the Mount.* From the JST it becomes clear that the Sermon on the Mount, delivered in the Holy Land, was not the identical discourse delivered by the Savior at the Nephite temple in the land Bountiful. Nor was it intended to be. The Joseph Smith Translation does not attempt to harmonize the two sermons word for word. The Sermon on the Mount, in the Old World, was principally a missionary-preparation discourse. It was the Apostles' MTC experience (Missionary Training Center). The JST additions to Matthew 5, 6, and 7 plainly show that Jesus gave the sermon in the Old World to prepare his disciples to be missionaries, to explain how they should act as missionaries, and to demonstrate what they should teach as missionaries. Here are some of the JST additions to the sermon. First from Matthew 6:25–27:

> And, again, I say unto you, go ye into the world, and care not for the world; for the world will hate you, and will persecute you, and will turn you out of their synagogues.
>
> Nevertheless, ye shall go forth from house to house, teaching the people; and I will go before you.
>
> And your heavenly Father will provide for you, whatsoever things ye need for food, what ye shall eat; and for raiment, what ye shall wear or put on.

Here is Matthew 7:9–11:

> Go ye into the world, saying unto all, Repent, for the kingdom of heaven has come nigh unto you.
>
> And the mysteries of the kingdom ye shall keep within yourselves; for it is not meet to give that which is holy unto the dogs; neither cast ye your pearls unto swine, lest they trample them under their feet.
>
> For the world cannot receive that which ye, yourselves, are not able to bear; wherefore ye shall not give your pearls unto them, lest they turn again and rend you.

The JST additions to Matthew 7:12–17 also report that Jesus supplied suggestions or "helps" to these apostolic missionaries on how to overcome objections they would encounter in their attempts to spread the gospel among the Jews.

> Say unto them, Ask of God; ask, and it shall be given you; seek, and ye shall find; knock, and it shall be opened unto you.
> For every one that asketh, receiveth; and he that seeketh, findeth; and unto him that knocketh, it shall be opened.
> And then said his disciples unto him, they will say unto us, We ourselves are righteous, and need not that any man should teach us. God, we know, heard Moses and some of the prophets; but us he will not hear.
> And they will say, We have the law for our salvation, and that is sufficient for us.
> Then Jesus answered, and said unto his disciples, thus shall ye say unto them.
> What man among you, having a son, and he shall be standing out, and shall say, Father, open thy house that I may come in and sup with thee, will not say, Come in, my son; for mine is thine, and thine is mine?

Contribution 16: *The JST makes it clear that Jesus knew who he was and testified of himself more often than is recorded in other New Testament versions.* It may seem obvious to some, even redundant to others, to say that Jesus knew who he was and often testified of that truth. But this is a significant controversy in the scholarly world because the information in the other versions of the New Testament is regarded by some as ambiguous. That is, they believe the authentic parts of the New Testament never really show Jesus saying that he is the Messiah. However, the JST dispels any ambiguity or question by showing that Jesus testified of his messiahship throughout his ministry, in many different places to many different people. The following examples are instructive.

To Nicodemus he said: "He who believeth not is condemned already, because he hath not believed in the name of the only begotten Son of God, *which before was preached by the mouth of the holy prophets; for they testified of me*" (JST, John 3:18). To his disciples in Galilee he testified:

"I am he of whom it is written by the prophets; follow me, and I will make you fishers of men" (JST, Matthew 4:18). To the Pharisees in Perea: *"Then said Jesus unto them,* The law and the prophets *testify of me; yea, and all the prophets who have written, even* until John, *have foretold of these days. . . . And why teach ye the law, and deny that which is written; and condemn him whom the Father hath sent to fulfil the law, that ye might all be redeemed?"* (JST, Luke 16:17, 20.)

There are many other clarifications, additions, and corrections in the JST New Testament which bring the ministry and identity of our Savior into clearer focus. We see that the gospel of the first century is the same gospel we have today. We are brought closer to Jesus by studying the Joseph Smith Translation than by any other version of the Bible. The JST provides powerful insights into the whole purpose and meaning of the Lord's mission. A major contribution to be appreciated is the way the JST explains Jesus' use of parables as well as the interpretations it provides for those parables.

In an important and fitting conclusion to the earthly ministry of Jesus, the JST restores to us the final words uttered by the Savior as a mortal. The KJV simply states that Jesus cried with a loud voice and yielded up the ghost. But the JST tells us exactly what was on the mind of the Lord as he was ready to pass through the veil: "Jesus when he had cried again with a loud voice, *saying, Father, it is finished, thy will is done,* yielded up the ghost" (JST, Matthew 27:54). What a magnificent detail to have restored to us! What a tragedy if it had been lost! Right up to the end, the Savior of humankind was thinking about the Father's plan and purpose.

Explaining Doctrines of the Plan of Salvation

The JST New Testament makes invaluable contributions to our understanding of specific facets of the plan of salvation. I mention only some of the major ones.

Contribution 17: *The JST New Testament teaches the doctrine of Elias in a new, more complete, and surprising way.* Because of the JST, we understand more fully that:

— Elias is an office; there is an Elias of preparation and an Elias of restoration (JST, John 1:20–28; JST, Matthew 17:13–14);

— John the Baptist was an Elias of preparation; Jesus and Elijah were Eliases of restoration (JST, John 1:20–28; JST, Matthew 17:13–14);

— the term *Elias* was often used by the Jews to mean Elijah;

— in his role as Elias and as a spirit personage, John the Baptist was on the Mount of Transfiguration along with Moses, Elijah, Jesus, the chief Apostles, and God the Father (JST, Mark 9:3–5; JST, Matthew 17:10–14). This was where keys of power *and* knowledge were restored, and Jesus was strengthened against his forthcoming suffering. Who better to help strengthen the Savior than the one specifically called to prepare his way, and the one who had preceded him in death?

— from translating the book of Revelation, Joseph Smith learned that John the Revelator is also a promised Elias (D&C 77:9, 14).

In summary, Elder Bruce R. McConkie taught: "Elias is a composite personage. The expression must be understood to be a name and a title for those whose mission it was to commit keys and powers to men in this final dispensation."[18] Indeed, these mighty prophets—these Eliases—of ancient times have all come back to restore keys and powers in this dispensation of fulness.

Contribution 18: *The JST New Testament provides a more complete explanation of the Second Coming and the end of the world than is found in any other text or document, outside of modern revelations.* Among other things, we learn from the JST where Jesus was on different occasions when he gave instructions about his second coming. We learn why he gave the specific instruction he did (that is, what questions he was responding to). We learn that Jesus gave a detailed summary of the signs of his second coming, and that he made a clear distinction between the destruction of Jerusalem in A.D. 70 (an "end of the world" of sorts) and similar conditions which would be seen at his second coming. From the JST we understand that it was Jesus and not Paul who first said "the coming of the Lord is as a thief in the night" (compare JST, Luke 12:44 with 1 Thessalonians 5:2). Paul had learned the exact words of Christ and simply used them to teach in a dramatic way.

The JST brings out a truth about the coming of the Lord that cannot be found anywhere else in scripture.

> *For, behold, he cometh in the first watch of the night, and he shall also
> come in the second watch, and again he shall come in the third watch.*
>
> *And verily I say unto you,* He hath already come, *as it is written of him;
> and again when* he shall come in the second watch, or come in the third
> watch, *blessed are those servants when he cometh,* that he shall find so
> *doing;*
>
> *For the Lord of those servants shall gird himself, and make them to sit
> down to meat, and will come forth and serve them.* (JST, Luke 12:41–43.)

This is an important concept. Every generation should watch for
Christ's coming, for he comes in *every* generation, or in every "watch
of the night." Such knowledge provides a powerful incentive that
helps motivate individuals to live righteously in a consistent manner
and thus be prepared to meet the Lord always, whether in life or
death. The righteous will then receive the approbation of the Lord.

In addition, specific clarifications in the JST show us that after
the Ascension the Apostles, especially Peter and Paul, had a clear understanding about the timetable of the Second Coming. They were
not confused, as the KJV sometimes leads us to believe. For example,
Paul did not compare the high priest's entering the holy place with
Christ's appearing at the "end of the world" to suffer for sins, as the
KJV states. Rather, as the JST specifies, Paul wrote that Jesus came in
the meridian of time to suffer for sins (JST, Hebrews 9:26). In the KJV,
Peter is quoted as saying "the end of all things is at hand" (1 Peter
4:7). But the JST reads: "But *to you,* the end of all things is at hand"
(JST, 1 Peter 4:7).

Of course, the retranslation of Matthew 24 (now Joseph Smith—
Matthew in the Pearl of Great Price) constitutes one of the most substantial doctrinal contributions found in the JST New Testament. It is
also a discussion topic in itself. Suffice it to say that a major change
this chapter makes in comparison to the KJV is its rearrangement of
verses. This is significant because events and descriptions are placed
in a more chronological sequence. The destruction of Jerusalem and
the temple in A.D. 70 are placed first, followed by the rise of false mes-

siahs (such as Bar-Cocheba in A.D. 135, and other pretenders). The signs of the times and events associated with the Second Coming and the inauguration of the Millennium are placed last. Viewed together, the following references provide us with an invaluable resource on the coming of the Lord: JST, Matthew 24; Joseph Smith—Matthew; JST, Matthew 13:39–44; JST, Luke 21:15; JST, Luke 12:41–57; JST, Luke 17:36–40; JST, 2 Thessalonians 2:2, 7–9; JST, 1 Corinthians 10:11; JST, 1 Peter 4:7.

Contribution 19: *The JST clarifies both Paul's teachings and the early Church's instruction regarding marriage and women.* Perhaps Paul's teachings on marriage and women have been his most misunderstood. It is important to note that 1 Corinthians, where many of the major difficulties appear, was not the earliest correspondence Paul sent to the Church members at Corinth. As the text itself makes clear, 1 Corinthians is a response to questions the Corinthians had already sent to Paul, after having received his first letter. So two previous pieces of correspondence have been lost. First Corinthians is a follow-up letter. Also, 1 Corinthians is missing important clarifications which only the JST restores. These clarifications often give the context of Paul's remarks. The best example is 1 Corinthians 7.

The KJV implies that it was Paul who said, "It is good for a man not to touch a woman" (1 Corinthians 7:1). The JST clarifies this with the addition of a single word, which then indicates that it was the Corinthian Saints who wrote to Paul "*saying,* it is good for a man not to touch a woman" (JST, 1 Corinthians 7:1). Another major clarification in the JST indicates that when Paul is talking about abstinence from marriage, he is talking about specific situations lasting for specified periods, most particularly missionary service. This then harmonizes with what Paul teaches just a few chapters later: "Nevertheless neither is the man without the woman, neither the woman without the man, *in the Lord*" (1 Corinthians 11:11, emphasis added; see also Hebrews 13:4).

Many other inconsistencies in 1 Corinthians are also resolved in the JST. One interesting insight is provided in 1 Corinthians 14:33–34. While the KJV has Paul telling women that they should keep silent in church, the JST changes the word *speak* to *rule.* Women may teach, counsel, testify, exhort, preach, preside over an auxiliary organization when so called, and lead out with their example (which they frequently do). But they are not to assume the rule of the Church. That is contrary to the Father's plan, as Joseph Smith testified.[19]

Contribution 20: *The JST New Testament teaches the fulness of the doctrine of repentance, linking it explicitly to the Atonement and harmonizing it with other Restoration scriptures.* The JST emphasizes that forgiveness and remission of sins comes by baptism *only* after faith in Christ and sincere repentance (JST, Matthew 3:38; JST, Matthew 12:26). Of the several passages that bear on the matter, perhaps the clearest is the following: "Verily I say unto you, All sins *which men have committed, when they repent,* shall be forgiven them; *for I came to preach repentance* unto the sons of men. And blasphemies, wherewith soever they shall blaspheme, *shall be forgiven them that come unto me, and do the works which they see me do. But there is a sin which shall not be forgiven.* He that shall blaspheme against the Holy Ghost, hath never forgiveness; but is in danger of *being cut down out of the world. And they shall inherit* eternal damnation." (JST, Mark 3:22–24.)

The JST also adds a major teaching of the Savior's concerning the repentance of little children, the power of his atonement, and the nature of the fall of Adam. Matthew 18:2 records that while Jesus was teaching his disciples in Galilee, he "called a little child unto him." He then used the child to help illustrate a central aspect of his mission: "For the Son of Man is come to save that which was lost, *and to call sinners to repentance; but these little ones have no need of repentance, and I will save them*" (JST, Matthew 18:11).

Just as does the Book of Mormon, the JST teaches that Jesus came to redeem everyone and everything, all of which were lost (utterly unredeemable) due to the Fall and the nature of mortality. Christ's atonement made redemption possible. In order to be fully redeemed all individuals must repent, except little children who need no repentance. They are "redeemed from the foundation of the world" through the Atonement (D&C 29:46).

One chapter later (Matthew 19:13), this doctrine is reemphasized. After Jesus and the Twelve had gone from Galilee to Judea, the people brought their children to the Savior, requesting that he bless the little ones. Matthew tells us that the disciples rebuked those who had brought forth their children. The disciples issued the rebuke not because they thought little children were a bother to Jesus (as the KJV seems to imply), but because, as the JST demonstrates, they were trying to apply the new doctrine they had just learned; namely, that little children will be saved unequivocally, as Jesus had taught earlier. They didn't need to be blessed to enjoy salvation. Of course, the Savior did some more teaching by blessing the children and commending the child-like virtues of faith, trust, and guilelessness. This new information fits in perfect harmony with what has been revealed by other prophet-authors. It is also a powerful witness to the compassion of our Lord.

Contribution 21: *The JST emphasizes the transforming power of the Atonement by clarifying the true nature and character of the Apostle Paul in Romans chapter 7.* The Epistle to the Romans is perhaps Paul's greatest doctrinal treatise in the New Testament. Reading chapter 7 without the clarifications and insights restored through the Prophet Joseph Smith is a depressing enterprise. Christian theologians and philosophers have been left to conclude that the Apostle Paul, and by extension all humans, are depraved, helpless creatures who are compelled to give in to their carnal natures and forced to muddle around in their inherently sinful circumstances.

The Joseph Smith Translation of Romans 7 presents quite a different picture. To be sure, the fall of Adam was powerful in its effects, and yes, every human being unquestionably inherited the effects of that fall. But far more powerful than the fall of Adam was the atonement of Jesus Christ! Its power is the power to take humankind out of the grasp of the Fall, as well as the grasp of Satan, and transform the human soul into something divine.

The KJV reports one of Paul's introspective moments as follows: "For we know that the law [of Moses] is spiritual: but I am carnal, sold under sin. For that which I do I allow not: for what I would, that do I not; but what I hate; that do I." Paul further laments, "For I know that in me (that is, in my flesh,) dwelleth no good thing: for to will is present with me; but how to perform that which is good I find not." (Romans 7:14–15, 18). This whole passage is indeed an enigma, for elsewhere Paul spent much of his ministry teaching the inferiority of the law of Moses compared with the transcendent qualities of the gospel, owing to the Atonement. Here he seems to be praising the law of Moses and demeaning the influence of the higher or gospel law which he accepted when he became a Christian.

We are thankful that we have the JST. Here is the way it changes the passage so as to emphasize Paul's true understanding of the power of Christ's gospel to reform all of us, to free us from the enticement and stain of sin: "For we know that the *commandment* is spiritual; but *when I was under the law, I was yet* carnal, sold under sin. *But now I am spiritual;* for that which *I am commanded to do, I do; and that which I am commanded not to allow,* I allow not. *For what I know is not right I would not do; for that which is sin,* I hate. . . . For I know that in me, that is, in my flesh, dwelleth no good thing; for to will is present with me, but to perform that which is good I find not, *only in Christ.*" (JST, Romans 7:14–16, 19.)

From another KJV passage in Romans one receives the impression that Paul wished he could have been separated from Christ for the sake of his Jewish associates. "For I could wish that myself were accursed from Christ for my brethren, my kinsmen according to the flesh" (Romans 9:3). But the JST makes it clear that these were his feelings before his conversion to and knowledge of Christ: "For *once I could have wished* that myself were accursed from Christ, for my brethren, my kinsmen according to the flesh" (JST, Romans 9:3). A careful reading of the JST New Testament reveals that after his conversion, one finds in the writings of Paul only profound praise for the gospel of Jesus Christ.

The Joseph Smith Translation makes the atonement of Christ so much more necessary and majestic than any other religious document or text can, except for the Book of Mormon. The personal reflections of the Apostle Paul, as presented in the JST, are an excellent example of both the transforming power of the Atonement and the confusion that arises when plain and precious truths get distorted, the influence of prophetic inspiration being lacking in the translation process.

Contribution 22: *The JST clarifies the person of Melchizedek and the high priesthood.* Much confusion has arisen in the world about the figure of Melchizedek, some of it due to the King James Version. The JST of Hebrews 7:3 makes clear that it was not Melchizedek who was "without father, without mother, without descent, having neither beginning of days, nor end of life" (KJV Hebrews 7:3). Rather, it was the high priesthood to which Melchizedek was ordained: *"For this Melchizedek was ordained a priest after the order of the Son of God, which order was* without father, without mother, without descent, having neither beginning of days, nor end of life" (JST, Hebrews 7:3). The same verse goes on to explain the significance of ordination to this priesthood for all those who accept it as Melchizedek did: *"And all those who are ordained unto this priesthood are* made like unto the Son of God, *abiding* a priest continually."

Later in the same chapter the JST makes a profound contribution to our understanding of a major difference between the Aaronic and Melchizedek priesthoods. The KJV of Hebrews 7:19 reads: "For the law [of Moses] made nothing perfect, but the bringing in of a better hope did; by the which we draw nigh unto God." Compare that statement with the magnificent additions found in the JST: "For the law [of Moses] *was administered without an oath* and made nothing perfect, but *was only* the bringing in of a better hope; by the which we draw nigh unto God. Inasmuch as *this high priest* was not without an oath, *by so much was Jesus made the surety of a better testament."* (JST, Hebrews 7:19.)

The priesthood associated with the law of Moses, the lesser or Aaronic Priesthood, truly is not equal to the perfecting priesthood of the full gospel. As the JST indicates, this difference can be seen in the fact that the Melchizedek Priesthood is received with an oath, while the Aaronic Priesthood is not. The JST testifies of the inferior nature of the law of Moses as compared with the gospel of Jesus Christ: "For the law was given *through* Moses, but *life* and truth came *through* Jesus Christ. *For the law was after a carnal commandment, to the administration of death; but the gospel was after the power of an endless life, through Jesus Christ, the Only Begotten Son, who is in the bosom of the Father."* (JST, John 1:17–18.)

Perhaps we can now more fully appreciate the stress which is placed upon the phrase "oath and covenant" of the priesthood (see D&C 84:39), and the distinction it denotes. The phrase refers to the procedure by which men may place themselves under God's tutelage, obtain the very power which he himself possesses, and become perfect like him. The phrase immediately distinguishes the power of God (the Melchizedek Priesthood) from the lesser or Aaronic order. Oaths convey a sense of fulness and perfection. Covenants are indeed two-way promises between man and God. But oaths are solemn promises to fulfill covenants. Oaths are made by invoking witnesses, and particularly in previous ages were often consummated by the oath-taker swearing by his own life that the terms and obligations of the oath would be met. If one honors the oath and covenant of the Melchizedek Priesthood, God's reciprocal promise is no less than exaltation.

Contribution 23: *The JST New Testament helps us to understand how faith, works, grace, and justification operate together for our salvation.* There seems to be some argument among Christians regarding what it is that saves us. The JST lays to rest the dispute. Just as the Book of Mormon harmonizes the concepts of faith, grace, and works, teaching that we cannot completely ignore righteous conduct in the saving process, so too the JST integrates the three doctrines in a relationship not clarified by other versions of the New Testament.

An important statement is found in JST, Romans 4:16: "Therefore *ye are justified* of faith *and works, through* grace, to the end the promise might be sure to all the seed; not to *them* only *who are* of the law, but to *them* also *who are* of the faith of Abraham; who is the father of us all." We are justified, or brought back into a right relationship with God, because several principles operate together: faith, repentance, baptism, continuing righteous actions, and ultimately the mercy of Christ as manifest in the Atonement. In other words, "it is by grace that we are saved, after all we can do" (2 Nephi 25:23). Without Christ, and his sacrifice, we would never be redeemed. We cannot perform enough good works to merit salvation on our own. But neither can we be redeemed by ignoring the commandments, doing nothing, or acting wickedly. As the JST says: "But to him that *seeketh not to be justified by the law of works*, but believeth on him who justifieth *not* the ungodly, his faith is counted for righteousness" (JST, Romans 4:5).

Contribution 24: *The JST New Testament teaches the antiquity of the gospel.* As with the JST Old Testament, the JST New Testament helps us to see that the preaching of the gospel did not commence with the ministry of Jesus in the Holy Land. Nor did the preaching of the gospel begin even at the time of Adam. The gospel we possess is much older. The opening verse of John's "Testimony" expresses it in these words: "In the beginning was the *gospel preached through the Son. And the gospel was the* word, and the word was *with the son, and the Son was with God,* and *the Son* was *of God*" (JST, John 1:1). In the KJV, this verse is worded so as to speak only of the Son as existing in the beginning with God. The JST plainly declares that both the Son and the gospel were in the beginning with the Gods! The gospel was the Father's plan.

Contribution 25: *The JST New Testament refines our perspective on mortality in comparison to eternity.* Life is short and sometimes difficult. We may even wonder at times if our righteous efforts and sacrifices in obedience are noticed. The JST gives us renewed confidence that the Lord cherishes and prizes nothing more highly than our obedience. Nothing will be rewarded as greatly as our loyalty to God. The KJV of Matthew 16:25–26 reads: "For whosoever will save his life shall lose it: and whosoever will lose his life for my sake shall find it. For what is a man profited, if he shall gain the whole world, and lose his own soul?"

The Joseph Smith Translation of these verses provides us with the Savior's expanded perspective on the purpose of mortality. Earth life is a probationary period of testing; eternity hangs in the balance. Nothing is nearly as important as one's commitment to the Savior: "*Break not my commandments for to save your lives;* for whosoever will save his life *in this world,* shall lose it *in the world to come.* And whosoever will lose his life *in this world,* for my sake, shall find it *in the world to come. Therefore, forsake the world, and save your souls;* for what is a man profited, if he shall gain the whole world, and lose his own soul? (JST, Matthew 16:27–29.) The corresponding section in Mark teaches the same basic lesson, but with a slightly different emphasis: "For whosoever will save his life, shall lose it; *or whosoever will save his life, shall be willing to lay it down for my sake; and if he is not willing to lay it down for my sake, he shall lose it.* But whosoever shall *be willing to* lose his life for my sake, and the *gospel,* the same shall save it." (JST, Mark 8:37–38.)

Perhaps no mortal better exemplified these verses than the Prophet Joseph Smith, the very one who gave us this remarkable and meaningful new translation of the scriptures. May the Prophet's translation inspire us to be more like the Savior and the disciples the Prophet came to know so well as a result of his translating.

Conclusion

Many other doctrines of the plan of salvation are clarified and elaborated upon in the Joseph Smith Translation of the New Testament. They include the nature of the Sabbath, the sacrament, Satan, casting pearls before swine, turning the other cheek, the nature of sin and temptation, who has seen God, and the death of Judas Iscariot. A careful study of the changes made in the JST reveals that the New Testament teaches doctrine with clarity and power. When compared with doctrinal concepts found in other volumes of scripture, the JST New Testament demonstrates a complete harmony and continuity.

May I plead with us to use the JST New Testament with vigor in all we do, particularly as we study the New Testament. We can read and teach from it with complete confidence, knowing it is the word of the Lord. I know it is given by the Lord to us because he cares about us so deeply. As he said to Joseph Smith, just before the Prophet embarked on the translation of the New Testament, "Great things await you" (D&C 45:62).

I believe that when we read and teach from the JST we place ourselves on firm doctrinal ground. We are blessed with restored portions of uncorrupted text in this age of great confusion. When we study the JST New Testament we not only honor the Prophet after whom the translation is called but we also honor our God.

I believe with all my heart that if we will use the JST, a spirit and power will come over us such as we have not felt in a long time. We will develop a renewed appreciation and witness of the Prophet Joseph Smith. But more important, we will come to understand and love the Savior as never before.

Notes

1. Donald Q. Cannon and Lyndon W. Cook, eds., *The Far West Record* (Salt Lake City: Deseret Book Co., 1983), p. 23.

2. In Dean C. Jessee, comp., *The Personal Writings of Joseph Smith* (Salt Lake City: Deseret Book Co., 1984), p. 248.

3. HC 1:238.

4. In Robert J. Matthews, *Plainer Translation*, p. 267.

5. TPJS, pp. 369–71.

6. TPJS, p. 181.

7. See the introductory heading to section 76.

8. See the summary heading at the beginning of the section.

9. Figures for the changes are taken from Matthews, *Plainer Translation*, p. 425.

10. *Journal of Discourses* 5:83–84.

11. Kenneth L. Woodward, "The Death of Jesus," *Newsweek* (4 April 1994), p. 49.

12. The first three Gospels are called synoptic, after the Greek *synoptikos* ("to see alike"), and present their information in a similar way, using common phraseology and similar main points.

13. See Robert W. Funk, Roy W. Hoover, et al., *The Five Gospels: The Search for the Authentic Words of Jesus* (New York: Macmillan Publishing Company, 1993).

14. See Marcus J. Borg, "Jesus in Four Colors," *Bible Review* (December, 1993), p. 10.

15. Robert W. Funk, Roy Hoover, et al., *The Five Gospels*, p. 7, emphasis added.

16. TPJS, p. 392.

17. TPJS, p. 181.

18. Bruce R. McConkie, *Mormon Doctrine*, 2d ed. (Salt Lake City: Bookcraft, 1966), p. 221.

19. See TPJS, p. 212; Bruce R. McConkie, *Doctrinal New Testament Commentary*, 3 vols. (Salt Lake City: Bookcraft, 1966–73), 2:387.

6

The Joseph Smith Translation and the Doctrine and Covenants

LARRY E. DAHL

What is the relationship of the Joseph Smith Translation of the Bible and the Doctrine and Covenants? To investigate that question is an exciting venture, leading to a better appreciation of the role of the Prophet Joseph Smith in restoring the fulness of the gospel, important insights into the history of The Church of Jesus Christ of Latter-day Saints, better comprehension of the process of revelation, and a clearer understanding of the text of the Doctrine and Covenants— and more! The "more" includes such eternally significant things as an increased faith in the Lord Jesus Christ; wonderment and gratitude for the love of God, the great plan of redemption, and the restoration of the gospel in this dispensation; respect and love for the Prophet Joseph Smith; and, perhaps, as important as any benefit, encourage- ment to forge ahead with commitment and optimism, seeking "to bring forth and establish the cause of Zion" (D&C 6:6).

To begin, let us consider the following words of Robert J. Matthews, the acknowledged authority in the Church today on the JST:

> The work that the Prophet Joseph did in making a new translation of the Bible resulted in much more than the single production of a manuscript of the Bible. In the process of the translation the Prophet re- ceived many revelations about various subjects which have greatly added

to the scripture and doctrine of the church in this dispensation. In fact, the revelations that came in the process of the Bible translation are better known and more widely used than the translation itself.

Many of the revelations that comprise the Doctrine and Covenants have a direct relationship to the translation of the Bible which the Prophet Joseph was making at the time the revelations were received. They consist of two kinds: (1) directions or instructions to the Prophet about the Bible translation and (2) doctrinal revelations given to the Prophet while he was engaged in the translation process.[1]

To help us better understand the relationship of the JST and the Doctrine and Covenants we will first address category 1. We will examine the verses of each revelation that refer directly to the JST, and provide some commentary about the context and significance of each entry. Then we will briefly discuss category 2, citing examples of different dimensions of doctrinal relatedness of the JST and the revelations in the Doctrine and Covenants. Finally, we will summarize and highlight the purposes and importance of the JST as identified in the Doctrine and Covenants. And because we will be focusing directly on the purposes and importance of the JST at the end of the paper, we will not pay particular attention to such matters as we review, in order, the various sections in which the JST is mentioned.

As we proceed it will be helpful to note what words are used in the revelations to refer to the JST. The Lord refers to the project as "my scriptures" (35:20; 42:56; 93:53), "the fulness of my scriptures" (42:15; 104:58), "the work of translation" (73:4; 76:15), "translation of the prophets," referring to the Old Testament (90:13), and "the new translation of my holy word" (124:89). Hence it appears that it is appropriate to call it a "translation," even though the Prophet Joseph was not, at least at this early date, acquainted with the ancient languages used in writing the original Bible manuscripts and did not have those manuscripts at his disposal. Other terms in common usage to refer to the JST, though these are not found in the Doctrine and Covenants, include "Inspired Translation," "Inspired Version," "Inspired Revision," and "Holy Scriptures." *Holy Scriptures* is the title given the publication of the JST by the Reorganized Church of Jesus Christ of Latter Day Saints. They have published four major editions of the work, 1867, 1944, 1974, and 1991. The Church of Jesus Christ of Latter-day Saints has not published the complete text of the JST. In the Pearl of Great Price, however, and in the footnotes and the "Joseph Smith Translation" appendix to the LDS edition of the King James Version of the Bible, it has provided access to most of the textual changes having doctrinal significance.

Category One: Instructions About the JST

Section 35

The first direct Doctrine and Covenants mention of a translation of the Bible is in section 35. Sidney Rigdon had been converted and baptized in the Kirtland area in November 1830.[2] He then travelled to Fayette, N.Y., to meet Joseph Smith. Arriving early in December 1830, Sidney asked the Prophet to enquire of the Lord concerning his (Sidney's) duties, and D&C 35 was given. In the revelation the Lord called Sidney Rigdon to be a scribe for Joseph in the Bible translation: "And a commandment I give unto thee—that thou shalt write for him; and the scriptures shall be given, even as they are in mine own bosom, to the salvation of mine own elect" (D&C 35:20).

The translation had been in progress at least since the previous June, with Oliver Cowdery and John Whitmer serving as scribes. Thus, prior to the arrival of Sidney Rigdon in December 1830, the visions of Moses (Moses 1) and Genesis chapters 1 through 4 (KJV) had been completed. After his appointment by revelation to be the Prophet's scribe in the translation, Sidney Rigdon "did most, but not all, of the original scribal work thereafter until the translation was 'finished' on July 2, 1833."[3] John Whitmer, officially appointed Church historian and scribe for the Prophet Joseph in March 1831 (D&C 47) three months after the arrival of Sidney Rigdon, continued to be involved in the JST, mainly in transcribing (copying) the original manuscripts. He also served as scribe for some of the original manuscripts in the New Testament—Matthew 26–Mark 8. Others who may have been involved in a limited way include Emma Smith and Frederick G. Williams.[4]

Section 37

The next revelation mentioning the JST came shortly after Sidney Rigdon was appointed scribe, still in December 1830. The Lord revealed that the Church "should assemble together at the Ohio" (D&C 37:3) and instructed Joseph and Sidney: "Behold, I say unto you that it is not expedient in me that ye should translate any more until ye shall go to the Ohio" (D&C 37:1). Obedient to the Lord's call, they left New York the "latter part of January," arriving in Kirtland, Ohio, "about the first of February."[5]

Section 41

Within days of their arrival in Ohio, another revelation was received that pertains to the JST. Dated 4 February 1831, it says: "And again, it is meet that my servant Joseph Smith, Jun., should have a house built, in which to live and translate" (D&C 41:7). Was such a house built for Joseph Smith, in which to live and translate? Yes. Isaac Morley owned a farm on the northeast edge of Kirtland. He was generous in allowing Church members gathering to Ohio to settle on his land. In response to the Lord's instruction a small home (either a log cabin or a frame house) was built on the Morley farm for Joseph and Emma, where they lived for six months.[6]

Section 42

Just five days after D&C 41 came D&C 42, 9 February 1831. Concerning the JST this revelation says:

> And again, the elders, priests and teachers of this church shall teach the principles of my gospel, which are in the Bible and the Book of Mormon, in the which is the fulness of the gospel.
> And they shall observe the covenants and church articles to do them, and these shall be their teachings, as they shall be directed by the Spirit.
> And the Spirit shall be given unto you by the prayer of faith; and if ye receive not the Spirit ye shall not teach.

JOSEPH SMITH TRANSLATION—
CHRONOLOGY

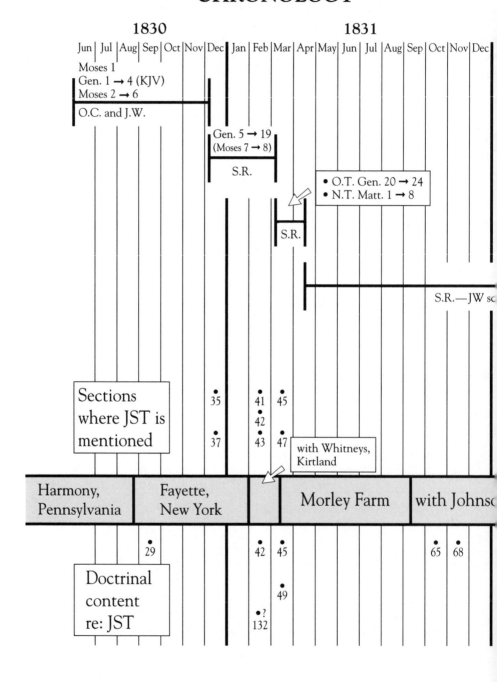

1830

Jun | Jul | Aug | Sep | Oct | Nov | Dec

Moses 1
Gen. 1 → 4 (KJV)
Moses 2 → 6

O.C. and J.W.

Gen. 5 → 19
(Moses 7 → 8)

S.R.

1831

Jan | Feb | Mar | Apr | May | Jun | Jul | Aug | Sep | Oct | Nov | Dec

- O.T. Gen. 20 → 24
- N.T. Matt. 1 → 8

S.R.

S.R.—JW sc

Sections
where JST is
mentioned

•35   •41   •45
       •42
•37   •43   •47

with Whitneys,
Kirtland

Harmony,
Pennsylvania

Fayette,
New York

Morley Farm

with Johns

•29

•42   •45

•65   •68

Doctrinal
content
re: JST

•49

•?
132

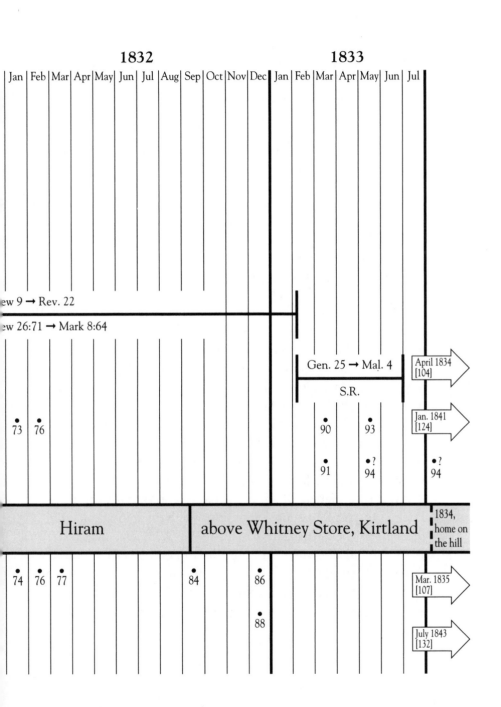

1832   1833

Jan | Feb | Mar | Apr | May | Jun | Jul | Aug | Sep | Oct | Nov | Dec | Jan | Feb | Mar | Apr | May | Jun | Jul

ew 9 → Rev. 22

ew 26:71 → Mark 8:64

Gen. 25 → Mal. 4   April 1834
                       [104]
        S.R.

•   •   •   •   Jan. 1841
73   76   90   93   [124]

                                         •   •?   •?
                                         91   94   94

Hiram   above Whitney Store, Kirtland   1834, home on the hill

•   •   •   •   •   Mar. 1835
74 76 77   84   86   [107]

                                           •
                                           88

                                                             July 1843
                                                             [132]

And all this ye shall observe to do as I have commanded concerning your teaching, until the fulness of my scriptures is given. . . .

Thou shalt ask, and my scriptures shall be given as I have appointed, and they shall be preserved in safety;

And it is expedient that thou shouldst hold thy peace concerning them, and not teach them until ye have received them in full.

And I give unto you a commandment that then ye shall teach them unto all men; for they shall be taught unto all nations, kindreds, tongues and people.

Thou shalt take the things which thou hast received, which have been given unto thee in my scriptures for a law, to be my law to govern my church;

And he that doeth according to these things shall be saved, and he that doeth them not shall be damned if he so continue. (D&C 42:12–15, 56–60.)

These verses clearly portray the importance of the JST in the mind of the Lord. The implication of *until* in verse 15 is that once the translation is done, it is to be used in teaching the gospel. Perhaps that injunction is something those of us in the modern Church should more closely follow. It seems that Latter-day Saints should make a special effort to know and share how the JST informs, corrects, enhances, and adds to our understanding of the gospel, beyond the translations of the Bible generally available.

The instruction in verse 57 about not teaching the new translation until it is received in full seems to apply to teaching it to the world, not to the Church, for verse 59 indicates that the truths revealed through the JST are to be used to govern the Church. Perhaps it was this revelation which prompted Joseph Smith to refuse W. W. Phelps's request for permission to print the New Translation serially in the Church newspaper. In a letter to W. W. Phelps dated 21 April 1833, the Prophet wrote: "It is not the will of the Lord to print any of the New Translation in the *Star*; but when it is published, it will all go to the world together, in a volume by itself; and the New Testament and the Book of Mormon will be printed together."[7]

Section 43

Still in February 1831, along with section 41 calling for a house to be built for Joseph and the verses in section 42 we have just considered, came section 43, offering the elders of the Church a conditional blessing:

> And if ye desire the glories of the kingdom, appoint ye my servant Joseph Smith, Jun., and uphold him before me by the prayer of faith.
>
> And again, I say unto you, that if ye desire the mysteries of the kingdom, provide for him food and raiment, and whatsoever thing he needeth to accomplish the work wherewith I have commanded him;
>
> And if ye do it not he shall remain unto them that have received him, that I may reserve unto myself a pure people before me. (D&C 43:12–14.)

Webster's 1828 *American Dictionary of the English Language* and modern dictionaries agree that one of the meanings of the word *appoint* (v. 12) is to "furnish; equip with things necessary." That seems to be the intent of these verses. Joseph Smith needed, in addition to a house, the faith and prayers of Church members, and provisions of "food and raiment" so that he could accomplish what the Lord had commanded him to do. An important part of what he had been commanded to do was to make a new translation of the Bible. If the elders supplied the needed provisions, they were promised the glories of the kingdom, or the mysteries of the kingdom; if they did not, they would lose their tie to the Prophet and not be numbered among the people of the Lord—a pure people he reserves unto himself. Looking closely at verses 12 and 13, it appears the conditional promise is given twice, perhaps for emphasis.

From February 1831 to the martyrdom of Joseph Smith in 1844 repeated calls went out in sermons, epistles, and notices in Church newspapers for funds to assist in completing and publishing the scriptures, including the JST. In addition, certain brethren were appointed by the First Presidency "to go throughout the Church" appealing for contributions.[8] One has to wonder what blessings did not come to the Church in those critical years that could have come had the members been more willing to help with needed resources. And in the same breath, so to speak, one has to wonder what blessings could now come to the Church if, as a people, we paid more attention to the JST than we currently do.

Section 45

The date of 7 March 1831 brought section 45, the sixth revelation in three months (December 1830 to March 1831) to include instructions concerning the JST (sections 35, 37, 41, 42, 43, and 45). After revealing to Joseph Smith some of what he told his disciples on the Mount of Olives in A.D. 33 about the impending destruction of Jerusalem and the signs of his second coming (D&C 45:15–59), the Lord added: "And now, behold, I say unto you, it shall not be given unto you to know any further concerning this chapter, until the New Testament be translated, and in it all these things shall be made known; wherefore I give unto you that ye may now translate it, that ye may be prepared for the things to come (D&C 45:60–61).

What is meant by "this chapter"? It does not seem to have a context, or a referent in this revelation. It is interesting to note that in the first printing of this revelation in the Book of Commandments[9] (chapter 48, verse 54) the wording was, "it shall not be given unto you to know *any further than this* until the new testament be translated." Given the words *chapter* and *New Testament*, and noting that the occasion is the Savior explaining to his disciples in A.D. 33 about the destruction of Jerusalem and the signs of his coming to the earth in glory, it all points to Matthew 24 being "this chapter." When and why was the wording of the revelation changed? The change came in the first edition of the Doctrine and Covenants in 1835, after the translation of the New Testament was "finished," perhaps to relate section 45 to that "chapter" in the New Testament—Matthew 24—which deals with the same content. The connection may have seemed so obvious to the brethren preparing the revelations for publication that they didn't see the need for specifying which "chapter" was meant.

After learning what they did from section 45, Joseph Smith and Sidney Rigdon must have looked forward anxiously to the "further" knowledge awaiting them through the translation of the New

Testament, which they were now instructed to begin. In fact, from the New Testament manuscripts we can tell that they began the very next day, 8 March 1831. From then until April 5 they worked on the Old Testament and the New Testament concurrently. In that month's time they translated Genesis 20–24 and Matthew 1–8. They then laid the Old Testament aside, apparently until the New Testament was "finished," nearly two years later. Under the date of 2 February 1833, the Prophet recorded, "I completed the translation and review of the New Testament, on the 2nd of February, 1833, and sealed it up, no more to be opened till it arrived in Zion."[10] The reason for sending it to Zion (Independence, Jackson County, Missouri) was that the Church printing press, under the direction of W. W. Phelps, was there, and they were anticipating publishing the complete text of the translation.

Section 73

The next revelation that speaks of the JST is section 73. It was received 10 January 1832, ten months after D&C 45. It reads: "Now, verily I say unto you my servants, Joseph Smith, Jun., and Sidney Rigdon, saith the Lord, it is expedient to translate again; and, inasmuch as it is practicable, to preach in the regions round about until conference; and after that it is expedient to continue the work of translation until it be finished" (D&C 73:3–4).

Though the Prophet and Sidney Rigdon had worked diligently at the translation since the previous spring, there had been several interruptions—conferences, a missionary journey to Missouri in July and August, Joseph and Emma's move from the Morley farm to Hiram, Ohio, in September, and most recently an assignment from the Lord in early December to "proclaim unto the world in the regions round about [Kirtland], and in the church also, for the space of a season" to "confound your enemies" (D&C 71:2, 7). Of that assignment, Joseph reported:

> From this time [3 December 1831] until the 8th or 10th of January, 1832, myself and Elder Rigdon continued to preach in Shalersville, Ravenna, and other places, setting forth the truth, vindicating the cause of our Redeemer; showing that the day of vengeance was coming upon

this generation like a thief in the night; that prejudice, blindness and darkness filled the minds of many, and caused them to persecute the true Church, and reject the true light; by which means we did much towards allaying the excited feelings which were growing out of the scandalous letters than being published in the *Ohio Star,* at Ravenna, by the before-mentioned apostate, Ezra Booth.[11]

After this five-week hiatus it was time to translate again. The Prophet and Sidney Rigdon were instructed of the Lord to continue with the translation "until it be finished." Clearly, the Lord wanted this work done; it was an important priority. But why was it so important? Robert J. Matthews has suggested, and I believe rightly so, that the translation of the Bible had at least two major purposes: (1) to restore to the earth precious truths of the gospel which were once in the scriptural record, or should have been, and (2) to tutor Joseph Smith, "giving him knowledge and understanding that he did not possess beforehand," resulting "in the spiritual education of the Prophet."[12] A wonderful example of the translation contributing to both these purposes is the next revelation discussed here, section 76.

Section 76

It was 16 February 1832. Joseph and Emma were living with the John Johnson family on their farm in Hiram, Ohio. Sidney Rigdon lived in a home within a few blocks of the Johnson home. They were busily engaged in translating the New Testament, and on this day they were considering chapter 5 of John. Several verses in the revelation provide some context:

> For while we were doing the work of translation, which the Lord had appointed unto us, we came to the twenty-ninth verse of the fifth chapter of John, which was given unto us as follows—
> Speaking of the resurrection of the dead, concerning those who shall hear the voice of the Son of Man:
> And shall come forth; they who have done good, in the resurrection of the just; and they who have done evil, in the resurrection of the unjust.
> Now this caused us to marvel, for it was given unto us of the Spirit.

And while we meditated upon these things, the Lord touched the eyes of our understandings and they were opened, and the glory of the Lord shone round about. (D&C 76:15–19.)

What caused them to marvel? The translation of the verse is nearly the same as the KJV of John 5:29, except that the terms *life* and *damnation* in John are replaced with *the just* and *the unjust* in D&C 76. Something more had to be happening. It is clear that the translation of John 5:29 was "given" to them by the Spirit. Perhaps it was the Spirit that also caused them to "marvel" and to "meditate upon these things," leading to the opening of their understandings, and to their privilege to see and hear the marvelous things they witnessed as the vision of the glories burst upon them. The translation of one short verse of scripture was the catalyst for their experiencing a vision lasting probably one and one-half hours—as long as a full-length movie.[13] What they were marvelling about and meditating upon is possibly identified in Joseph Smith's introduction to section 76 in the *History of the Church*. He said:

> Upon my return from Amherst conference, I resumed the translation of the Scriptures. From sundry revelations which had been received, it was apparent that many important points touching the salvation of man, had been taken from the Bible, or lost before it was compiled. It appeared self-evident from what truths were left, that if God rewarded every one according to the deeds done in the body the term "Heaven," as intended for the Saints' eternal home must include more kingdoms than one. Accordingly, on the 16th of February, 1832, while translating St. John's Gospel, myself and Elder Rigdon saw the following vision.[14]

Whether that principle was on their minds before they translated John 5:29, or whether the wonderment struck them as they translated the verse by the power of the Spirit, is not said. They may have wondered about such things previously and then had the question impressed upon them in a powerful way during the process of translation of verse 29. Whatever may be true in that regard, the results of their efforts were marvelous, for us and for them. The revelation gives us important truths about the eternal possibilities awaiting mankind in the world to come—truths which were not known by the religious world in 1832 and, we sadly note, are not understood and accepted by most today. The reality of those truths, and the vision that brought them, led the Prophet Joseph to proclaim:

> Nothing could be more pleasing to the Saints upon the order of the kingdom of the Lord, than the light which burst upon the world through the foregoing vision. Every law, every commandment, every promise, every truth, and every point touching the destiny of man, from Genesis to Revelation, where the purity of the scriptures remains unsullied by the folly of men, go to show the perfection of the theory [of different degrees of glory in the future life] and witnesses the fact that that document is a transcript from the records of the eternal world. The sublimity of the ideas; the purity of the language; the scope for action; the continued duration for completion, in order that the heirs of salvation may confess the Lord and bow the knee; the rewards for faithfulness, and the punishments for sins, are so much beyond the narrow-mindedness of men, that every honest man is constrained to exclaim: "It came from God."[15]

Again, it should be remembered that all of this came as a result of the inspired translation of one verse of scripture in the Bible.

Section 90

After the vision of the glories received in February 1832, nothing more is said about the JST in the text of the revelations in the Doctrine and Covenants for a period of one year, until March 1833. Then came section 90. Concerning the JST this revelation says: "And when you have finished the translation of the prophets, you shall from thenceforth preside over the affairs of the church and the school" (D&C 90:13).

The Prophet was translating "the prophets," or the Old Testament, having finished the New Testament a month earlier—2 February 1833. It should be remembered that work on the JST began with the Old Testament and proceeded through Genesis chapter 24. Then work on the Old Testament was laid aside for nearly two years, from early April 1831 to February 1833, until the New Testament was completed. By the time section 90 was received on 8 March 1833, it seems the expectation was that the translation of the Old Testament would also soon be completed and that Joseph Smith and Sidney Rigdon could then devote themselves to their First Presidency duties identified in this revelation—presiding over the Church and the school (meaning the School of the Prophets, called for in section 88 a few months earlier); receiving "revelations to unfold the mysteries of the Kingdom;" studying, learning, and becoming "acquainted with all good books, and with languages, tongues, and people;" and setting in order their own houses (D&C 90:13–18).

Section 91

The very next day, 9 March 1833, section 91 came. Concerning this revelation, in his history the Prophet wrote: "Having come to that portion of the ancient writings called the Apocrypha, I received the following."[16] The revelation is six short verses:

> Verily, thus saith the Lord unto you concerning the Apocrypha—There are many things contained therein that are true, and it is mostly translated correctly;
> There are many things contained therein that are not true, which are interpolations by the hands of men.
> Verily, I say unto you, that it is not needful that the Apocrypha should be translated.
> Therefore, whoso readeth it, let him understand, for the spirit manifesteth truth;
> And whoso is enlightened by the Spirit shall obtain benefit therefrom;
> And whoso receiveth not by the Spirit, cannot be benefited. Therefore it is not needful that it should be translated. Amen. (D&C 91:1–6.)

In the 1828 edition of the King James Bible which Joseph Smith and Sidney Rigdon were using for the translation, the Apocrypha was located between the Old and New Testaments.[17] If they were still in the process of translating "the prophets" on March 8, how could they "come to that portion of the ancient writings called the Apocrypha" by March 9, the very next day? Obviously they could not have completed translating the rest of the Old Testament in one day. In fact, that they did not do so is clear from a revelation two months later, which told them to hasten the work (D&C 93:53). How then did they "come to" the Apocrypha on March 9?

It may be that the instruction in section 90 to finish the translation of the prophets, then turn to other things, led Joseph and Sidney to consider carefully the amount of translating they had yet to do. During that consideration, possibly on March 9, once they had thumbed through the Old Testament (from whatever page had been completed in the translation by March 8) to the end of Malachi, they would have "come to" the Apocrypha. Where did it fit? Was it to be considered part of "the prophets?" Should it be translated? These kinds of questions may have arisen in their minds, and elicited from the Lord the revelation we know as section 91. And such a scenario could account for the dating of that section as March 9, even though they had not yet completed the translation of the prophets of the Old Testament.

Section 93

We have already made brief mention of section 93 as having been received in May 1833. Here Joseph Smith was instructed to hasten the translation. The pertinent verse reads: "And, verily I say unto you, that it is my will that you should hasten to translate my scriptures, and to obtain a knowledge of history, and of countries, and of kingdoms, of laws of God and man, and all this for the salvation of Zion. Amen." (D&C 93:53.)

Hasten they did, completing the work on 2 July 1833. A letter "To the Brethren in Zion," written by Sidney Rigdon and signed by the First Presidency, dated 2 July 1833, contains the following statements about the JST: "We are exceedingly fatigued, owing to a great press of business. We this day finished the translating of the scriptures, for which we returned gratitude to our Heavenly Father. . . . Having finished the translation of the Bible, a few hours since. . . ."[18]

Section 94

There is some question about the dating of the next revelation to mention the JST—section 94. The earliest manuscript copies date it 2

August 1833, but later printings, including the section headings in all editions of the Doctrine and Covenants, have dated it May or 6 May 1833.[19] For our purposes the dating is not critical; it is the message of the revelation that is important. By the time section 94 was received the focus had shifted from *translating* the Bible to *printing* the translation. The revelation calls for two buildings to be built, in addition to the temple, and in close proximity to the temple in Kirtland. On the first lot south of the temple, an office building for the First Presidency was to be erected. The revelation then says: "And again, verily I say unto you, the second lot on the south shall be dedicated unto me for the building of a house unto me, for the work of the printing of the translation of my scriptures, and all things whatsoever I shall command you" (D&C 94:10).[20]

Section 104

Without doubt, the Lord desired the translation of the Bible to be printed. This desire was underscored the following April 1834 when the Lord said: "And for this purpose I have commanded you to organize yourselves, even to print my words, the fulness of my scriptures, the revelations which I have given unto you, and which I shall, hereafter, from time to time give unto you—for the purpose of building up my church and kingdom on the earth, and to prepare my people for the time when I shall dwell with them, which is nigh at hand" (D&C 104:58–59).

Verse 58 can be seen as evidence that the translation of the scriptures comprises revelations given of the Lord, and is given equal billing to that of the revelations which had been given to that time, and which would be given thereafter—an important truth concerning how the Lord views the JST.

An interesting bit of further evidence of the serious intent to publish the translation is found in the manuscript copy of section 104. Though not part of the canonized, published accounts of the revelation, this portion speaks of obtaining a copyright of the new translation, along with copyrights for the Book of Mormon and the "Articles and Covenants," or the revelations to be printed in the Doctrine and Covenants. The information appears in the manuscript copy between

verses 59 and 60 of section 104, and reads: "Therefore, a commandment I give unto you, that ye shall take the books of Mormon and also
the copy-right, and also the copy-right which shall be secured of the
Articles and Covenants in which covenants all my commandments
which it is my will should be printed, shall be printed, as it shall be
made known unto you; and also the copy-right of the new translation
of the scripture; and this I say that others may not take the blessings
away from you which I have conferred upon you."[21]

Section 124

The final direct reference to the JST in the Doctrine and
Covenants comes in section 124, dated 19 January 1841, nearly seven
years after section 104. The focus is still the publication of the JST.
The pertinent verse is directed to William Law, who is called in this
revelation as a counselor in the First Presidency, to serve with Joseph
Smith and Sidney Rigdon. The instruction concerning William Law
is: "If he will do my will let him from henceforth hearken to the counsel of my servant Joseph, and with his interest support the cause of the
poor, and publish the new translation of my holy word unto the inhabitants of the earth" (D&C 124:89).

With all the troubles that followed the Prophet and the Church
in Kirtland and Missouri from 1834 through 1839, and with the pressures of trying to reestablish a community of Saints, this time in
Nauvoo, the new translation of the Bible had not yet been published
as a whole. The intent to publish it as a complete text "unto the inhabitants of the earth," however, was still very much a matter of concern. That intent continued with the Prophet Joseph Smith, unful-
filled, to the end of his life in 1844.[22] Only extracts of the translation
were published before the Prophet died: *The Evening and the Morning
Star* published the early chapters of Genesis in 1832–33; excerpts were
quoted in the *Lectures on Faith* in 1834; a separate broadsheet of the
translation of Matthew 24 was published sometime between 1832 and
1837; and the *Times and Seasons* published the visions of Moses (Moses
1) in 1843.[23] The publication of the JST as a complete text waited
until 1867, when it was done by the Reorganized Church of Jesus
Christ of Latter Day Saints. As mentioned earlier, The Church of

Jesus Christ of Latter-day Saints has never published the JST as a complete text, but it has provided access to significant changes in the text in the Pearl of Great Price and through the footnotes and the Joseph Smith Translation appendix in the LDS edition of the Bible, 1979 to the present.

Category Two: Doctrinal Relatedness

There are at least three dimensions of doctrinal relatedness between the JST and the Doctrine and Covenants: 1) whole sections of the Doctrine and Covenants on doctrinal themes received in response to questions arising out of the translation; 2) doctrinal items revealed during the translation of the Bible which appear in the Doctrine and Covenants, either near the time of the translation, or sometime later; and 3) doctrinal information revealed to the Prophet in a section of the Doctrine and Covenants which later appears in the translation of the Bible. It may be helpful to cite examples of each of these dimensions of doctrinal relatedness and to provide a brief commentary. Before doing so, however, a word of caution is in order.

We are here discussing the principle of a prophet of God receiving revelation. And that process does not confine itself to mortal methodologies. It is generally agreed in academia, by those who adopt the historical method, that if two or more documents contain the same ideas or wording, the documents have an interdependency, or derive from a common source document. Confidence that such interdependency exists increases with every added similarity of ideas, diction, and style. The principle is reasonable, and seems to work well in the world of secular scholarship as one attempts to sort out the interdependency and source of written documents, the provenance of which is not clearly known. And the principle works as well in the world of religious scholarship, if one is willing to accept revelation from God as the original source of several interdependent documents or, just as possible, the independent source of a number of documents which contain similar ideas, words, and style.

It seems to me important that we accept revelation from God as the source of both the Joseph Smith Translation and the Doctrine and

Covenants, as well as other documents which may contain similar doctrines, words, and style—i.e., the Book of Mormon, the Pearl of Great Price, and entries in the history of the Church reporting the messages received from Moroni, John the Baptist, or others. Therefore, as we examine the similarity of content between the JST and the Doctrine and Covenants, the dating of the information received, and the possible interdependence of these documents, we must be careful to remain somewhat tentative in our conclusions. Some connections are known because they are so stated in the historical record. Other connections seem obvious enough to speak of them with a good degree of confidence. Still others fall into the "possible" category—interesting but uncertain connections. With these cautions in mind, let us proceed to point to examples, and briefly discuss the previously mentioned three dimensions of doctrinal relatedness between the JST and the Doctrine and Covenants.

Whole Sections of the D&C

We have already pointed out that section 76, the vision of the glories, was received in answer to questions arising from the translation of one verse in the Bible, John 5:29. Other whole sections of the Doctrine and Covenants which are definitely tied to the JST include sections 74, 77, and 91. Each of these revelations the Prophet introduced with a statement that it came in connection with the translation:

> [D&C 74] Upon the reception of the foregoing word of the Lord [D&C 73, 10 January 1832], I recommenced the translation of the Scriptures, and labored diligently until just before the conference, which was to convene on the 25th of January. During this period, I also received the following, as an explanation of [1 Corinthians 7:14].[24]

> [D&C 77] About the first of March, in connection with the translation of the Scriptures, I received the following explanation of the Revelation of St. John.[25]

> [D&C 91—Under the date of 9 March 1833] Having come to that portion of the ancient writings called the Apocrypha, I received the following.[26]

A close comparison of the dates for sections 77 and 91 with the chronology of the translation of the Bible shows that the revelations probably did not come at the same time the Prophet was in the process of translating the particular part of the Bible to which the revelations relate. We simply do not have sufficient information, either from the manuscripts of the translation or from the history of the Church, to explain all the details of sequence and the reasons thereof. It has previously been suggested how section 91 might have come when it did. Concerning section 77, it may be that questions about John the Revelator's vision arose in the minds of the two brethren, even though they were not translating the book of Revelation at that time. In response to such questions, the Prophet may have asked the Lord for answers and recorded those answers under the date they were received. Such a possibility may explain why section 77, which contains answers to questions about the book of Revelation, the last book of the New Testament, was received in March 1832, eleven months before the New Testament was finished.

Two other sections of the Doctrine and Covenants, 7 and 113, are wholly devoted to explaining biblical passages but may or may not have ties to the JST. They fall into the "possible" category—interesting but uncertain connections.

Section 7 was received in April 1829 while Joseph Smith, with Oliver Cowdery as scribe, was translating the Book of Mormon. In his history the Prophet introduced this section as follows:

> During the month of April I continued to translate, and he to write, with little cessation, during which time we received several revelations. A difference of opinion arising between us about the account of John the Apostle, mentioned in the New Testament, as to whether he died or continued to live, we mutually agreed to settle it by the Urim and Thummim and the following is the word which we received: Revelation given to Joseph Smith, Jun., and Oliver Cowdery, in Harmony, Pennsylvania, April, 1829, when they desired to know whether John, the beloved disciple, tarried on earth or died. Translated from parchment, written and hid up by himself.[27]

What connection might section 7 have to the JST? Section 7 was first published in 1833 (apparently as received in April 1829) as chapter

6 in the Book of Commandments. When it was published in the 1835 Doctrine and Covenants as section 33, however, it included additional wording. The original wording and the added portion are shown in the following quotation, the italicized words indicating what was added in the 1835 printing:

And the Lord said unto me, John, my beloved, what desirest thou? *For if ye shall ask, what you will, it shall be granted unto you.* And I said *unto him,* Lord, give unto me power *over death,* that I may *live and* bring souls unto thee. And the Lord said unto me, Verily, verily, I say unto thee, because thou desiredst this thou shalt tarry till *(until)* I come in my glory, *and shall prophesy before nations, kindreds, tongues and people.*

And for this cause the Lord said unto Peter, If I will that he tarry till I come, what is that to thee? For he desiredst of me that he might bring souls unto me; but thou desiredst that thou might speedily come unto me in my kingdom. I say unto thee, Peter, this was a good desire, but my beloved has *desired that he might do more, or a greater work, yet among men than what he has before done; yea, he has* undertaken a greater work; *therefore, I will make him as flaming fire and a ministering angel: he shall minister for those who shall be heirs of salvation who dwell on the earth; and I will make thee to minister for him and for thy brother James: and unto you three and I will give this power and the keys of this ministry until I come.*

Verily I say unto you, ye shall both have according to your desires, for ye both joy in that which ye have desired.[28]

Many of the added words simply make clear the meaning of the original. The last part of the second verse, however, adds information. Perhaps this added information represents words spoken by the Savior to Peter, which words John did not record on the parchment which he "hid up by himself." When and under what circumstances did Joseph Smith learn of this added information? It could have been during the translation of the Bible.[29]

Section 113, dated March 1838, explains the true meaning of terms used in Isaiah chapter 11 and interprets certain phrases in Isaiah 52:1–2. There is no indication in the JST manuscript of Isaiah to indicate that this information was received during the translation of the Old Testament. And the information in section 113 does not require any textual changes in the biblical verses. Did Joseph Smith learn these things by revelation in 1838 when the questions were raised, or did he answer the questions raised in 1838 with information he earlier received, possibly during the translation of the Bible? We do not know.

Which Came First?

Though an exhaustive study comparing when certain doctrines appeared in the JST and when they appeared in the Doctrine and Covenants is yet to be done, even a quick perusal shows some convincing parallels and possibilities. Sometimes the Prophet learned things during the translation of the scriptures which soon or later appear as part of a revelation in the Doctrine and Covenants. Less often, but noticeable, Joseph Smith received a revelation about something before that doctrine was addressed as part of the JST. We will cite examples of each case, hopefully stimulating interest in others to find more such connections.

Items Learned in the Translation Which Later
Appeared in the Doctrine and Covenants

An early example of items learned during the translation of the Bible appearing in a revelation in the Doctrine and Covenants is section 29. This revelation was received in September 1830. Just before, and at this same time, Joseph Smith was translating the early chapters of Genesis (Moses 1–5). Verses 31–41 of this section speak of a spiritual and a temporal creation, Satan's rebellion and fall in the pre-earth life, and pre-earth agency of mankind. These same items are central to Moses 1–5. (Jumping ahead for a moment, it is interesting to note that section 29 also contains information that seems to be pre-JST; i.e., verses 7–8 about the elect gathering to one place, verses 14–21 regarding the signs preceding the Second Coming, and verses 46–50 concerning the spiritual status of little children. Those doctrines are dealt with in Moses 6–7, which were not translated till three or four months after section 29 was received.)

Other parts of the Doctrine and Covenants which reflect information that might have been revealed earlier to the Prophet during the translation of the Bible include sections 42 and 104, containing the basics of the law of consecration; sections 68, 84, 88, 102, and 107, which speak of priesthood matters in terms of ancient councils, priesthood genealogies, keys and powers; and section 132, which responds to the question of plural marriage among the ancient patriarchs.[30]

Time and space does not permit extended commentary on each of these; perhaps two examples will suffice. The first is section 68. Often Latter-day Saints point to section 68 as the source for the age of accountability of children being eight years old. Actually that doctrine is of ancient origin, which the Prophet learned at least ten months before section 68 was received. The JST text of Genesis 17:11 reports the Lord's words to Abraham: "And I will establish a covenant of circumcision with thee, and it shall be my covenant between me and thee, and thy seed after thee, in their generations; that thou mayest know for ever that children are not accountable before me until they are eight years old."

The second example concerns information in section 107, verses 53–56. It tells of Adam calling his righteous posterity into the valley of Adam-ondi-Ahman three years before his death, of his giving them his last blessing, and his predicting "whatsoever should befall his posterity unto the latest generation" (D&C 107:56). We know that D&C 107 contains information received at different times between 1831 and 1835.[31] The recording of verses 53–56 took place in March 1835, but that may not be the time when Joseph Smith learned about this special meeting. Though he did not identify when he learned of it, Joseph Smith tells of actually *seeing* the event. He said: "I saw Adam in the valley of Adam-ondi-Ahman. He called together his children and blessed them with a patriarchal blessing. The Lord appeared in their midst, and he (Adam) blessed them all, and foretold what should befall them to the latest generation."[32]

It is possible, and in my view even probable, that the Prophet saw this vision of Adam in the valley of Adam-ondi-Ahman during the early phases of the translation of the Bible.

Items Learned in the Doctrine and Covenants
Before Consideration in the JST

Sections 45, 65, and 86 of the Doctrine and Covenants are three examples of information being made known in revelations before those same ideas or doctrines were treated as part of the translation of the Bible.

We have earlier noted that D&C 45 reveals an account of the Savior's instructions to his disciples in A.D. 33 about the impending destruction of Jerusalem and the signs of his second coming, and that the revelation came before the Prophet translated Matthew 24 in the New Testament, which addresses the same topics. Another interesting parallel between the earlier information in section 45 and the later New Testament translation is the clarification of the expression "times of the Gentiles" (in D&C 45:25–31 and JST, Luke 21:25, 32).

Section 65 gives an interpretation of the stone in Daniel's vision (Daniel 2:44–45) which was cut out of the mountain without hands and rolled forth until it filled the whole earth. This section was received in October 1831, about one and one-half years before the Prophet would have translated the book of Daniel in the Old Testament.

Our final example is section 86, which reverses the order of gathering of the wheat and the tares in the parable recorded in Matthew 13. The KJV of the parable has the tares gathered first, then the wheat. Section 86, however, says: "Therefore, let the wheat and the tares grow together until the harvest is fully ripe; then ye shall first gather out the wheat from among the tares, and after the gathering of the wheat, behold and lo, the tares are bound in bundles, and the field remaineth to be burned" (D&C 86:7).

The published version of the JST has the same sequence of gathering (wheat first, then tares) as section 86, but there is a good possibility that the section 86 revelation came first and influenced the textual change in the Bible translation. Evidence for that conclusion is as follows: NT 1 manuscript shows that when Joseph Smith translated Matthew 13:30, in the spring of 1831, he made no textual changes. NT 2, written a few weeks later, also shows no changes. Sometime

later, date unknown, the KJV wording was lined out in the NT 2 manuscript and a note was pinned over the verse. The note reads: "gather
ye together first the wheat into my barn, and the tares are bound in
bundles to be burned."[33] Not knowing just when the note was pinned
to the manuscript, we cannot say for certain that section 86, which
was received in December 1832, came before the note was written,
but the possibility is strong.

Undoubtedly a careful examination of dates and manuscripts
would uncover dozens, perhaps even hundreds, of textual connections
between the JST and the Doctrine and Covenants.

Conclusion

We conclude with a brief review of what the Doctrine and
Covenants says about the purpose and importance of Joseph Smith's
translation of the Bible. The following quotations are from sections of
the Doctrine and Covenants where the context is clearly referring to
the JST:

> . . . And the scriptures shall be given, even as they are in mine own
> bosom, to the salvation of mine own elect (35:20).

> . . . Then ye shall teach them unto all men; for they shall be taught
> unto all nations, kindreds, tongues and people (42:58).

> And he that doeth according to these things shall be saved, and he
> that doeth them not shall be damned if he so continue (42:60).

> . . . Now translate it, that ye may be prepared for the things to come
> (45:61).

> For while we were doing the work of translation, which the Lord
> had appointed unto us . . . it was given unto us of the Spirit. (76:15, 18.)

> . . . And all this for the salvation of Zion (93:53).

> For the purpose of building up my church and kingdom on the earth,
> and to prepare my people for the time when I shall dwell with them,
> which is nigh at hand (104:59).

What more needs to be said about the purpose and importance of the Joseph Smith Translation? Perhaps the Prophet himself capsulized the true significance of this work when he said "except the Church receive the fulness of the Scriptures that they would yet fall."[34] I believe that what is said there about the Church applies to each of us individually. It is my hope that all of us will catch the vision of the value of the Joseph Smith Translation of the Bible and reap the rich rewards promised those who take it seriously.

Notes

1. *Plainer Translation*, p. 255.

2. Sidney Rigdon was living in Mentor, Ohio, just a few miles north and a little east of Kirtland.

3. *Plainer Translation*, p. 92. See pp. 91–95 for a discussion of the scribes for the New Translation.

4. See *Plainer Translation*, pp. 67, 94–95. See also D&C 25:6 and D&C 90:19.

5. HC 1:145.

6. The sources for the information about living accommodations for Joseph and Emma Smith include the following: Karl Ricks Anderson, *Joseph Smith's Kirtland: Eyewitness Accounts* (Salt Lake City: Deseret Book Co., 1989), pp. 31–41, 153; Donna Hill, *Joseph Smith the First Mormon* (New York: Doubleday & Company, Inc., 1977), pp. 130–31; Linda King Newell and Valeen Tippetts Avery, *Mormon Enigma: Emma Hale Smith* (New York: Doubleday & Company, 1984), pp. 38, 39, 41, 44, 45, 50; Preston Nibley, *History of Joseph Smith by His Mother, Lucy Mack Smith* (Salt Lake City: Bookcraft, n.d.), p. 237; Keith W. Perkins, "The Prophet Joseph Smith in 'the Ohio': The Schoolmaster," in Larry D. Porter and Susan Easton Black, editors, *The Prophet Joseph: Essays on the Life and Mission of Joseph Smith* (Salt Lake City: Deseret Book Company, 1988), pp. 90–114. (In addition to

the works cited above, the author had conversations with and received documentary evidence from Karl Anderson (30 December
1994) and Keith Perkins (23 December 1994), two recognized authorities on Kirtland, regarding the dates and places and other particulars
of Joseph and Emma's homes while in Kirtland.

7. HC 1:341. This instruction is reminiscent of earlier and later
injunctions about revealed information: see for example Moses 1:42;
D&C 19:21–22; D&C 76:113–16. It should be noted that previous to
this letter from the Prophet, excerpts from the new translation had already been published in the *Star*, in August 1832, and March and
April 1833. Also, later, in 1834 and in 1843, the publishing of excerpts was evidently approved by the Prophet. See *Plainer Translation*,
p. 52.

8. See *Plainer Translation*, pp. 41–48.

9. The first effort to publish a compilation of revelations received by Joseph Smith was made in 1833, under the title of Book of
Commandments. In July 1833 a mob "demanded the discontinuance
of the Church printing establishment in Jackson County. . . . The
house of W. W. Phelps, which contained the printing establishment,
was thrown down, the materials taken possession of by the mob, many
papers destroyed, and the family and furniture thrown out of doors."
(HC 1:390.) Only a few copies of the Book of Commandments were
preserved.

10. HC 1:324.

11. HC 1:241. See pp. 238–41 for context.

12. *Plainer Translation*, p. 53.

13. See Larry E. Dahl, "The Vision of the Glories: D&C 76," pub-
lished in Robert L. Millet and Kent P. Jackson, editors, *Studies in
Scripture, Volume One: The Doctrine and Covenants* (Sandy, Utah:
Randall Book Co., 1984), pp. 279–308.

14. HC 1:245.

15. HC 1:252–53.

16. HC 1:331.

17. "The copy of the King James Version used by the Prophet in
making the New Translation of the Bible is a large pulpit-style edition
containing the Old and New Testaments and the Apocrypha. Printed
in 1828 by the H. and E. Phinney Company at Cooperstown, New

York, it measures nine inches in width, eleven inches in length, about two and one-half inches in thickness, and weighs at present about half an ounce under five pounds. It is bound with heavy, stiff lids covered with brownish-yellow leather. On the flyleaf, in the large handwriting of Joseph Smith, occupying nearly the whole page, is written:

> The Book of the Jews and the property of
> Joseph Smith Junior and Oliver Cowdery
> Bought October the 8th 1829 at Egbert B. Grandins
> Book Store Palmyra Wayne County New York
>
> Price $3.75
>
> Holiness to the Lord" (*Plainer Translation*, p. 56.)

18. HC 1:368–69. For additional discussion see *Plainer Translation*, pp. 38–39.

19. For sources and discussion of the dating of D&C 94 see Robert J. Woodford, "The Historical Development of the Doctrine and Covenants," Ph.D. Dissertation, Brigham Young University, 1974, pp. 1222–27; Lyndon W. Cook, *The Revelations of the Prophet Joseph Smith* (Provo, Utah: Seventy's Mission Book Store, 1981), pp. 195–97.

20. The two buildings called for in D&C 94, an office building for the First Presidency and a printing office, each to be 55' x 65', were not built. One building, 30' x 38', which served both purposes, was built in November 1834. The lower floor was used for the school for the elders and the upper story housed the printing press. "The building was attached to satisfy a judgment in late 1837, and on 16 January 1838 the whole printing apparatus and office were burned to the ground." See Cook, *The Revelations of the Prophet*, pp. 196–97.

Keith W. Perkins believes the printing office was built on land immediately west of the Temple, rather than on the second lot south of the temple, as D&C 94 called for. One of the guides at the Kirtland Temple explained to Keith that the gardeners had turned up quite a quantity of type on that particular land just west of the temple. He also showed Keith some of the type. See the "Kirtland Village 1837" map, *Ensign*, January 1979, p. 41. (Information based on a personal conversation between the author and Keith Perkins, 1–20–95).

21. "Kirtland Revelation Book," under the date of 23 April 1834. A double underlined note appears at the end of the revelation in the KRB: "Recorded by O. Hyde 18 Augt. 1834 upon this Book." See also Cook, *The Revelations of the Prophet*, p. 212.

22. See *Plainer Translation*, pp. 41–52.

23. See *Plainer Translation*, p. 52.

24. HC 1:242.

25. HC 1:253.

26. HC 1:331.

27. HC 1:35–36.

28. 1972 reprint of the Book of Commandments by Herald House, the Publishing Division of the Reorganized Church of Jesus Christ of Latter Day Saints, p. 18; and 1971 reprint of the 1835 Doctrine and Covenants by Herald House, pp. 160–61.

29. The question may be asked: "If the Prophet received the added information during the translation of the Bible, he would have known that information before the printing of the Book of Commandments in 1833. Why was not the change made in that printing?" Perhaps the answer lies in the fact that the decision to print a compilation of revelations was made in November 1831, and the selection of revelations to be printed made soon thereafter. It may be that it simply did not occur to those involved in the process, including the Prophet, to check each revelation against all that had been learned in the meantime.

30. The section heading for D&C 132 indicates that "the doctrines and principles involved in this revelation had been known by the Prophet since 1831." For a discussion of evidence that this is so see the Introduction to volume 5 of the *History of the Church*, pp. xxix-xxxiv, written by Elder B. H. Roberts.

31. See Cook, *The Revelations of the Prophet Joseph*, pp. 215–16.

32. HC 3:388. This information is published in the history under the date of July 1839. Ronald K. Esplin suggests, based on William Clayton's Journal, that it fits better into an 1841 context. See Esplin, "An Historical Analysis of Brigham Young's Teachings on Adam and Creation," unpublished manuscript, p. 13.

33. See *Plainer Translation*, p. 82.

34. The statement is attributed to Joseph Smith in the minutes of a conference of the Church in Orange, Ohio, 25 October 1831. The clerk of the conference was Oliver Cowdery. The minutes are published in Donald Q. Cannon and Lyndon W. Cook, editors, *Far West Record: Minutes of The Church of Jesus Christ of Latter-day Saints, 1830–1844* (Salt Lake City: Deseret Book Company, 1983), pp. 19–24. The same quotation is given in *Teachings of the Prophet Joseph Smith*, compiled by Joseph Fielding Smith (Salt Lake City: The Deseret News Press, 1956), p. 9, but there the word *fail*, rather than *fall*, is used. In the original handwritten minutes, the word in question (*fall* or *fail*) is located on the line directly underneath the word *except*, and the stem of the *p* falls exactly in line with what is either an *i* or an *l*. It is very difficult, therefore, to determine whether the word is *fall* or *fail*. It could be either. Perhaps it matters little which word is accepted; they both convey the same basic meaning.

7

The Joseph Smith Translation, the Pearl of Great Price, and the Book of Mormon

ROBERT L. MILLET

M y colleague Larry Dahl has dealt at some length with the relationship of the Joseph Smith Translation of the Bible (JST) to the Doctrine and Covenants. It is a remarkable thing indeed to realize how the translations and revelations provided an interdependent learning process for the Prophet Joseph Smith and the Church, and how it is that revelations obtained through one sphere of prophetic activity impacted the choice Seer's capacity to receive them in another sphere. In this presentation I would like to discuss, first of all, the relationship of the JST to the Pearl of Great Price, and then something that is not so obvious, namely, the relationship of the inspired translation of the Bible to the Book of Mormon.

The JST and the Pearl of Great Price

Most of us know the historical setting for the fourth book in our canon of scripture, the Pearl of Great Price. Elder Orson Pratt was followed by a young Apostle, Franklin D. Richards, as president of the European Mission. Elder Richards discovered a paucity of printed material among the Latter-day Saints in England and chose to prepare a mission tract to bring under one cover some of the gems from our doctrinal and historical reservoir. In July 1851 the pamphlet entitled Pearl of Great Price came off the press. In this first edition, among other things were excerpts from the JST of the early chapters of Genesis and Matthew 24. The Genesis material was not organized as we have it now in our book of Moses, but rather consisted of extensive extracts, first from the prophecy of Enoch (parts of what we know as Moses 6 and 7) and also much of what is in Moses 1–5 and parts of Moses 8. These were piecemeal and not in chronological order. Brother Richards seems to have drawn upon his own collection of Church periodicals in which some of Joseph Smith's Bible translation had appeared, some from *The Evening and the Morning Star* (1831–33), the *Times and Seasons* (1843), possibly from the *Lectures on Faith* (in the 1835 edition of the Doctrine and Covenants), and more recently from the *Millennial Star* (1851). In addition Elder Richards must have had access to an independent manuscript of the JST of Matthew 24. It is interesting that the JST of Genesis in the first edition of the Pearl of Great Price represents an earlier version of the Prophet's work, which has been drawn from Old Testament Manuscript 2.

No doubt many of the British Saints began to share their scriptural treasure with the Saints in America as the former gathered to the United States. In 1876 Elder Orson Pratt, then the Church historian, was asked to prepare new editions of the Book of Mormon and the Doctrine and Covenants. He also prepared the first American edition of the Pearl of Great Price, which was presented to and accepted by the Church as a part of the standard works at the October 1880 general conference. In regard to the JST of the Genesis material, Elder Pratt supplied the missing parts of the translation, organized it, and called it the "Visions of Moses" (Moses 1) and the "Writings of Moses" (Moses 2–8). The Reorganized Church of Jesus Christ of Latter Day Saints had published, for the most part, the Prophet's latest translation work with the Old Testament (what we know as Old Testament Manuscript 3) in their first edition of the JST in 1867. Elder Pratt drew upon the printed JST for the Moses material.

The Prophet's continuing work with the manuscripts of the JST is an evidence of the line-upon-line, precept-upon-precept manner in which insights and additional inspiration came to Joseph Smith.

There can be no question but that on some occasions the exact wording came into the Prophet's mind; the differences, however, between
earlier and subsequent JST emendations suggest that very often Joseph
Smith was required to labor with a concept, to struggle in his effort to
arrive at a choice of words to convey what he had come to know by
revelation. Let me note just two of the textual differences in the
Moses material between Elder Richards's 1851 edition and Elder
Pratt's 1878 edition. Others are readily available in the Matthews
book, "A *Plainer Translation*," chapter 11.

Perhaps the most quoted scriptural passage in the history of
Mormonism is Moses 1:39. The wording we know so well comes from
Old Testament Manuscript 3, the Prophet's latest work: "For behold,
this is my work and my glory—to bring to pass the immortality and
eternal life of man." If, however, we were to obtain a copy of the 1851
edition of the Pearl of Great Price and read this passage, we would
read what is found in Old Testament Manuscript 2: "Behold, this is my
work to my glory, to the immortality and eternal life of man." Though
there is something to be said to recommend the earlier rendition—
namely, a seeming stress upon the fact that God grows in glory
through the glorification of his children, a doctrinal point the Prophet
later made in the King Follett Sermon[1]—the more familiar version is
to be preferred for its clarity.

In what might be called the revelation of the gospel to Adam, we
find these words of God to Adam in the latest version of the translation (Old Testament Manuscript 3): "Therefore I give unto you a
commandment, to teach these things [the Fall and the Atonement]
freely unto your children, saying: that by reason of transgression
cometh the fall, which fall bringeth death, and inasmuch as ye were
born into the world by water, and blood, and the spirit, which I have
made, and so became of dust a living soul, even so ye must be born
again into the kingdom of heaven, of water, and of the Spirit, and be
cleansed by blood, even the blood of mine Only Begotten; that ye
might be sanctified from all sin, and enjoy the words of eternal life in
this world and eternal life in the world to come, even immortal glory"
(Moses 6:58–59).

The earlier version of this passage (Old Testament Manuscript 2)
was rendered as follows: ". . . inasmuch as they were born into the

world by the fall which bringeth death, by Water and Blood and the Spirit, which I have made, and so become of dust a living soul, even so ye must be born again of Water and the Spirit, and be cleansed by Blood, even the Blood of mine Only Begotten, *into the mysteries of the kingdom of heaven*" (emphasis added). What exactly the Prophet Joseph had in mind and why he chose to remove the phrase "into the mysteries of the kingdom of heaven" in the final version of this passage is not known.

The JST and the Book of Mormon

Surely the translation of the Book of Mormon was an excellent preparation for the translation of the Bible. For one thing, the Prophet's immersion in the spirit of revelation, his acquaintance with the workings of the Holy Ghost, and his intense study of the prophetic word and how it should be rendered—all of these must have expanded his mind and heart and provided a spiritual and doctrinal foundation for subsequent translation activity with the Bible and later with the book of Abraham. In addition, some matters of doctrine, clarified in the Book of Mormon, would have been foundational for his study of the Bible. For example, the Book of Mormon is a powerful witness of the reality of the fall of Adam and Eve, of the plight of fallen mankind, and of the absolute necessity for redemption in Christ. But nowhere does the Book of Mormon suggest a type of Calvinistic or Lutheran notion of human depravity. This would certainly have an effect on the way Joseph smith altered the seventh chapter of Romans or the second chapter of James. It is clear from the Book of Mormon that we are saved ultimately by the grace of Christ, but that our good works (including the receipt of the ordinances) are necessary for salvation as our part of the gospel covenant. Such clarifications are made in JST alterations in Romans 4. The Book of Mormon prophets offer consistent witness of the fact that no person's salvation is secure independent of personal acceptance of the gospel plan (including faith in Jesus Christ and repentance from sin), receipt of the ordinances, and faithful endurance to the end. That knowledge would surely have made a difference when the Prophet Joseph encountered passages in the King James

Bible that suggested the possibility of predestination or unconditional election of individuals to eternal life, or reprobation of individuals to damnation.[2]

One of the most interesting aspects of the Book of Mormon is the impact of scripture on the Nephites. The brass plates had a tremendous influence on the way they behaved and on what they believed and taught. For our purposes it is worth noting a fascinating similarity in subject and specific language between the brass plates and the JST. In the words of Robert J. Matthews: "The Book of Mormon is . . . related to the Prophet's Bible translation in an interesting way: the Nephite scripture serves as evidence that the Joseph Smith Translation is indeed a work of restoration—the revealing anew of plain and precious truths once enjoyed anciently." Further, "It is very clear that the contents of the JST, having received the touch of restoration through the hand of the prophet of God, resemble the doctrinal content of the brass plates more fully than [does the Bible]."[3] We will now consider several specific examples wherein the texts of the two works will be compared.

1. *The Fall of Lucifer.* One of the most profound doctrinal sections of the Book of Mormon is Lehi's counsel to his sons just before his death. For our purposes the account begins as follows: "And I, Lehi, according to the things which I have read, must needs suppose that an angel of God, *according to that which is written*, had fallen from heaven; wherefore, he became a devil, having sought that which was evil before God. And because he had fallen from heaven, and had become miserable forever, he sought also the misery of all mankind." (2 Nephi 2:17–18, emphasis added.) Biblical references to the fall of Lucifer in premortal times are, of course, scarce (Isaiah 14; Revelation 12), and are only to be recognized and understood as a result of modern revelation on the subject.

The Joseph Smith Translation of Genesis 3:1–5 (also known in our canon of scripture as Moses 4:1–4) is an account of the Grand Council in heaven wherein the plan of the Father was discussed by the spirits, Jehovah was selected and acknowledged as the Savior and chief advocate of the plan, and Lucifer was cast from heaven for rebelling against the will of Almighty Elohim. Lehi pointed out that the diabolical one "became a devil, having sought that which was evil before God." The JST is remarkably specific about his malevolent motives: "He came before me [God], saying—Behold, here am I, send me, I will be thy Son, and I will redeem all mankind, that one soul shall not be lost, and surely I will do it; wherefore, give me thine honor." Regarding Lehi's observation that Satan had "sought also the misery of all mankind," we note from the JST that "he became Satan, yea, even the devil, the father of all lies, to deceive and to blind men, and to lead them captive at his will, even as many as would not hearken unto my voice."

2. *Creation, Fall, and Atonement.* From the same chapter in the Book of Mormon (2 Nephi 2) we are able to learn invaluable truths through Lehi's teachings concerning the plan of salvation. Lehi explained to his sons that "if Adam had not transgressed he would not have fallen, but he would have remained in the garden of Eden. And all things which were created must have remained in the same state in which they were after they were created; and they must have remained forever, and had no end." (2 Nephi 2:22.) The great Nephite patriarch is here alluding to the paradisiacal and Edenic state, the *spiritual* state, a state in which nothing was yet subject to death (see also Alma 11:45; D&C 88:27; 1 Corinthians 15:44), a state which applied to man and all forms of life on earth before the Fall. From the Prophet Joseph Smith's inspired translation of Moses' account of the Creation we learn a similar truth. In speaking of the things on the earth in the morn of creation, the Lord said that "it was spiritual in the day that I created it; for it remaineth in the sphere in which I, God, created it" (JST, Genesis 2:11; Moses 3:9).

Being in an immortal, spiritual state, Adam and Eve "would have had no children." Lehi added, "wherefore they would have remained in a state of innocence, having no joy, for they knew no misery; doing no good, for they knew no sin." After acknowledging the hand of the omniscient God in the plan of life, Lehi concluded that "Adam fell that men might be; and men are, that they might have joy" (2 Nephi 2:23–25). The JST provides an expanded biblical account of Adam and Eve's retrospective thinking in regard to the events in the Garden of Eden. Having learned by the ministry of angels (see Alma 12:29–32; JST, Genesis 4:5–8 [Moses 5:5–8]) of the mission of the Messiah and the redemption possible through repentance, Adam blessed God, began to prophesy concerning all the families of the earth, and expressed gratitude for the eternal benefits of the Fall. "And Eve, his wife, heard all these things and was glad, saying: Were it not for our transgression we never should have had seed, and never should have known good and evil, and the joy of our redemption, and the eternal life which God giveth unto all the obedient." (JST, Genesis 4:9–11; Moses 5:9–11.) It was Enoch who later observed simply that "because that Adam fell, we are" (JST, Genesis 6:49; Moses 6:48).

Jacob, drawing upon the teachings of his father (and thus the doctrines on the brass plates), taught: "For as death hath passed upon all men, to fulfill the merciful plan of the great Creator, there must needs be a power of resurrection, and the resurrection must needs come unto man by reason of the fall; and the fall came by reason of transgression: and because man became fallen they were cut off from the presence of the Lord" (2 Nephi 9:6). This language is unmistakably close to the divine directive to Adam contained in the inspired translation of Genesis: "Therefore I give unto you a commandment, to teach these things freely unto your children, saying: that by reason of transgression cometh the fall, which fall bringeth death, and inasmuch as ye were born into the world by water, and blood, and the spirit, which I have made, and so became of dust a living soul, even so ye must be born again into the kingdom of heaven" (JST, Genesis 6:61–62; Moses 6:58–59).

3. *The Origin of Secret Combinations.* In the book of Helaman we are introduced to one Kishkumen, the originator among the Nephites of a secret band of men bent upon wealth and power. After the death of Kishkumen this secret combination continued its escapades of evil under Gadianton and thereafter came to be known as the Gadianton robbers (Helaman 1–2). In writing of this abominable group, Mormon observed that "those secret oaths and covenants [of the Gadianton bands] did not come forth unto Gadianton from the records which were delivered unto Helaman [Alma had commanded Helaman to keep the particulars of these oaths from public knowledge—see Alma 37:27–32]; but behold, they were put into the heart of Gadianton by that same being who did entice our first parents to partake of the forbidden fruit—yea, that same being who did plot with Cain, that if he

would murder his brother Abel it should not be known unto the world. And he did plot with Cain and his followers from that time forth." (Helaman 6:26–27.)

The biblical account of the murder of Abel is extremely brief, only six verses long (Genesis 4:3–8, and the only motive it contains for murder is implied—jealousy as a result of the Lord's acceptance of Abel's sacrifice. Further, there is no mention of Satan's involvement in the story. From the JST we gain an insight into Cain's personality as a result of his response to the counsel of his parents and the Lord: "Who is the Lord that I should know him?" We learn further that "Cain loved Satan more than God," and thereby chose to follow the devil and thus reject divine counsel. Cain entered into an oath of secrecy with Satan and became "master of this great secret, that I may murder and get gain. Wherefore Cain was called Master Mahan [perhaps "Master Mind"], and he gloried in his wickedness." Others entered into league with Lucifer and perpetuated this perversity. "For, from the days of Cain, there was a secret combination, and their works were in the dark"; therefore, we learn that "the works of darkness began to prevail among all the sons of men." (JST, Genesis 5:5–42; Moses 5:16–55.)

4. *The Prophecies of Joseph.* In delivering his parting counsel to his son Joseph, the prophet Lehi took occasion to quote (or read) from the writings of the patriarch Joseph, the one who had been sold into Egypt. In discussing this record, Nephi observed: "And now, I, Nephi, speak concerning the prophecies of which my father hath spoken, concerning Joseph, who was carried into Egypt. For behold, he truly prophesied concerning all his seed. And the prophecies which he wrote, there are not many greater. And he prophesied concerning us, and our future generations; and they are written upon the plates of brass." (2 Nephi 4:1–2.) Joseph's prophecies (as contained in the Book of Mormon via the brass plates) consist of predictions concerning such matters as: (1) the ministry of Moses as a seer and deliverer; (2) the ministry of a "choice seer" of the lineage of Joseph to be raised up in the last days—Joseph Smith; (3) the "growing together" of the writings of Joseph and Judah in order to confound false doctrines, lay down contentions, and establish peace among and bring knowledge to the descendants of Joseph; (4) the choice latter-day seer to be named

after his father, his father's name being Joseph; (5) that which comes
forth by the hands of the latter-day seer to bring many to salvation;
(6) Moses to be given a spokesman; (7) a spokesman to be provided
for the representative of the fruit of the loins of Joseph; and (8) many
in the last days to remember the covenants of the Lord unto the ancient fathers (2 Nephi 3).

These prophecies of Joseph have no biblical counterpart whatsoever. The JST contains an account of these prophecies with many
verses almost identical to that given in the Book of Mormon.
Additional details contained in the JST are: (1) the Messiah is known
as Shiloh (Genesis 49:10); and (2) the name of the spokesman of
Moses is to be Aaron. It is interesting to note that in the JST account
there is no mention of a scribe for the "choice seer" of the latter days.
(JST, Genesis 50:24–35.)

5. *Abraham's Knowledge of the Messiah.* Nephi, the son of
Helaman, taught clearly that "all the holy prophets, from [Moses']
days even to the days of Abraham," bore fervent witness of the coming of Jesus Christ, the Lord Omnipotent. Nephi then exclaimed:
"Yea, and behold, Abraham saw of his coming, and was filled with
gladness and did rejoice." (Helaman 8:16–17.) Though we have biblical episodes wherein Abraham heard the voice of the Lord and received revelations, we have no single account on record where the father of the faithful beheld the Savior in vision. And yet there is
evidence in the New Testament of this very thing. Jesus, in speaking
to those who opposed him and who claimed special status via their
Abrahamic descent, said: "Your father Abraham rejoiced to see my
day: and he saw it, and was glad" (John 8:56). It would appear, therefore, that such a prophetic vision was had by Abraham, but that the
episode has been lost from our present biblical collection.

A marvelous restoration of an ancient event is found in the
Prophet's translation of the fifteenth chapter of Genesis. The Lord
Jehovah had just explained to Abraham concerning his eventual land
inheritance in Canaan:

> And Abram said, Lord God, how wilt thou give me this land for an
> everlasting inheritance?
> And the Lord said, Though thou wast dead, yet am I not able to give
> it thee?

And if thou shalt die; yet thou shalt possess it, for the day cometh, that the Son of Man shall live; but how can he live if he be not dead [reference here seems to be to the doctrine and promise of resurrection]? he must first be quickened.

And it came to pass, that *Abram looked forth and saw the days of the Son of Man,* and was glad, and his soul found rest, and he believed in the Lord; and the Lord counted it unto him for righteousness. (JST, Genesis 15:9–12, emphasis added.)

6. *The Ministry of Melchizedek.* In speaking to the people in the city of Ammonihah, Alma and Amulek preached sound and powerful doctrine on such vital matters as the Creation, the Fall, the Atonement, and the Resurrection (Alma 11–12). Then Alma began a sermon on the priesthood and stressed the importance of the high priesthood in attaining the rest of the Lord. As an example of those who had been faithful in times past in magnifying callings in the priesthood (and had thereby been sanctified by the Spirit—D&C 84:33), Alma referred to Melchizedek and the people of Salem. "Now this Melchizedek," he observed, "was a king over the land of Salem; and his people had waxed strong in iniquity and abomination; yea, they had all gone astray; they were full of all manner of wickedness." Alma then explained that "Melchizedek did establish peace in the land in his days; therefore he was called the prince of peace, for he was the king of Salem; and he did reign under his father." And then, by way of summary, Alma stated: "Now, there were many before him, and also there were many afterwards, but none were greater; therefore, of him they have more particularly made mention." (Alma 13:1–9.)

It seems that on some scriptural record the writers prior to Alma had made mention of this king of Salem, and had given enough detail of his successful ministry to allow Alma to utilize him as a notable example of what could be done via righteousness. As is commonly known, however, such detail is not to be had in our present Bible. There is passing reference to Melchizedek in Genesis (chapter 14), as well as a strange allusion to Melchizedek by Paul in Hebrews 7:3 (he is identified as being "without father, without mother, without descent, having neither beginning of days, nor end of life"), but we must turn to the JST to learn specifically of this ancient character. In this inspired restoration we learn that Melchizedek "was a man of faith, who wrought righteousness," one ordained after that order of priesthood which "came, not by man, nor the will of man; neither by father nor mother; neither by beginning of days nor end of years; but of God." This account explains that those who were faithful to the covenant of the high priesthood obtained an oath from God, an immutable promise from the Almighty, that they would have power to subdue the elements and even come up into the presence of God. "And men having this faith, coming up unto this order of God, were," like Enoch the ancient prototype, "translated and taken up into heaven. And now, Melchizedek was a priest of this order; therefore he obtained peace in Salem, and was called the Prince of peace. And his people wrought righteousness, and obtained heaven, and sought for the city of Enoch which God had before taken." (JST, Genesis 14:26–34.)

Conclusion

I would like to conclude in a rather unusual way. I want to discuss briefly my personal odyssey with Joseph Smith's translation of the Bible.

In the fall of 1969 I walked the BYU campus one evening. I was a new transfer student, knew no one at the university, and was a bit homesick. I roamed the campus, did a lot of thinking, and drew a few conclusions about the future. For some reason I happened into the Joseph Smith Building and made my way into the auditorium. There were about fifty to one hundred people listening to what appeared to be a special lecture. I sat down, mostly to rest for a few moments. The man at the pulpit spoke of the Inspired Version of the Bible, something that I think I had heard my father refer to a time or two. I listened intently. I do not remember a single concept presented that night, but I still remember what I felt as I sat there. There came into my heart the firm realization that what this man, a Brother Robert Matthews, was speaking about was important and that I should learn all I could about the subject. I sensed that, for some strange reason, what he had to say would one day be an important part of my life's work.

I managed in the next few years to learn something of the Inspired Version of the Bible; a few of my Religion teachers here made passing reference to it. After I had finished the master's degree we moved to Idaho to work with LDS Social Services. While I was there I was asked to participate in an Education Days program. I sat in awe as Lynn McKinlay spoke of the mighty change of heart. I was deeply impressed as a Brother Max Caldwell explained different aspects of the gospel with great power and persuasion. And once again my spiritual appetite was whetted as Robert Matthews discoursed on the importance of the Inspired Version. I spoke to him at some length after the program, and he referred me to several of his own publications on the subject. He also indicated that he had completed a book on the subject that would soon be released by BYU Press. I devoured all I could find until the book, "A *Plainer Translation*," was available. Then I began my study in earnest. Not only did I discover many of the monumental doctrinal contributions of what we now call the Joseph Smith Translation (JST), but I then saw for the first time what an integral part of the Prophet Joseph's overall ministry this work really was.

By the time I began teaching in the Church Education System, I had read Brother Matthews's book two or three times. My teaching of the Old and New Testaments took on a new meaning, and I would like to think my students were able to see some things they might not have seen had I not been made acquainted with this valuable scriptural resource. When I was reassigned to the institute adjacent to Florida State University, one of the first things I did was to offer a course in the JST, which of course caused me to search deeper and deeper, both theologically and historically. When it was time to prepare my dissertation prospectus I indicated that I wanted to do a dissertation on the role of Joseph Smith as Translator, Biblical Critic, and Scriptural Exegete (arrangements had even been made for Bob Matthews to serve on my committee).

Providentially, my committee chair suggested that such a topic might be worthy of a lifetime of study but was a bit steep for a dissertation. But my interests in the JST continued, and Bob and I carried on a correspondence over several years. I treasure those letters, because of my affection and admiration for Bob, but also because of the answers he provided for many of my queries. When I was hired at BYU in 1983, Bob graciously suggested that I teach a course in the JST. I have tried to do that as regularly as possible. During that time I have been thrilled to witness the joy of discovery and the anchoring of testimony in the eyes and hearts of many of my students. They are not the same since they have undertaken a serious study of Joseph Smith's translation of the Bible. Nor am I. Like the Book of Mormon, the JST has a spirit all its own, one that testifies that Joseph Smith was all that he said he was, and more. It is indeed one of the great evidences of his prophetic calling.

I bear witness that as a result of my discovery of the JST there has come into my life a light, a power, and a clarity of thought that I am convinced could have come in no other way. I now see the Doctrine and Covenants and the history of the Church with new eyes. I now testify of Joseph Smith as a translator with a zeal and a perspective that I did not have before. I feel closer to him. There is a fire in my bones that drives me to assist my students in gaining a like witness.

My challenge to us all is this: If you have not heretofore taken the JST seriously, if it has not become more than a distant acquaintance, if for one reason or another you have not afforded it the prominent doctrinal or historical position that it surely deserves, then prayerfully consider the need to expand your horizons. I attest that you will never regret having done so. It just may be the beginning of a sublime encounter with light and truth, which light and truth are the very glory of God.

Notes

1. See TPJS, pp. 347–48; see also D&C 132:31, 63.

2. For example, see JST, Exodus 4:20–21; 7:1–3, 13–14; 14:17; JST, Acts 13:48; JST, Romans 8:29–30. See also TPJS, p. 189.

3. *Bible*, p. 153.

8

Hard Questions About the Joseph Smith Translation

ROBERT L. MILLET

There are questions, recurring questions, about the Joseph Smith Translation of the Bible (JST) that deserve at least partial answers. Robert J. Matthews addressed several of the most frequently asked questions in his book, "A *Plainer Translation.*" I would like to review and expand upon a few of those, pose a few others, and offer some possible answers. I will refer occasionally to the comments of Elder Bruce R. McConkie, who had a great love and appreciation for the inspired translation.

1. *Why did Joseph Smith translate the Bible?* First and foremost, he was commanded of God to do so. We do not have within our possession the specific revelation authorizing and commanding this work, only reference to the fact that it was so appointed (D&C 42:56; 76:15). The Prophet referred to this labor as a "branch of [his] calling"[1]

Second, the work proved to be an important part of Joseph Smith's spiritual education. The Prophet did not translate the Bible primarily on the basis of what he already knew; he learned great and important truths in the process. He wasn't, as some have suggested, merely "Mormonizing the Bible"; a moment's reflection suggests that there would have been very little Mormon doctrine with which to Mormonize the Bible in June of 1830.

Third, the work of translation illustrates a concept of revelation that has great relevance for all members of the Church. Revelation often comes line upon line to prophets, just as it does to you and me. The fact that Joseph Smith worked and revised and prepared the manuscripts of the JST from 1830 until the time of his death demonstrates this principle.

Fourth, it is worth noting that over 50 percent of the revelations in the Doctrine and Covenants were received during the time period associated with the formal work of Bible translation. As Brother Dahl has already pointed out, a number of revelations that we now have in the Doctrine and Covenants (including sections 74, 76, 77, 86, 91, 132) came as a direct result of the translation. A number of other revelations in the Doctrine and Covenants are tied to the work with the Bible directly because of the instructions within the revelation regarding the JST (e.g., D&C 25:6; 35:20; 37:1; 42:15, 56–57; 45:60–61; 47:1; 73:3; 90:13; 93:53; 94:10; 104:58; 124:89). It is important also for us to recognize that revelation in the form of biblical revisions was being received at the same period that revelation in the Doctrine and Covenants was being received; the same spirit of inspiration was at work with Joseph the Seer.

When the full picture of the Restoration is unveiled, perhaps then we will come to appreciate an even greater impact of the JST on this final dispensation. In the meantime we can only surmise concerning other sections of the Doctrine and Covenants and their possible relation to the translation.

2. Did the Prophet actually finish the work of translation? The answer to this question is a clear-cut "Yes and No." He finished it in the sense that he gave attention to every book in the Old and New Testaments. (He did not make changes in every book, but he did consider every book.) He did not finish it in the sense that he made every change or clarification that ever would be made. President George Q. Cannon observed: "Joseph did not live to give to the world an authoritative publication of these translations. But the labor was its own reward, bringing in the performance a special blessing of broadened comprehension to the Prophet and a general blessing of enlightenment to the people through his subsequent teachings." President Cannon also noted: "We have heard Brigham Young state that the Prophet before his death had spoken to him about going through the translation of the scriptures again and perfecting it upon points of doctrine which the Lord had restrained him from giving in plainness and fulness at the time of which we write [1832]."[2]

Elder Joseph Fielding Smith wrote in 1914 that the Prophet "revised, as it is, a great deal more than the world can, or will, receive. In the 'translation' of the scriptures, he gave to the world all that the Lord would permit him to give, and as much as many of the members of the Church were able to receive. He therefore finished all that was required at his hands, or, that he was permitted to revise, up to July, 1833, when he discontinued his labors of revision."[3] Finally, Elder Bruce R. McConkie wrote: "In many passages all necessary changes were made; in others he was 'restrained' by the Spirit from giving the full and clear meaning. As with all revealed knowledge, the Lord was offering new truths to the world, 'line upon line, precept upon precept. . . .' Neither the world nor the saints generally were then or are now prepared for the fulness of biblical knowledge."[4]

3. *Why has the Church hesitated over the years to use the JST?* Meaning no disrespect, I simply suggest that for many years we were ignorant of both the process and the product. Over the years we have been a bit prejudiced, have assumed that the Reorganized Church of Jesus Christ of Latter Day Saints made changes in the Prophet's work. Robert Matthews's groundbreaking work with the original manuscripts helped to dispel these myths.

Some have suggested that we should not use the JST because the Prophet never finished the work. They utilize the following scripture for support: "It is expedient that thou shouldst hold thy peace concerning [the translations], and not teach them until ye have received them in full" (D&C 42:57). This simply cannot mean, as some have concluded, that Joseph and the Saints were not to teach that which was found in the JST until all changes that were ever to be made in the Bible were made. Earlier in that same revelation, section 42, the Lord had directed that the elders, priests, and teachers of the Church were to teach the principles of the gospel, as found in the Bible and the Book of Mormon. In addition, the Saints were to "observe the covenants and church articles to do them, and these shall be their teachings, as they shall be directed by the Spirit. . . . And all this ye shall observe to do as I have commanded concerning your teaching, *until the fulness of my scriptures is given.*" (D&C 42:12–15, emphasis added.) "At that time," Elder McConkie has noted, "they had only the imperfect King James Version of the Bible and the near-perfect Book of Mormon. These were their only scriptural sources for the principles of the gospel. When the Joseph Smith Translation of the Bible—included in this revelation [D&C 42] under the designation 'fulness of my scriptures'—came forth, then teachers were to use it and the various additional direct revelations. This, then, is a command to teach the changes and additions now found in the so-called Inspired Version."[5]

As indicated, Joseph Smith was not permitted to make every possible change. The fact is, the Prophet did teach from the new translation during his ministry, and many parts of the JST were published during his lifetime—in *The Evening and the Morning Star,* the *Lectures on Faith,* and the *Times and Seasons.*[6] He obviously did not perceive the Lord's command to be other than a warning against sharing the "mysteries of the kingdom" prematurely with those unprepared to receive them. (The Prophet did ask that William W. Phelps not print the New Translation in a serial format in *The Evening and the Morning Star.*[7] He had plans of publishing it all as a unit; see also Moses 1:42; 4:32.) Again from Elder McConkie, who had such strong feelings on this matter:

> True, the Joseph Smith Translation, though completed to the point that the early Brethren were going to publish it at one time, has not been completed in the full and true sense. But for that matter neither has the Book of Mormon. I am as anxious to read and study what is in the sealed portion of the Book of Mormon as I am to give the same attention to those parts of the Bible yet to be revealed.
>
> I am clear in my mind that the sealed portion of the Book of Mormon will not come forth until the Millennium. The same thing is undoubtedly true of the fulness of the Bible, though some additions could well be made before that time.
>
> Of what will the Bible consist when it is perfected?
>
> Surely it will contain the writings of Adam and Enoch and Noah; of Melchizedek and Isaac and Jacob; and certainly Abraham wrote much more than the Prophet found on the Egyptian papyrus. The Book of Abraham in our Pearl of Great Price is obviously a restored biblical record.

Does anyone think we have all of the words of Isaiah or Jeremiah or Malachi? And are there not prophets and apostles without number, whose names we do not even know, who have recorded their teachings and testimonies?[8]

4. *How do we explain the fact that the Prophet made certain changes in the Bible during the years of the translation—between 1830 and 1833— and then later used the language from the King James Version to make a differing doctrinal point?* First of all, this illustrates the gradual unfolding of truth through the translation; not everything of theological significance came forth through the translation or by 1833, and perhaps, as suggested earlier, the Lord only made known through his latter-day Seer what he wanted the Saints to know at the time. This opens the door to the fascinating concept that a passage of scripture may be rendered in more ways than one. In short, an alteration need not invalidate the original KJV passage.

For example, Malachi 4:5–6 is as true as it can be, even though Moroni's rewording of this scripture (see Joseph Smith—History 1:38–39) adds a doctrinal dimension that is not apparent in the original. Hebrews 11:40 was altered in the JST to reflect its doctrinal context and thus lays stress upon the requisite suffering of those who gain faith unto life and salvation. Later, however, when the Prophet had come to know by vision and revelation of the possibility of the redemption of the dead—principally through the vision of the celestial kingdom (D&C 137)—Hebrews 11:40 was used in an entirely new way. And so it is with Revelation 1:5–6. The addition in the JST of a comma, so as to make the passage read, "And hath made us kings and priests unto God, his [Christ's] Father," reflects a beautiful truth. But in later years the Prophet learned—principally from his translation of the Egyptian papyri[9]—of the plurality of Gods, and thus the KJV ("and hath made us kings and priests unto God *and* his [God's] Father") took on new meaning.

5. *What do we conclude when the JST differs from the same passage in the Book of Mormon, such as in the Sermon on the Mount?* This is a tough one. I cherish the Book of Mormon. It has a place in my heart like no other book of scripture, and I enjoy teaching its truths more than anything else. But I must add that I am convinced that the JST

has clarifications and insights that in some cases even surpass those found in the Book of Mormon.[10] The translation of the Book of Mormon served as an excellent spiritual preparation for the translation of the Bible; the Prophet's maturity, as well as the readiness of the Saints, may well have made it possible for additional insights to come through the JST that may not have come through the translation of the golden plates.

I do not know whether the Prophet and his scribe utilized a King James Bible when they translated the Book of Mormon and am not aware of anyone now living who knows for sure. If in fact they did use the Bible, and if and when the Prophet sensed by revelation that the message on the golden or brass plates was sufficiently close to what was had in the KJV, he may have decided to simply go with the translation language most familiar to the people. He obviously did not sit down and copy everything from the Bible, given the hundreds of differences between the passages in the Bible and those in the Book of Mormon. Robert Matthews pointed out some years ago: "One thing is certain: Joseph Smith himself was aware that he had rendered these various passages different yet felt free to do so and apparently also felt that his rendition was necessary. Our task, therefore, is not one of trying to decide when or if the Prophet was right but rather of achieving his level of spiritual understanding so that we can appreciate the additional insight he is unfolding to us."[11]

6. *What of those times when the changes in the JST do not seem to fit the context, or alter the context, or when they seem to give the text a different flavor entirely? What do we conclude when we find that our most ancient Old and New Testament texts do not reflect the changes from the JST?* This is an interesting question. For example, the JST of Romans 13 alters the discussion from our civic responsibility to pay taxes to our religious responsibility to consecrate of our means for the building of the kingdom of God. Because we are uncertain as to what change falls into what category—restoration of text, restoration of events or words not previously recorded, prophetic commentary, harmonization of text with other passages—we are not really at liberty to say whether the KJV or the JST is historically correct. In this case, is Joseph Smith playing "fast and loose" with sacred scripture? Or is it possible he is trying to tell us something about the context, the setting, or the origi-

nal meaning that is not clear from extant texts? I would be very careful about dismissing outright something of this type from the Prophet because it doesn't fit the text or texts or contexts with which we are most familiar and thus most comfortable.

A very important example is Romans 7 on the power of Christ to change men's souls. The King James Version conveys an idea of human depravity and suggests—as Luther or Calvin would later do—that Paul believed that men and women do not even have the capacity to choose good. As Latter-day Saints we know better than that, or we should. The JST echoes the same doctrine as the Book of Mormon—that we are able to overcome the flesh and to face human weakness only in and through the transforming powers of Jesus Christ. If we teach only the KJV we risk confusing the students on the nature of the Fall and the Atonement; through the JST, Paul's message is illuminated and even corrected by modern revelation. In Matthew 9 the Prophet's alterations of the text introduce a most interesting concept: that Jesus had rejected the baptism of the Pharisees. In Luke 16 the Prophet's alterations in the text tie together at least three otherwise disparate and unrelated concepts, all as a background to the parable of the rich man and Lazarus. Isn't it just possible that Joseph Smith is restoring historical and doctrinal information that may be had in no other way?

Is our trust in the traditional available texts so certain that we would be willing to dismiss or ignore what Joseph Smith delivered because it strikes a discordant chord with what we may have learned elsewhere? Are we absolutely confident that what we now have is what once was, so far as ancient texts and manuscripts are concerned? President J. Reuben Clark, Jr., posed the following interesting question: What if the Greek texts toward which scholars feel such reverence were to be found to be only translations of Aramaic texts? That means they would be "in fact only a translation of the Aramaic words used by the Savior," and thus "it would seem that the whole critical structure built by the Extreme Textualists would crumble to the ground, because the words, the Greek words, upon which they comment and surmise, . . . are not the words of Jesus at all."[12] We must not turn a deaf ear to the warning Elder McConkie issued in 1984: "Those who turn to the original tongues for their doctrinal knowledge have a

tendency to rely on scholars rather than prophets for scriptural interpretations. This is perilous; it is a sad thing to be numbered with the
wise and the learned who know more than the Lord."[13]

7. *What do we make of the fact that some feel comfortable accepting the
parts of the JST that are in the canon of scripture (the standard works),
such as the book of Moses and Joseph Smith—Matthew, but feel less in-
clined to accept the other JST alterations?* There is no question but that
we are firmly committed to the canon, the standard works, and that
these books of scripture serve as the rule of faith and practice for the
Latter-day Saints; they are binding upon us. At the same time, if any
people in all the wide world should have reason to be nervous about
sealing the canon, it is the Latter-day Saints. For us nothing is more
fixed, set, and established than the eternal fact that the canon of
scripture is open, flexible, and expanding. What is scripture one day
may become part of the canon the next, as was the case in 1976 with
the vision of the celestial kingdom (D&C 137) and the vision of the
redemption of the dead (D&C 138). These were, according to the definition provided in modern revelation (D&C 68:3–4), *scripture* from
the time they were given; they were just as true before they were canonized in 1976. The same is so in regard to the entire JST before it was
printed by the Reorganized Church.

Further, in our study or our inquiry after the mind and will of the
Lord we as a people are not bound by a single collection of sacred
books. We are called upon to "live by every word . . . of God" (D&C
84:44), to open ourselves to new truths as they may come forth
through proper channels. The addresses delivered by the President of
the Church at general conference are not in the canon, nor are such
official doctrinal declarations of the First Presidency as "The Origin of
Man" (November 1909) or "The Father and the Son" (June 1916),
but they certainly represent the mind and will and voice of the Lord
to the Saints; the members of the Church are expected to "give dili-
gent heed to the words of eternal life" (D&C 84:43) as they come
from the lips of the Lord's anointed servants. Does anyone really believe that what is said in scripture by Alma or Paul or John the
Beloved is any more binding on the Saints in our day than President
Ezra Taft Benson's messages on the Book of Mormon or President

Howard W. Hunter's plea for greater Christian charity and more devoted service in the temples?
President Spencer W. Kimball declared:

> Since . . . 1820, additional scripture has continued to come, includ-
> ing the numerous and vital revelations flowing in a never-ending stream
> from God to his prophets on the earth. Many of these revelations are
> recorded in . . . the Doctrine and Covenants. Completing our Latter-day
> Saint scriptures is the Pearl of Great Price, another record of revelation
> and translated writings of both ancient and modern prophets.
>
> There are those who would assume that with the printing and bind-
> ing of these sacred records, that would be the "end of the prophets." But
> again we testify to the world that revelation continues and that the
> vaults and files of the Church contain these revelations which come
> month to month and day to day. We testify also that there is, since 1830
> when The Church of Jesus Christ of Latter-day Saints was organized, and
> will continue to be, so long as time shall last, a prophet, recognized of
> God and his people, who will continue to interpret the mind and will of
> the Lord.[14]

In writing on the subject of the biblical canon, the respected
scholar F. F. Bruce observed:

> There is a distinction between the canonicity of a book of the Bible
> and its authority. Its canonicity is dependent upon its authority. For
> when we ascribe canonicity to a book we simply mean that it belongs to
> the canon or list. But why does it so belong? Because it was recognized as
> possessing special authority. People frequently speak and write as if the
> authority with which the books of the Bible are invested in the minds of
> Christians is the result of their having been included in the sacred list.
> But the historical fact is the other way about; they were and are included
> in the list because they were acknowledged as authoritative.
>
> For example, when Moses came down from Mount Sinai and told
> the people all the words he had received from God, reading them from
> the "book of the covenant" in which he had written them, the people
> answered: "All that the Lord hath spoken will we do" (Exodus 24:7).
> That is to say, they acknowledged that the words they heard from Moses'
> lips were the words of God, and therefore absolutely authoritative and

binding. But we can hardly say that they recognized these words as *canonical*, for the idea of a list or collection of such writings lay still in the future. Or when, in New Testament times, Paul wrote to the Christians at Corinth, "If any man thinketh himself to be a prophet, or spiritual, let him take knowledge of the things which I write unto you, that they are the commandment of the Lord" (1 Corinthians 14:37), no doubt those members of the Church whose spiritual sense was alert acknowledged the written words of Paul as the commandments of Christ Himself. But the idea of a New Testament canon was still to take shape. Both logically and historically, authority precedes canonicity."[15]

We have within our own history examples of doctrines or practices that were in effect long before the actual revelation was a part of the canon. For example, the Latter-day Saints were gathering Israel—bringing people into the kingdom through conversion—even before the Church was officially organized. But the keys of the gathering of Israel were not actually conferred until the coming of Moses to the Kirtland Temple in April of 1836. In fact, those keys formalized and empowered a work that was already well under way. Joseph Smith seems to have learned of eternal and plural marriage as early as 1831, as a result of his inspired translation of Genesis. Plural marriage was introduced to some of the Saints in Nauvoo. It remained for Elder Orson Pratt to deliver the first public discourse on the subject in 1852. The revelation we now have as section 132 of the Doctrine and Covenants was first recorded on 12 July 1843 but was not included in the Doctrine and Covenants until 1876. The practice continued until after the Manifesto of President Wilford Woodruff in 1890 called for its cessation.

Elder McConkie noted in 1984 that the JST

> contains various additions, deletions, and emendations to the King James Version. But most importantly it contains the book of Moses and the twenty-fourth chapter of Matthew as published in the Pearl of Great Price.
>
> These portions have been formally canonized by us, which should establish that any changes made by the Prophet are true and should be used. Does anyone think that the pure revelation found in Genesis 14 about Melchizedek or in Genesis 50 about the Nephites and Joseph

Smith and the latter days is any less a revelation that Moses 1? Does anyone think the [JST of the] first chapter of John's Gospel is of any less
worth than the twenty-fourth chapter of Matthew's?[16]

As the Saints of the Most High, we are under obligation to receive all that God sees fit to deliver. It would be tragic to deny ourselves additional light and truth through holding to a technicality to
which the Lord does not hold. "And now, verily I say unto you, that as
I said I would make known my will unto you, behold I will make it
known unto you, not by the way of commandment, for there are many
who observe not to keep my commandments. But unto him that keep-
eth my commandments I will give the mysteries of my kingdom, and
the same shall be in him a well of living water, springing up unto everlasting life." (D&C 63:22–23.)

8. *Is it that critical that we turn to the JST in our teaching? Are not
most of the doctrinal contributions found elsewhere in the standard works?*
There are, of course, some doctrines or principles from the JST that
are made known in other modern revelations. There are some, however, that are taught principally, and in some cases only, in the JST.
The following concepts represent only a fraction of what might be
cited from the JST of the Old Testament alone (or in some cases also
from the book of Moses in the Pearl of Great Price):

— The spirit creation and the spiritual creation (JST, Genesis
    1–2);
— The premortal existence of mankind (JST, Genesis 3);
— The revelation of the gospel of Jesus Christ to Adam by heav-
    enly messengers; the baptism, confirmation, and ordination of
    Adam (JST, Genesis 5–6);
— The call and prophetic ministry of Enoch, and the ultimate
    translation of Enoch and his people; God's covenant with
    Enoch (later confirmed with Noah) that he would never again
    destroy the earth by water; the prophetic insight that the Lord
    would in the last days flood the earth with the Book of
    Mormon and the message of the Restoration, all as a part of
    the establishment of Zion and the New Jerusalem (JST,
    Genesis 6–7);
— The gospel teachings of Noah and his sons (JST, Genesis 8);

— The deeper meaning of the token of the rainbow, namely, the
return of the city of Enoch in the last days (JST, Genesis 9);
— The ministry of Melchizedek and the translation of inhabitants of the city of Salem (JST, Genesis 14);
— The age of eight days established as the time of circumcision as
a token that children become accountable before God at eight
years; the false practice of infant baptism in the days of
Abraham; the false notion introduced anciently that the blood
of the righteous Abel had been shed for sins (JST, Genesis 17);
— The prophecies of Joseph of old regarding the Messiah, Moses,
Aaron, and Joseph Smith, Jr., an account more extensive than
that contained in the Book of Mormon (JST, Genesis 50; compare 2 Nephi 3);
— That the name Jehovah was known from the beginning (JST,
Exodus 6);
— That the first set of tablets given to Moses contained divine
instructions for establishing the holy order of God, including
the fulness of the blessings of the priesthood, while the second
set did not (JST, Exodus 34; Deuteronomy 10).

These doctrines are important. They constitute some of the singularly Latter-day Saint theological perspectives. We could list scores of
additions, occasional deletions, and clarifications from the JST of the
New Testament pertaining to

1. the ministry of John the Baptist;
2. some of the doctrinal teachings of the Baptist;
3. the teachings and doings and personality of Jesus;
4. the doctrine of Elias;
5. how our Lord prepared the Twelve for their preaching ministry;
6. what it means to take up our cross;
7. the call and writings of the Apostle Paul;
8. what the Saints in the first century did and did not believe in
regard to the imminence of the Second Coming;
9. what John the Beloved taught and meant in his Apocalypse.

It seems a shame (almost a *crime*) to ignore such insights when
they are readily available to the Saints. Why be content with what we
have in an imperfect Bible when we can bask in a greater light?

9. *If we are teaching about the Bible, how are we to use the JST? Is not the course of study primarily a search of what the KJV has to offer?* I believe we are asked to teach the gospel, as found in the Bible. Agreed, we are to teach the text of the scripture, but if there are clarifying principles or doctrines in the Book of Mormon, the Doctrine and Covenants, the book of Abraham, or the sermons and writings of modern prophets, we are to draw upon them. Likewise, we are to use the JST to clarify and expand the students' understanding of the KJV. Otherwise we shortchange the students. As Robert Matthews observed: "Too often we make the faulty assumption that the established scriptures are the ultimate source of doctrine, rather than revelation. This was the basic argument Jesus had with the Jews in John 5:39, wherein Jesus told the Jewish rulers that they had placed their confidence in the written scriptures instead of listening to him. For both Jesus and Joseph Smith, the Bible was a teaching tool rather than the basic source of their information."[17]

10. *What exactly is the JST and how does it compare with the Book of Mormon, the Doctrine and Covenants, or the Pearl of Great Price?* I will be brief here. The JST is one of many sources of divine truth, one of several ways by which the God of heaven has begun his "restitution of all things" (Acts 3:21) and, more specifically, his restoration of plain and precious truths in these last days. In my mind it holds a place at least as important as the other books of scripture given in our dispensation and is deserving of our ponderings and prayerful attention.

Conclusion

In Joseph Smith we have a man who walked in the light of God's revelation, who was intimately acquainted with those prophets and seers we read about. We have a man who was in a sense a walking and talking Urim and Thummim, one for whom the veil was all but gone. We honor the Book of Mormon, and we treasure the revelations in the Doctrine and Covenants. But I feel duty bound to read, study, teach, and emphasize all of the translations and revelations of Joseph Smith. An acceptance of Joseph Smith's work transcends what is currently known or available in the world of scholarship and thus enters the world of faith. If we cannot for the present time understand how he translated Reformed Egyptian from golden plates, we must still receive his work in all patience and faith. If we cannot reconcile the text of the book of Abraham with what scholars translate from the facsimiles or the few papyri fragments in our possession, we must still receive his work in all patience and faith. If we find that the Prophet's Bible translation does not fit with extant Hebrew or Greek manuscripts, we must still receive his work with all patience and faith.

"Search diligently," the Lord implored in a modern revelation, "pray always, and *be believing*, and all things shall work together for your good, if ye walk uprightly and remember the covenant wherewith ye have covenanted one with another" (D&C 90:24, emphasis added). In the words of Elder Neal A. Maxwell: "It is [my] opinion that all the scriptures, including the Book of Mormon, will remain in the realm of faith. Science will not be able to prove or disprove holy writ. However, enough plausible evidence will come forth to prevent scoffers from having a field day, but not enough to remove the require- ment of faith. Believers must be patient during such unfolding."[18]

The Lord does not ask that we suspend all mental activity, that we compromise our integrity, or that we rely upon cunningly devised fables. What he does ask is that we be willing to exercise faith, to be- lieve in the reality of the unseen, and to trust in things beyond the works of our own hands or the wisdom of our own discoveries. If we are true and faithful to what we believe and know in our hearts, the Lord will yet open our minds and bring forth great discoveries in the land. If, on the other hand, we let what we have discovered by study alone limit our faith and commitment, we close ourselves to a vital realm of reality and block the hand of God. Our study must always be tempered by faith if we desire to be loyal to the work of Joseph Smith.

A few years ago the editors of the *Encyclopedia of Mormonism* were faced with a very practical question: To what extent should the JST be used in the encyclopedia? The question was forwarded by Daniel H. Ludlow, the editor-in-chief, to Elders Neal A. Maxwell and Dallin H. Oaks, advisors to the project. Elder Maxwell responded as follows:

I have conferred with Elder Dallin Oaks concerning our discussion on the Joseph Smith Translation. You and the other editors should feel perfectly free to use the Joseph Smith Translation whenever desirable and possible. The Brethren 'crossed the bridge' concerning the use of the Joseph Smith Translation when they approved (and strongly endorsed) the use of excerpts from the Joseph Smith Translation in the footnotes of the LDS publication of the Bible in 1979, and even provided a special section for more lengthy excerpts.

I do not know of any of the present First Presidency or Quorum of the Twelve who question in any way the use of such quotations from the Joseph Smith Translation in the *Encyclopedia of Mormonism* as would be appropriate and useful. I believe they would be disappointed if you did not use the Joseph Smith Translation extensively. As you may have noted, I frequently use the Joseph Smith Translation in my own writings, as do others of my brethren. (Used by permission.)

Joseph Smith's translation of the Bible stands as a beacon of light to which we would do well to give heed as we seek to gain that more sure knowledge of the word of prophecy. On two different occasions the Lord spoke of the Bible translation as a work which would contribute to the salvation of souls. To Sidney Rigdon he said: "And a commandment I give unto thee—that thou shalt write for him; and the scriptures shall be given, even as they are in mine own bosom, to the salvation of mine own elect" (D&C 35:20). To Frederick G. Williams the Savior declared: "Now I say unto you, my servant Joseph Smith, Jr. is called to do a great work and hath need that he may do the work of translation for the salvation of souls."[19] In the form of a warning, the Prophet Joseph Smith declared at a conference in Orange, Ohio, that God "had often sealed up the heavens because of covetousness in the Church." He added that "the Lord would cut short his work in righteousness and except the Church receive the fulness of the Scriptures that they would yet fail."[20] That we may receive wholeheartedly this vital work, view it in its proper place in the grand scheme of the Restoration, and learn and live by its truths, is my sincere prayer.

Notes

1. HC 1:238.

2. George Q. Cannon, *Life of Joseph Smith the Prophet* (Salt Lake City: Deseret Book Co., 1986), p. 148, note.

3. "Joseph Smith's 'Translation' of the Scriptures," *Improvement Era*, April 1914, p. 595.

4. Bruce R. McConkie, *Mormon Doctrine*, 2d ed. (Salt Lake City: Bookcraft, 1966), p. 384.

5. Bruce R. McConkie, "The Doctrinal Restoration," in *The Joseph Smith Translation: The Restoration of Plain and Precious Things* (Provo: BYU Religious Study Center, 1985), p. 3.

6. See *Plainer Translation*, p. 52.

7. See HC 1:341.

8. "The Doctrinal Restoration," p. 15.

9. See TPJS, p. 373.

10. See Bruce R. McConkie, "The Bible—A Sealed Book," in *Doctrines of the Restoration* (Salt Lake City: Bookcraft, 1989), p. 291.

11. *Ensign*, September 1981, p. 17.

12. From "The King James Version of the Bible," address to CES personnel, 7 July 1954.

13. "The Bible—A Sealed Book," pp. 284–85.

14. Conference Report, April 1977, p. 115, emphasis added.

15. F. F. Bruce, *The Books and the Parchments* (Westwood, New Jersey: Fleming H. Revell Co., 1963), pp. 95–96. See also F. F. Bruce, *The New Testament Documents: Are They Reliable?* (Grand Rapids, Michigan: William B. Eerdmans, 1974), p. 27.

16. "The Doctrinal Restoration," p. 15.

17. *Ensign*, September 1981, p. 16.

18. Neal A. Maxwell, *Plain and Precious Things* (Salt Lake City: Deseret Book Co., 1983), p. 4.

19. Revelation given to Frederick G. Williams, 5 January 1834; in Joseph Smith Collection, Letters 1834, in LDS Church Archives.

20. TPJS, p. 9. See also Donald Q. Cannon and Lyndon W. Cook, eds. *The Far West Record* (Salt Lake City: Deseret Book Co., 1983), p. 23, in which the account reads ". . . except the church receive the fulness of the Scriptures that they would yet *fall*."

9

The Eternal Worth of the Joseph Smith Translation

ROBERT J. MATTHEWS

We have already had seven hours of concentrated instruction by capable and enthusiastic scholars, one of whom is an ordained Apostle, prophet, seer, revelator, and special witness for the Lord Jesus Christ. All of the presenters have labored for the love of the Lord and their devotion to the work. They have assembled much more information than time would permit them to use, but the printed papers will contain this additional information.

A Proper Name for This Gathering

There has been much said about the spirit of revelation, and the importance of the holy scriptures. I have seriously wondered what the proper name is for this kind of a gathering. Is it a seminar? A conference? A symposium? The printed program states that this is a symposium; but I am not sure that term is strong enough. Dictionary definitions are as follows:

A *seminar* is a group of university students engaged in advanced study and original research. That definition is only partly applicable to us, because not all in attendance are university students.

A *conference* is defined as the act of consulting together, usually in a formal manner for the purpose of "dispensing and exchanging information." It involves intensive instruction, emphasizing practical

experience and demonstration, as well as theory. I believe that definition comes very close to our experience the past two days.

A *symposium* consists of "a series of articles delivered or con-
tributed on some subject." We have done that. Symposia originally included eating and drinking. We have drunk of the Spirit and have
partaken of the bread of life in this symposium.

I also checked the meaning of some other words that have relevance to this gathering.

A *feast* is "an elaborate meal prepared for some special occasion,
and for a number of guests." It is a banquet; "an unusually delicious or
abundant meal." The word *feast* emphasizes "the abundance, fulness,
and richness of the food." It carries with it also the idea of "rich sur-
roundings accompanied with joy and pleasure." I hope you feel that
we have been feasting throughout these sessions. Nephi says we must
"press forward, feasting on the word of Christ" (2 Nephi 31:20). On
this occasion we have not merely sipped, but have had opportunity to
feast on some of the words of Christ that have not been available to
the world, but are given to us through the Prophet Joseph Smith.

One more definition: *celebration*. A celebration is "to observe with
proper ceremony or festivities and dignity. To make known publicly;
to proclaim; to praise and to honor, to laud, and to commemorate."
We have tried to do that. We have celebrated the work of the Lord as
brought forth by the Prophet Joseph Smith, who was an instrument in
the Lord's hands. We have praised the Lord and have lauded both the
Prophet Joseph Smith and the JST.

Now, which of these terms best fits this gathering? It would take
all of them. This has been a seminar, a conference, a symposium, a
feast, and a celebration in which we have all participated. The spirit
of testimony has characterized this gathering almost as a revival. I
trust what has been accomplished here will bear spiritual fruit for
many individuals for years to come.

Our Individual Opportunity

We talk frequently of the "restoration of the gospel" in a past
tense, as though it has already taken place. In one sense it has taken

place, for the priesthood and the keys need only be restored one time to the Prophet, but a knowledge of the Restoration first began to occur in the lives of those brethren and sisters who were there a century and a half ago with the Prophet Joseph. A knowledge of the Restoration must continue to take place in the lives of individuals—in each one of us. The Restoration must become a reality and be meaningful to every person individually, in our hearts, and in our minds, and in our knowledge, and in our feelings. I do not think we can stand aloof from the JST and still partake of the complete restoration.

Elder Bruce R. McConkie has cogently declared concerning the JST:

> Let me speak plainly. Satan hates and spurns the scriptures. The less scripture there is, and the more it is twisted and perverted, the greater is the rejoicing in the courts of hell. . . .
>
> May I be pardoned if I say that negative attitudes and feelings about the Joseph Smith Translation are simply part of the devil's program to keep the word of truth from the children of men.
>
> Of course the revealed changes made by Joseph Smith are true—as much so as anything in the Book of Mormon or the Doctrine and Covenants.
>
> Of course we have adequate and authentic original sources showing the changes—as much so as are the sources for the Book of Mormon or the revelations.
>
> Of course we should use the Joseph Smith Translation in our study and teaching. Since when do any of us have the right to place bounds on the Almighty and say we will believe these revelations but not those? . . .
>
> Perhaps these are some of the final great questions we should ask: *Is the restored word true? Is it the mind and will and voice of the Lord? Does the Joseph Smith Translation, as it now stands and without more, have divine approval, and should we use it?*
>
> By way of answer let us ask: Is the Book of Mormon true and should we use it? We all know it is true, even though there is more of it to come.
>
> Is the divine word in the Doctrine and Covenants true? Of course, even though new revelations lie ahead.
>
> Is the book of Abraham true? Yes, but it is not complete; it stops almost in midair. Would that the Prophet had gone on in his translation or revelation, as the case may be.

Yes, the Inspired Version is inspired. Yes, the Joseph Smith Translation of the Bible is holy scripture. In one sense of the word it is the crowning part of the doctrinal restoration. At least it sets the pattern and marks the way as to how the doctrinal rivers of the past shall yet flow into the ocean of the present, as shall surely be in the fulness of times.[1]

The Joseph Smith Translation, or Inspired Version, is a thousand times over the best Bible now existing on earth. It contains all that the King James Version does, plus pages of additions and corrections and an occasional deletion. It was made by the spirit of revelation, and the changes and additions are the equivalent of the revealed word in the Book of Mormon and the Doctrine and Covenants.

For historical and other reasons, there has been among some members of the Church in times past some prejudice and misunderstanding of the place of the Joseph Smith Translation. I hope this has now all vanished away.[2]

What Is the Proper Name of the Joseph Smith Translation?

The Prophet Joseph Smith's translation of the Bible has been known by several names. Joseph Smith consistently called it the New Translation. The published version by the RLDS church has been called Holy Scriptures, Inspired Version, and for many years has popularly been called the Inspired Version. Some have preferred "Inspired Revision." The Church of Jesus Christ of Latter-day Saints has officially labelled it the Joseph Smith Translation, abbreviated as JST.

An interesting situation regarding the name developed in the 1970s when the committee was preparing the new editions of the scriptures. There needed to be some consistent and easily identifiable abbreviation or initials by which this important work could be identified in the footnotes. Since Joseph Smith called it the New Translation, that was considered; but it would be abbreviated to NT, and that could easily be mistaken as meaning New Testament. Inspired Version abbreviates to IV, which could be mistaken for a roman numeral four. So eventually the term *Joseph Smith Translation* was decided upon and was approved by action of the Brethren in a temple meeting. It is the official and formal name for this work in this Church. Although this occurred in the middle 1970s, it took a while to adapt our thinking and usage from Inspired Version to Joseph Smith Translation. But now even some of our RLDS acquaintances occasionally refer to the work as the JST.

A few years ago in a fireside meeting in Detroit, I had given about a forty-minute demonstration of the help the JST can be in understanding the Bible. In closing I explained to the congregation about the various titles and why the term JST was finally selected, just as I have done in this meeting today. A medical doctor stood up and graciously made the remark that he felt the letters IV would have been best, since in medical circles IV also refers to intravenous feeding, which revitalizes many people, and the Joseph Smith Translation does the same for us spiritually. A year or so ago some BYU students came into the classroom, and said, "Brother Matthews, pronounce J-S-T." I replied, "It means Joseph Smith Translation." They said, "We know that, but pronounce it." So after a little hesitation, I said, "Gist." They laughed and said, "That's what the JST does, it gives us the gist of the scriptures."

This reminds me of an event that happened in Pasadena, California, more than thirty years ago. I was speaking about the JST to a group of university students in a Friday noon forum. The meeting had been advertised on several campuses, and a number of non-LDS students were in attendance, besides many LDS institute students. The JST was not so well known among our own people in those days as it is today. After I had explained to the students what the JST was, why Joseph Smith had made the corrections, and given quite a few examples, a young lady (obviously not LDS) stood and asked a question. She was polite, but obviously a little perplexed and surprised. She said, with an incredulous tone to her voice, "Mr. Matthews, do you mean that Mr. Joseph Smith made corrections to the Bible!" I had been saying that very thing for about half an hour, and the idea was just beginning to come across to her. I thought to myself, "This young woman almost missed the point." But before I had time to respond, one of our own students jumped up and said, "Yes! But nothing very important." She almost missed the point, and he had missed it entirely.

The JST Is a Strong Witness for
the Lord Jesus Christ

The title of this address is "The Eternal Worth of the JST." Above all else the Joseph Smith Translation of the Bible is a witness for the Lord Jesus Christ, not only in the New Testament but also in the Old Testament. Time will not permit a complete recitation of these things, but I will cite a few of the most specific instances where the JST is unmistakably informative about the mission of Jesus Christ. For example, early in JST Genesis there is an account of the premortal Grand Council and the opposition of Satan to Christ and to the Father. Early on we learn who Satan is and what kind of a being he is. We also learn in that same instance of the call of Jesus in the premortal councils to be the Creator and the Savior.

Continuing this subject, the JST clearly shows that Adam and Eve after the Fall understood the need for a Redeemer and had the complete assurance that a Redeemer would come. Adam was baptized, and he also testified of the resurrection, knew the purpose of animal sacrifice, and held the Holy Priesthood. He knew of the innocence of little children because of the atonement of Christ. Adam taught all these things to his children. All of the patriarchs from Adam to Melchizedek knew of these same things, held the same priesthood, taught the same gospel, and practiced the same ordinances. The record specifically says that Enoch saw a vision of Jesus lifted up on the cross, and also saw the resurrection, and events in the spirit world. He also knew of the second coming of Jesus to the earth in the last days, and of the Millennium. Likewise Noah taught the gospel in his day, proclaiming the redeeming power of Jesus Christ, and declared to the people that they must be baptized and receive the Holy Ghost. The JST shows that Noah was a prophet of God, and not just a weather prophet.

The same is true of Melchizedek, and of Abraham, and Joseph, and Moses. In the JST all of them were preachers of the gospel of Jesus Christ. None of the things I have just mentioned are in any other Bible—all of these things are in the JST, and can be found in JST, Genesis chapters 1–17 and chapters 49–50. There is not another Old Testament in this world, that we have access to, that teaches these things.

The JST New Testament contains everything about Christ that other Bibles have and in addition strengthens and clarifies what Jesus was like and what he taught. There is not another New Testament like this anywhere in the world that we know about.

In all of these items the JST not only *informs* us about Jesus, it *praises* and *exalts* him.

The JST Is a Symbol

Not only is the JST a fruitful source of revealed doctrinal truth; it is also a symbol of the way revelation can come from God to man. The Prophet Joseph received revelation when he read the scripture and inquired of the Lord for understanding. This thing is a pattern. We have many such examples. The First Vision occurred in 1820 in response to prayer, after Joseph read James 1:5–7. John the Baptist came and bestowed the Aaronic Priesthood on Joseph Smith and Oliver Cowdery in 1829 after they had read about baptism in the Book of Mormon and then inquired of the Lord concerning it. Doctrine and Covenants 76 also was received in this same pattern. The revelation about the postmortal spirit world came to President Joseph F. Smith in 1918 after he read 1 Peter 3:18–20 and meditated upon the meaning. This great revelation is now recorded as Doctrine and Covenants 138. When father Lehi was given a book of sacred writing he read therefrom, and "as he read, he was filled with the Spirit of the Lord" (1 Nephi 1:12), and he began to prophesy.

In each of these instances divine wisdom and information came to a human being after he had read and meditated upon the scripture. This process has also happened to millions of others, who have received revelation as they have read and prayed. Revelation from God is priceless, of untold worth. As mortals we live our entire lives with limited experience and with fragments of knowledge, but when we receive a revelation from the Lord we have tapped into the source of all the knowledge, wisdom, and experience of the eternities. We may not be given the whole of it, but whatever we receive by divine revelation is given out of the background and perspective of all the knowledge, wisdom, and experience that dwells in the Lord who gives the revelation.

So while the JST is not all that we will ever know, or need to know, about the Bible, it offers more than any other Bible and is the tangible symbol of the method by which more light will be received. It is a symbol not only of the eighth article of faith but also of the ninth.

I don't think we will get much more restoration of books of the Bible until we thoroughly make use of what we already have.

Confirmation from Archaeological Sources

The material that is unique to the JST, that which is not had in any other Bible or known manuscript or source, is not bland. There is a difference between a statement of doctrine and a statement telling about an actual event. The JST is direct and straightforward, and offers information that claims to be historical fact. For instance, the JST states that Adam offered the firstlings of his flock as a sacrifice to the Lord and that one day an angel came and asked him why he did so. Adam said he did not know why, but that the Lord had commanded him to do it. The angel then explained that animal sacrifice was a similitude of the future sacrifice and atonement of the Only Begotten. This event is spoken of in a manner to lead the reader to believe that this event actually happened to Adam somewhere in time and at some place. No other source is known which tells about this event aside from the JST. Other similar, actual, particular, exclusive events are told about Noah, Abraham, Melchizedek, Moses, John the Baptist, and Jesus—specific things of a factual nature that are plainly spoken of in the JST, but for which there is no currently known corroborating evidence from any other source in the world.

I have often thought that someday a manuscript or a document of some kind may be found in a cave or somewhere which, when translated, will tell of some or all of these things. Such an archaeological find would no doubt get attention in the journals and newspapers, just as the Dead Sea Scrolls have done. If such specific information comes that so exactly talks of "new" things about Adam, Melchizedek, Moses, John, Jesus, and so on, it will be heralded as a source of new information, theretofore unknown in the religious communities of the world. Then, after a respectable time, someone will discover that the identical concepts have been in the JST ever since the early 1830s.

When we think of how perfectly certain aspects of the Word of Wisdom have been verified and confirmed by secular evidence, we wonder if the same will not also occur with the JST and also with the Book of Mormon. I realize that the salvation of souls does not come that way, since secular evidence is not the path of faith and repentance, but someday I expect the Lord will prove to the world that Joseph Smith was a true seer in everything that he did. Such tangible proof would help to leave the unbelieving world without excuse. The Lord has said that he will prove all his words (see 2 Nephi 11:3).

However, I do not expect that such secular and archaeological proof will come until the members of the Lord's own true church are avid and vigorous users of the JST. I do not think the Lord would embarrass his people. The RLDS church, which historically has been the promoter, now appears to be downgrading the JST. Their respect concerning it is waning, as reported by Dr. Sherry in this symposium. It may be that when we as a people have thoroughly become established and recognized (and perhaps even ridiculed by the worldly wise) as the users and believers of the JST without reservation, then the Lord will bring forth his strong reasons and tangible evidence in some such manner as I have just proposed. This is the way the Lord has worked in times past. We do not receive tangible evidence until after the trial of our faith.

I don't think the present Dead Sea Scrolls will provide this kind of verification of the JST or of other things given through the Prophet Joseph Smith. Maybe they will in a small way. But certainly the Dead Sea Scrolls do verify that there are many old records that were kept that offer valuable insights on life and culture of the Palestine area at the approximate time of Jesus. We can therefore expect there will yet be other records that will come to light in the timetable of the Lord. But we do not need to wait for the kind of proof which might be convincing to the world. We who believe may enjoy the light and knowledge right now without any further delay, through the records given us by Joseph Smith. This assurance is given us in Moses 1:40–41: "And now, Moses, my son, I will speak unto thee concerning this earth upon which thou standest; and thou shalt write the things which I shall speak. And in a day when the children of men shall esteem my words as naught and take many of them from the book which thou shalt write, behold, I will raise up another like unto thee; and they shall be had again among the children of men—among as many as shall believe."

Notice that the promise is that the Lord will raise up one like Moses, and the lost words of Moses will be had again "among as many as shall believe." Who is the man like Moses who will do this? It is Joseph Smith. What did he restore from Moses' writing? The JST of Genesis, Exodus, Leviticus, Numbers, Deuteronomy. Who are they who believe? It should be us.

The Industrial and Technological Revolutions, Information Highways, and the JST

We live in a world of rapidly advancing technological information. Historians tell of the Industrial Revolution in recent centuries, and we know from our own experience of the increased ways of travel, communication, and printing processes over just a few years ago. All this is occurring along the information highway. The Church President can get in touch with the Saints in Africa and Australia easier and in less time than President Brigham Young could contact the Saints in Utah County. And the President's audience can see his face on a screen and hear his voice without his ever leaving his office in Salt Lake City.

When we consider the theological and doctrinal views held by Christian believers in the centuries before the restoration of the gospel and compare that with the marvelous flood of light that has burst upon the earth through the instrumentality of the Prophet Joseph Smith, we must recognize that the advance of spiritual and doctrinal information, which gives us a knowledge of the purposes of God, has been as great as, if not greater than, advances in the technical revolution. Through the process of the translation of the Bible, the Lord revealed to Joseph Smith, and thus to us, much information about the purposes of God, the doctrine of Jesus Christ, the nature of

God, the nature of man, the Church in ancient times, the priesthood, man's premortal existence, the origin and fall of Lucifer, and many other basic, significant points of doctrine.

The Apollos Principle

Acts chapter 18 illustrates what I call the Apollos principle. You are familiar with the good man named Apollos. "And a certain Jew named Apollos, born at Alexandria, an eloquent man, and mighty in the scriptures, came to Ephesus." He had a lot going for him: a pleasing personality, good speech, and some formal education. He was eloquent; he was mighty. "This man was instructed in the way of the Lord." He was not crude or ignorant. Fervent in the Spirit, he spoke and "taught diligently the things of the Lord, knowing only the baptism of John." So there was a limitation to his understanding. He had all the other qualifications but lacked the one that was most important. He did not use the fulness of what had been revealed. He was using old sources. He had the physical ability, the mental ability, the charisma, the power of language; he was fervent, but he lacked a fulness of understanding that could have come to him by using the revelations.

"And he began to speak boldly in the synagogue; whom when Aquila and Priscilla had heard, they took him unto them, and expounded unto him the way of God more perfectly" (Acts 18:24–26). Apollos was not lacking in secular training, but he had not been trained in all aspects of the scriptures. He had many tools but not all the necessary sources.

I am going to paraphrase this passage into a modern context:

There was a certain person named Henry, born in Seattle, an eloquent man, mighty in the scriptures, who came to Utah. (We could substitute any name we wanted for Apollos, and we could have him or her come from Seattle or Bountiful instead of from Alexandria, if we wanted, and we could have him go to Provo to teach instead of to Ephesus.) This person was instructed in the way of the Lord. Being fervent in the Spirit, he (she) spake and taught diligently the things of the Lord, knowing only the King James Version, and he (she) began to speak boldly in the meetings of the Church. But when Tom and Sally (or any of us) heard him, they took him unto themselves and expounded unto him the way of God more perfectly from the Joseph Smith Translation. You can see that testimony, eloquence, and enthusiasm are not enough. We need the word of the Lord through Joseph Smith concerning the Bible. With the correct sources, all those other magnificent gifts will bear more nourishing fruit.

Why Was Not All of the JST Included in the LDS Edition of the Bible?

The question is often asked why not all of the corrections and additions of the JST were included in the LDS edition of the Bible. I can tell you. There were several factors that had a bearing on how much would be used. One major factor was that the RLDS church holds the original manuscript and the copyright, and it is unlikely that they would have given us complete access to it all. Another major item was space. There is a practical limit to how thick a book can be in relation to length and depth. We probably could have included a little more than we did, but space was an important consideration. I can distinctly remember Elder Bruce R. McConkie saying: "If we lack room, let's have a little more JST and a little less dictionary."

In making the selection of JST passages, the following guidelines were used:

1. Selections must be doctrinally significant.
2. Selections must contribute something not readily apparent in the other standard works, thus saving space for unique JST contributions.
3. Priority must be given to passages clarifying the mission of Jesus Christ, the nature of God, the nature of man, the Abrahamic covenant, the priesthood, the antiquity of the gospel, the work of the Lord in the last days, the gathering of Israel—especially the emphasis on the tribes of Joseph—and the latter-day restoration.

4. Selections that correct error or remove contradictions should be used.

These guidelines illustrate the breadth of subject matter in the JST.

On the basis of these guidelines almost every JST passage of doctrinal significance was selected. Since the book of Moses and Joseph Smith—Matthew in the Pearl of Great Price are extracts from the JST, these were not included in the LDS edition of the Bible. Thus the first JST footnote is found in Genesis 6:18. Earlier chapters in Genesis are simply cross-referenced to the book of Moses.[3]

Is There Anything of Doctrinal Value in the Printed JST That Is Not Yet in the Other Standard Works?

Since our "new" LDS edition of the Bible has many footnotes and cross-references, we could ask: Is there still anything of significance in the JST that has not been incorporated into the standard works? The answer is yes, there are some important things. For one thing, some of the flavor and context is lost with the footnoting process. Secondly, there are many one- or two-word JST features, especially conjunctions or interjections that seem insignificant in isolation but which in context influence the direction of a passage. The JST contains a great many of these, especially in the New Testament. Furthermore, there is a great amount of JST information pertaining to the Sermon on the Mount that did not get into the LDS Bible—because it is similar to the Savior's sermon in 3 Nephi 12–14—that would clarify the Bible sermon immeasurably, even beyond what 3 Nephi does. The eager and earnest student will still find much to be happy about by reading the entire JST, even beyond the current LDS Bible.

In closing I would ask: What would you give to know the Bible and the other scriptures as Joseph Smith knew them? Would you be willing to search all he has given us about it? Using the JST in our study is like sitting at the same table with the Prophet Joseph Smith, with the privilege of turning to him for counsel.

I am thankful for a testimony of the gospel: a testimony that Jesus is the true Savior and Messiah; that Joseph Smith was able to restore so much in his day; and that the President of the Church is the designated and rightful holder of the keys of the kingdom today. I am also aware that it is not enough just to know these things, for such knowledge carries with it a strong commitment and requirement to become familiar with the revelations and with the directions given by the Brethren.

Notes

1. Bruce R. McConkie, "The Doctrinal Restoration," in *The Joseph Smith Translation* (Provo: BYU Religious Studies Center, 1985), pp. 12, 14, 21.

2. Bruce R. McConkie, "The Bible—A Sealed Book," in *Doctrines of the Restoration* (Salt Lake City: Bookcraft, 1989), p. 289.

3. A more complete discussion of this matter is found in *Ensign*, June 1992, p. 29.

10

Questions and Answers Pertaining to the Joseph Smith Translation

ROBERT J. MATTHEWS

*D*uring the two-day symposium that generated the essays in this book, questions sometimes arose from the audience or were asked the presenters between sessions. On the first day, Robert J. Matthews invited the audience to submit questions in writing, promising to respond to them in the final session of the second day. Thirty-three questions were submitted. There was some duplication, and some items were automatically dealt with by the other lecturers. Following are the remaining questions and the responses from Brother Matthews.

1. *Am I to assume that it would be appropriate to quote from the JST in our classwork and in sacrament meeting?*

Response: The answer to this can only be yes. The fact that our recent editions of the standard works, especially the Bible, have copious footnotes from the JST makes it clear that the JST is a viable source for us to use. As Elder Neal A. Maxwell explained in a letter to Daniel H. Ludlow, 19 July 1990: "The Brethren 'crossed the bridge' concerning the use of the Joseph Smith Translation when they approved (and strongly endorsed) the use of excerpts from the Joseph Smith Translation in the footnotes of the LDS publication of the Bible in 1979, and even provided a special section for more lengthy excerpts. . . . As you may have noted, I frequently use the Joseph

Smith Translation in my own writings, as do others of my brethren."
(Used by permission.)

Earlier confirmation is found in the counsel of Elder Bruce R.
McConkie to a seminar of Regional Representatives, 2 April 1982.
Elder McConkie gave seven items. Numbers 2, 6, and 7 are:

> May I suggest for you and your families and all those with whom you
> labor in the kingdom, the following: . . .
>
> 2. Mark a new set of the Standard Works. Learn to use the footnotes
> and teaching aids in our new editions of the scriptures. Pay particular at-
> tention to the inspired changes made by the Prophet Joseph Smith in
> the Bible. Be sure any quotations you make include the new textual cor-
> rections. . . .
>
> 6. Expound the scriptures. Explain their meanings. Let others know
> what you know. Raise your voice in testimony.
>
> 7. Get others to go and do likewise with reference to all these
> things.

*2. Since the JST is important, why was it not included in its entirety in
the new scripture edition of 1979?*

Response: There were various reasons why the entire JST was not
included. Two of the most notable reasons are space limitations and
the fact that the RLDS church has the manuscript and a copyright. A
more detailed discussion on this can be found in the *Ensign*, June
1992, p. 29, and also in chapter 9 of this present book.

*3. Will the missionaries at some future time be encouraged to use the
JST in their work?*

Response: I think it unlikely that the missionaries will be encouraged to carry an edition of the present JST to use in proselyting.
However, the LDS edition of the Bible, which missionaries to English-
speaking peoples use, contains hundreds of footnotes and an appendix
of JST passages. As a missionary tool, for public relations reasons, a
Bible that the world at least tentatively accepts such as the King
James Version has advantages. The King James Version, by decision of
the First Presidency and the Twelve, is the accepted Bible of the
Church at this time.

As stated in Doctrine and Covenants 24:56–58, the doctrines and
principles revealed through the JST are to be taught eventually to all

peoples. Someday, in the timetable of the Lord, a correct and complete translation of the Bible will be had by the Church. See also the essay by Larry E. Dahl presented in this book.

4. *What do you think is the single most important doctrinal point received through the JST?*

Response: It is difficult to make such a choice. As to a precise passage, I would select Moses 1:39: "Behold, this is my work and my glory, to bring to pass the immortality and eternal life of man." This grand declaration of the work and purposes of God is of great worth and comprehension. As a basic concept, I suppose that one of the most significant attainments of the JST is the principle that the canon of scripture is on-going, and that revelation from God comes when one carefully reads and ponders the scripture.

5. *Have there been any new and striking ideas generated by this symposium that sparked new interest in Brother Matthews, who has spent a lifetime with the JST?*

Response: I have not encountered any completely new ideas, but I have been impressed with the depth of scholarship and the interpretations offered by the other presenters. These brethren have rounded out the ideas and put meat on the bare bones. Also I am impressed with the multiple witnesses that these presenters have become as to the worth of the JST.

6. *What percentage of the JST doctrines and concepts that have been presented in this symposium are in the RLDS publication but are not in the book of Moses, Joseph Smith—Matthew, or the footnotes of the LDS edition of the Bible?*

Response: I do not know an exact percentage, but almost all of the JST passages that are doctrinally significant are now in our new editions of the standard works.

7. *Can the RLDS publication of the* Holy Scriptures, Inspired Version *be relied upon as correct?*

Response: The RLDS publications of the Joseph Smith Translation of the Bible are quite correct. That is, they follow the manuscript quite well. In some cases there is ambiguity in the manuscripts, and also a choice of terms sometimes must be made because of multiple manuscripts. After examining the manuscripts and the RLDS printed editions, it is my judgment that the published work is a very good representation of what is contained in the manuscripts. There are some problems, but in my opinion these are minor compared with the wonderful information that is contained throughout the entire work.

8. *Which edition of the RLDS publication of the translation is most correct?*

Response: The first edition of 1867 had the most typographical and judgmental errors. The "new corrected edition" of 1944 was a significant improvement. Subsequent editions have been even more correct in minor details. None of the RLDS editions have carried what we call Moses chapter 1 as part of the Genesis text. All earlier editions placed that document as special introductory material. However, the most recent edition, 1991, has omitted this valuable Moses material even from the introduction.

9. *Please comment on the usability of the parallel edition published by the RLDS Herald House in 1970, which presents the New Translation in tandem with the King James Version.*

Response: The concept of a parallel edition is very helpful for easy reference. The type-style is clear and readable. A major disadvantage is that the researchers failed to include nearly 120 passages of correction. This was not intentional or mischievous, but it lessens the reliability and function of the book. There are also several other less serious problems. A complete discussion of this matter can be found in the Robert J. Matthews book, *"A Plainer Translation": Joseph Smith's Translation of the Bible, A History and Commentary* (Provo: BYU Press, 1985), pp. 198–200.

10. *Should the RLDS publication of Joseph Smith's translation be used in classes and speaking in the Church, or is it better to use the LDS edition of the King James Version containing JST footnotes?*

Response: The First Presidency has set the example by the statement issued in 1992 (*Ensign*, August 1992, p. 80), which defines the LDS edition of the King James Version and the supplementary aids contained therein as the proper text to be used in Church meetings and assignments in English-speaking situations. The footnotes and the appendix provide many JST passages that will be adequate in most cases. If teachers and speakers will follow this example, Church members will be able to get full value from the many JST passages now found in the standard works.

11. *To what extent was the JST completed or finished by the Prophet Joseph Smith?*

Response: It appears that the Prophet Joseph Smith had made about all the corrections that he intended to make in the Bible. It is true that the translation is not 100 percent complete, but he was making serious efforts to publish it. There is considerable evidence that not all necessary passages were corrected. Also the "lost books" of the Bible were not restored. However, the translation was far more extensive than many people have thought. This subject is dealt with in Elder Dallin H. Oaks's address in this volume.

12. *Should the JST as now constituted be accepted as scripture and on equal footing with the other material in the standard works?*

Response: The JST has never been officially and completely canonized as a standard work; however, parts of it have been included in the Pearl of Great Price and it is evident that Elder Bruce R. McConkie felt very comfortable about the worth of the JST in its entirety. See chapter 9 herein, "The Eternal Worth of the JST," which cites Elder McConkie on this matter.

13. *What is the amount of time spent by the Prophet Joseph Smith in translating the JST as compared with the time spent in translating the Book of Mormon?*

Response: It is impossible to give even a close approximation of days or hours occupied in translating the JST. However, as cited by several presenters in this symposium, Joseph Smith spent many hours and days in serious work with the Bible translation, and enjoyed many hours of refreshing inspiration. He wrote of being "weary" because of the work involved. In several revelations in the Doctrine and Covenants the Lord encourages the Prophet to continue until the work is "finished," and to "hasten" with the work. Everything about the history and content of the JST, including the 464 pages of handwritten manuscript, suggests a monumental task stretching over several years.

14. *Why are some passages in the Book of Mormon, which are "faithful" to the King James text, "corrected" in the JST?*

Response: This is a question that Joseph Smith could answer better than anyone else. As a starter we would of necessity believe that the Prophet must have known that he was creating this situation, yet he saw fit to do so. The answer may lie in the concept of an "adequate" translation as compared to a "plainer" translation, as suggested in Doctrine and Covenants 128:18. This subject is dealt with in greater detail in the *Ensign*, September 1981, pp. 16–17.

15. *Why did the Prophet not change Malachi 4:5–6 to conform to the words of Moroni as cited in Doctrine and Covenants section 2?*

Response: This is something Joseph Smith could answer to greater satisfaction than any of us could do. However, we note that he did not cause the same passage in 3 Nephi 24:5–6 to conform to Moroni's words, but rather it reads the same as the King James Version. It may be that Moroni was paraphrasing or interpreting, or giving inspired commentary. Likewise, the variations may reflect different levels of meaning inherent in the original statement of Malachi.

The key to understanding this matter may be found in Doctrine and Covenants 128:18, in which the Prophet explains that he could render "a plainer translation" when and if necessary. On this very subject Elder Bruce R. McConkie has said:

> As a matter of fact, Moroni did this same thing in his 1823 appearances to Joseph Smith. For instance, he so improved upon the promise of Elijah's return that it is like stepping from a pleasant twilight into the brilliance of the noonday sun. And yet, years later, with a full knowledge of the more perfect translation, Joseph Smith retained the King James language in the Book of Mormon [3 Nephi 25:5–6] and the Doctrine and Covenants [D&C 128:17] and his inspired rendition of the Bible [Malachi 4:5–6].
>
> Surely there is a message here. For one thing it means that the same passage of scripture can be translated correctly in more ways than one and that the translation used depends upon the spiritual maturity of the people.
>
> Similarly, the Sermon on the Mount in the Book of Mormon preserves, with a few improvements, the language of the King James Version. But, later, the Joseph Smith Translation renders much of this sermon in a way that excels even the Book of Mormon.[1]

16. *If the Prophet Joseph Smith had reworked the Book of Mormon after his work on the JST, do you think that the Savior's sermon recorded in*

3 Nephi 12–14 would read a little more like the JST and a little less like the King James Version?

Response: The whole process of translation as done by a prophet is difficult to define, but I suppose what is suggested in your question is true. Such a thought does not lessen the inspiration of the Book of Mormon translation but it does indicate that there may be levels of depth and completeness in any translation made by a prophet. As noted in the response to a previous question, the Prophet Joseph Smith surely must have realized what he was doing in such instances, yet he apparently felt that the change needed to be made to clarify the biblical text. The citation from Elder Bruce R. McConkie in the previous question applies to this question also.

17. *How does the Joseph Smith Translation compare with ancient Jewish Midrashic tradition and Kabbalistic teachings?*

Response: *Midrash* is a Hebrew term meaning "to expound or explain." *Kabbal* is Hebrew, meaning "to receive" or to have obtained divine knowledge beyond that which is common to man. There is no known direct tie between these and the JST, and thus it is not likely that agreement would be found, unless the Midrashic or Kabbalistic teaching preserved some thread of knowledge or interpretation that was lost to the mainstream. This is possible. However, so far as I know, such a comparison has not yet been pursued. A number of similarities were found in comparing non-canonical Jewish sources with the book of Abraham.[2] Perhaps a search with the JST would also be fruitful.

18. *Since not all of the JST is included in the LDS edition of the Bible (1979), will there be a time when more can be added?*

Response: Adding to a published product is not an easy task, because the pagination is already set, and every addition requires that something would have to be removed to make room. Perhaps someday an entire new edition will be made, but I could not guess when that would be done.

19. *I have heard that the book of Ecclesiastes was omitted from the JST. Why was it not included?*

Response: It is not Ecclesiastes but the Song of Solomon that was omitted. The JST Old Testament manuscript (page 97) states that "The Songs of Solomon are not inspired writings." However, what you may also have heard is that in the JST Old Testament manuscript there is no mention of the book of Ecclesiastes, one way or another, with no comment. This is probably an oversight. The printed JST has Ecclesiastes precisely as contained in the King James Version.

20. *Did Joseph Smith use the Urim and Thummim in translating the Bible?*

Response: The Urim and Thummim was apparently not used in the translation of the Bible. The following was given in the School of the Prophets in Salt Lake City, on 14 January 1871, by Elder Orson Pratt, and was recorded by the secretary of the school:

> He [Elder Pratt] mentioned that as Joseph used the Urim and Thummim in the translation of the Book of Mormon, he wondered why he did not use it in the translation of the New Testament. Joseph explained to him that the experience he had acquired while translating the Book of Mormon by the use of the Urim and Thummim had rendered him so well acquainted with the Spirit of Revelation and Prophecy, that in the translating of the New Testament he did not need the aid that was necessary in the 1st instance.[3]

21. *What percentage of the JST is included in the LDS edition of the Bible?*

Response: Nearly all of the JST passages with doctrinal content are in our standard works, such as the footnotes and appendix of the Bible, in the book of Moses, and in Joseph Smith—Matthew. This is actually a small percentage—less than 50 percent of the total number of unique corrections in the JST. However, many corrections in the JST consist of only one word and sometimes reflect only a shade or nuance of meaning and were not included in the 1979 LDS edition of the Bible. Furthermore, many JST passages that are consistent with the Savior's sermon in 3 Nephi 12–14 were excluded for space considerations. Almost all of the doctrinally significant JST passages are found in our present standard works.

22. *The original JST manuscripts contain some lined-out words. Why is this?*

Response: Sometimes after a passage was recorded, new light was received, and so a word was lined out and the correction was inserted interlinearly. Sometimes when writing the scribe made an error, and he simply lined out the error and rewrote the passage.

23. *You once told of seeing a fingerprint in the ink of the JST manuscript. Will you enlarge upon that item?*

Response: When examining the original JST manuscripts, often I used a magnifying glass to view lined-out words in greater detail. Once, when doing so, I came across an ink blot (of which there are several) on the manuscript and saw an unmistakable finger or thumb print in the ink blot. This would likely be Sidney Rigdon's print.

24. *What are the chances of the LDS church's obtaining the JST manuscript and publishing it?*

Response: I don't see any possibility of that, at least in the near future. The RLDS church has a strong sense of history and would want to retain the manuscript and the marked Bible as historical artifacts. Furthermore, I am sure that the LDS church would not want to publish the document until the Lord gave more revelation on the matter.

25. *There seems to be a changing of positions with regard to the JST. The RLDS church appears to be lessening its official interest, whereas in the LDS church interest is increasing. Why is this?*

Response: There does seem to be a trend such as you have noted. It may be a matter of timing. The RLDS church is concerned with its world image and has made overtures toward twentieth-century Protestantism. Concurrent with this trend has been an increased RLDS interest in such Bible translations as the New English Bible and the New International Version. The LDS church has hesitated in using the JST because until recently we did not have access to the JST manuscripts. Since the manuscripts have become available for research, and we have learned that the JST is published accurately, acceptance in the LDS church has increased. The "new" editions of the scriptures have encouraged greater use of the JST.

26. *Could you discuss the feelings of those who worked in the development of the current edition of the standard works in 1979 (Bible) and 1981 (Triple)? What was the rationale for retaining the King James Version?*

Response: I can tell you that all of us felt then and still feel now that it was a once-in-a-lifetime honor to be part of the team that produced the new editions of the standard works. We worked under the direction of members of the Twelve and the First Presidency. We knew that the hand of the Lord was in the project. We almost daily saw the inspiration of God direct the decisions of the Brethren. We felt inspiration in our own labors. There was harmony and unity of purpose among those engaged in the work. The King James Version was retained as the biblical text because the First Presidency so directed, and we all willingly agreed. The King James Version is doctrinally closer to the revelations received by the Prophet Joseph Smith than are the newer translations that have been made by the wisdom of man.

Notes

1. *Doctrines of the Restoration: Sermons and Writings of Bruce R. McConkie* (Salt Lake City: Bookcraft, 1989), pp. 290–91.

2. See Rabbi Nissim Wernick, "A Critical Analysis of the Book of Abraham in the Light of Extra-Canonical Jewish Writings," unpublished Ph.D. dissertation, BYU 1968, pp. 106–8.

3. Manuscript in the Church Historical Department.

APPENDIX

Changing Attitudes Toward Joseph Smith's Translation of the Bible

THOMAS E. SHERRY

Editors' Note:

This appendix represents an illustrated lecture that was delivered at a public symposium at Brigham Young University, as were the other chapters in this book. It is included as an appendix because of its special historical content of significance to all who are interested in Joseph Smith's translation of the Bible. The lecture was based on the author's dissertation: "Attitudes, Practices, and Positions Toward Joseph Smith's Translation of the Bible: A Historical Analysis of Publications, 1847–1987." Brigham Young University, Provo, UT: 1988. Results from a five-year update entitled "Joseph Smith's Translation of the Bible: A Bibliography of Publications, 1988–1992" were also employed. Both studies made an effort to contain every publication dealing with the JST during the period of consideration (the dissertation chronicled and examined 389 publications, while the 1988–1992 study contained 50 published entries).

Copies of the multi-volume, extensively documented work can be found in the LDS Church Historical Library in Salt Lake City; the Harold B. Lee Library at BYU; the Religious Education Library, Joseph Smith Building at BYU; and the RLDS Library and Archives in Independence, Missouri.

In 1830 Joseph Smith, Jr., embarked on a project which would have significant impact on him and all who would from that time forward measure this Prophet of the Restoration. This work would have a marked impact on his concept of scripture and revelation, as well as on the future of the Church. It would also prove to be one of the key-stones around which would be built future opinions others would have of him. He would be obedient to a divine directive to undertake a "new translation," or revision, of the Holy Scriptures. The translation would be drawn from a pulpit edition King James Version of the Bible purchased in 1829 by him and Oliver Cowdery.

This paper is an examination of many published statements concerning Joseph Smith's translation of the Bible (JST) from 1847–1992 (see Supplement A). Virtually since the dates of their organization, both The Church of Jesus Christ of Latter-day Saints (hereafter, LDS church) and the Reorganized Church of Jesus Christ of Latter Day Saints (hereafter RLDS church) have had official publishing organs. These publications have played a central role in the collective education and attitudinal development of members of both churches. While of less significance (due in part to more limited distribution), many unofficial church-related publications have given outlet for members of both Latter-day Saint faiths and others to express opinions and influence the development of attitudes toward the JST.

Joseph Smith considered the work of revision as an integral "branch of [his] calling" as Prophet of the restored Church of Jesus Christ, and that it was undertaken because of a divine directive (*History of the Church* 1:238, hereafter HC). He unquestionably viewed the work as a product of heavenly guidance, "made by the power of God," which would in part restore lost meaning and material to the sacred record and therefore be of importance to the salvation of mankind. (A more complete view of Joseph Smith's perception of his revision and how, according to Joseph, the Lord viewed the work is contained in Supplement B: The JST: A Fundamental Standard of Belief.) He labored on the revision rather consistently from 1830–1833, giving it intermittent attention thereafter until his death in 1844. Although it is clear that he intended to do so, the Prophet Joseph Smith was not able to officially publish the whole of his "new translation."[1]

The Bible revision manuscripts left by Joseph at his death in 1844 were obtained, and later published in 1867, by the Reorganized Church of Jesus Christ of Latter Day Saints. Entitled *Holy Scriptures* (subtitled in 1936 *Inspired Version*), the publication was adopted as the official Bible of the RLDS church.[2] At that time the LDS church neither accepted, officially employed, nor rejected that publication of the Bible.[3] Certain portions of the translation (from Genesis and Matthew) had earlier been published by Joseph Smith and were later included in the LDS standard work known as the Pearl of Great Price. But extensive use of the JST was not officially endorsed until the inclusion of parts of it in the 1979 LDS edition of the King James Bible.[4]

Three Questions of Attitude, Position, and Practice

The following analysis of the history of published writings dealing with the JST was, in part, aimed at the exploration of three questions: (1) What attitudes, positions, or practices towards the JST are reflected in the nature and content of LDS and RLDS church publications? (2) Do the published sources evidence any shifts in attitude, position, or practice regarding the JST over time in LDS or RLDS church publications? and (3) What attitudes are evidenced in other publications not officially sponsored by the two churches ?

Question One: What attitudes, positions, or practices towards the JST are reflected in the nature and content of LDS and RLDS publications?

Consistent repetition of certain themes is observed in official publications of each church during the first century of their separation. The RLDS church had its formal beginnings in the 1860s and the LDS church was not fully reestablished in its western home of Utah until a roughly equivalent date. For that first hundred-year period (through the 1950s) "baseline" attitudes and positions are rather easily established because of their persistent recurrence and lack of variant opinion. Elements of these baseline positions will now be explored from both RLDS and LDS publication perspectives. Space limits dictate that only a few published statements representative of each element be used even though their themes were repeated often. (See Supplement C for parallel column comparisons of each position.)

RLDS Position Through the 1950s

Five basic attitudes and church postures found consistently over the first century of RLDS publications were: 1) The work of revision was divinely commanded, guided, and completed; 2) The revision clarified and corrected many difficult or erroneous aspects present in other versions, and restored many plain and precious lost parts; 3) Having been divinely initiated, guided, and approved, the revision was a better product than those Bible versions limited to human scholarship; 4) Members should not disparage the King James Version or other versions but should use the Inspired Version in preference to them, particularly where differences occur; and 5) Divine commands to preserve, publish, and give to the world Joseph Smith's revision were accomplished by the RLDS church and hence mark it as the true church of the Restoration. Each of these elements will now be articulated through the published record:

1. *The work of revision was divinely commanded, guided, and completed:*

> Resolved, That we believe the Holy Scriptures . . . were translated by Divine Inspiration (RLDS Conference resolution, 1873).

> The scriptures were received in full as we will show by the revelations of God, and the testimony of Joseph Smith (Bailey, *Saints' Herald*, 1937).

> It was done by direct revelation from God (Ferris, *Saints' Herald*, 1950).

> I feel we can establish quite satisfactorily that the work was completed (Smith, *Saints' Herald*, 1955).

2. *The revision clarified and corrected many difficult or erroneous aspects present in other versions, and restored many plain and precious lost parts:*

We understand that [Joseph] used the King James translation, the Holy Spirit inspiring him to correct its errors and supply much missing matter (*Saints' Herald*, 1890).

The Inspired Translation does claim to be a correction by the spirit of revelation, and thus we have the words, or thoughts, as Jesus really gave them (Moler, *Saints' Herald*, 18 February 1903).

The primary purpose of revising the Scriptures was avowedly to restore those things lost (Yale, *Saints' Herald*, 1956).

3. *Having been divinely initiated, guided, and approved, the revision was a better product than those Bible versions limited to human scholarship:*

A perfect translation can only be had by the power of God . . . and this, we are happy to learn, is soon to be presented to the saints in the translation by the Martyr (Blair, *Saints' Herald*, 1867).

When the wisdom of the world had failed to produce a translation of God's word clear of absurdities and contradictions; God by direct inspiration gave a plain and more consistent version than had ever been rendered by man (Smith, *Saints' Herald*, 1879).

When the Lord guarantees that the Inspired Version [contains the Scriptures] "as they are in my own bosom," what greater guarantee do we need . . . ? (Ferris, *Saints' Herald*, 1950.)

4. *Members should not disparage the King James Version or other versions but should use the Inspired Version in preference to them, particularly where differences occur:*

We may think our version the better one; and we may frankly say so . . . but the elder who in his ministry attacks the Bible in asperity of speech, or manner . . . clearly misrepresents the church (Smith, *Saints' Herald*, 1895).

At no time should the Inspired Version be replaced in the pulpit with another where interpretation varies (Koury, *Saints' Herald*, 1961).

5. *Divine commands to preserve, publish, and give to the world Joseph Smith's revision were accomplished by the RLDS church and hence mark it as the true church of the Restoration:*

The Lord, had appointed the seer to translate . . . he now promises that the said translation "shall be preserved in safety;" from which we must conclude that He esteemed the hands of Emma, and the Reorganized Church the proper places for his "safety" (Blair, *Saints' Advocate*, 1884).

The Inspired Version of the Holy Scriptures identifies the Reorganized Church of Jesus Christ of Latter Day Saints as being the true church in succession (Bailey, *Saints' Herald*, 1937).

LDS Position Through the 1950s

Four persistent attitudes and practices of the LDS church regarding Joseph Smith's Bible revision were evidenced in the first century of publications: 1) The work of revision was divinely commanded and guided, but not completed; 2) The revision clarified and corrected many difficult or erroneous aspects present in other versions, and "restored many plain and precious" lost parts of the Bible record; 3) Since Joseph Smith did not complete his revision, the RLDS Inspired Version is an unauthorized publication; and 4) The King James Version is the standard Bible of the Church until such time as the Lord directs otherwise. Each of these elements is now briefly viewed through the published record:

1. *The work of revision was divinely commanded and guided, but not completed:*

Joseph the Seer, under divine inspiration, went through the whole volume of ancient scriptures, re-translating or re-vising the text by inspiration. But this work was not fully completed, and it was his intention to give it a careful examination, correcting all errors . . . and preparing it in such a shape that it would be a standard for the Church, before it should be published to the world. (Penrose, *Deseret Evening News*, 1881.)

The Lord commanded Joseph Smith to make a translation of the Bible by revelation. . . . The Prophet finished the work as far as the Lord required of him at that time. In the remaining eleven years of his life the Prophet further revised some passages and attempted to prepare the manuscript for publication. However, because of persecution and a lack of financial means this was not accomplished before his death. (Smith, 1969.)

2. The revision clarified and corrected many difficult or erroneous aspects present in other versions, and restored many plain and precious lost parts of the Bible record:

This inspired rendering of the verse by our lamented patriarch sheds a beautiful light on this passage heretofore shrouded in mystery and doubt (Smith and Anderson, *Improvement Era*, 1900).

The restorations by the Prophet are . . . further evidence that through inspiration the Prophet Joseph Smith made his changes on the authority of the original, now lost, manuscripts, and that these interpolations are not products of his own imagination. . . . Many plain and most precious facts have been restored. (Sperry & Van Wagoner, *Improvement Era*, 1940.)

3. Since Joseph Smith did not complete his revision, the RLDS Inspired Version is an unauthorized publication:

The work has not been published under the auspices of this Church and is, therefore, not held out as a guide (Penrose, *Deseret Evening News*, 1900).

4. The King James Version is the standard Bible of the Church until such time as the Lord directs otherwise.

We believe [the King James Version] will retain its place for a long time, and that among the Latter-day Saints it will not be discarded for any other version until the inspired translation or revision commenced by Joseph Smith shall have been completed, in a form acceptable to the Almighty and suitable for publication (Penrose, *Deseret Evening News*, 1881).

The King James or Authorized Version . . . has been the version accepted by this Church since it was organized (Clark, *Improvement Era*, 1954).

These baseline positions gave shape to nearly every article published through the 1950s and formed the foundation for certain attitudes and traditions about the JST and how each of the churches viewed the Prophet's work. In addition to their own "in-house" view, the perspective each church (LDS and RLDS) had toward the other's view of the work colored many publications. Inherent in some elements of both RLDS and LDS positions were seeds of potentially antagonistic response and ill will between the two churches.

Question Two: Do the published sources evidence any shifts in attitude, position, or practice regarding the JST?
This question was approached by asking whether in the literature each element of the pre-1960s RLDS and LDS positions regarding the JST found continued support through 1992, was modified, or was eliminated. As a matter of publication history, elements of each position did find significant attention in the increased number of publications (since the late 1960s) both for support in some cases and striking modification in others. Again, space limits a portrayal of the richness found in reviewing many related publications that articulate a position on each element. A few statements most representative of the latest attitudes and positions on each element through 1992 have been chosen. Following the cited examples, a summary discussion will overview this thirty-two-year chronicle of publications (1960–1992).

RLDS Position, 1960–1992

From the middle 1960s every formerly held element reflected in the attitudes and positions toward the Inspired Version begins to move through a transition of modification or elimination. A 1992 statement of attitudes and positions of the RLDS church, as reflected in official publications, would likely convey the following: 1) Joseph Smith *perceived* his work of Bible revision as divinely commanded, guided, and sufficiently complete to warrant publication plans; 2) Changes made in the revision represent what Joseph Smith *believed* to be inspired commentary, and grew out of his effort to clarify and correct the Bible text according to his nineteenth-century understanding and resources. Such changes probably do not represent actual restorations of ancient text; 3) The Inspired Version should not be considered categorically better than other Bible versions, particularly those produced by modern Bible scholarship; and 4) Members are encouraged to use the version of the Bible which best meets their particular needs. It will be noted that Element 5 of the formerly held position has not been mentioned in RLDS publications since 1966. Modification of each element is seen via chronological excerpts from publications during this period:

1. *Joseph Smith perceived his work of Bible revision as divinely commanded, guided, and sufficiently complete to warrant publication plans:*

Changes [in the Inspired Version] should not be accepted on the blanket assumption that every change marks inerrant improvement . . . it may be held upon formidable grounds that a number of passages have been weakened in meaning by the changes introduced (Department of Religious Education, *Position Papers*, 1967).

It seems apparent that there is to be found in the "New Testament" a set of premises which are based on unexaminable presuppositions that pose critical problems for responsible exegesis. . . . Accordingly, the "insights" which are to be found in the New Translation can be more responsibly viewed as Joseph Smith's commentary. (Luffman, *Restoration Studies III*, 1986.)

We do not know for certain if Joseph actually considered his efforts final . . . the manuscript cannot be considered complete . . . [and] shows signs of haste at some points (Foreword to 1991 Edition of *The Holy Scriptures*).

At least through the 1950s there was consistent support for the idea of a "completed" text produced through "direct revelation." From the 1960s on, the idea of completion, particularly as attached to the traditional 1833 date, is abandoned. Historical studies by researchers from both churches left little doubt that throughout Joseph's life he continued to make some revision in the manuscripts. The idea of direct revelatory guidance attendant to Joseph's work of revision was also brought under severe questioning in RLDS commentary during this period.

Beginning in the 1960s, official publications show a gradual change in definition and acceptance of the position that Joseph's revision was a revelatory product. Significant articles by RLDS church historians in 1961 (Davies) and 1971 (Howard), as well as by RLDS First Presidency member F. Henry Edwards in 1967, suggest a need for and begin to explore a re-defined view of the nature of Joseph Smith's inspiration and revelation. This redefinition moved away from a traditional acceptance of "propositional" or "plenary" inspiration to one of an "encounter" nature. Propositional or plenary inspiration had traditionally been defined as an act of God, revealing his mind and will through an earthly instrument (e.g., prophets), and thus being a statement of truth binding upon all accountable recipients (e.g., similar to the concept expressed in D&C 93:24: "knowledge of things as they are, and as they were, and as they are to come"). In the field of biblical criticism, propositional revelation is that which can be reduced to propositions, or, evidence which can be examined and tested. At contrast is inspiration, which grows out of a human "encounter" with something thought to be divine. Such encounters are not "up for public examination," as they simply reflect the private experience of an individual, and are not binding on other persons.[5]

Consequent upon evolving thought on this issue, RLDS publications have come to reflect uncomfortableness with the concept of propositional revelation, and hence they prefer to accept that Joseph "thought" he was translating by divine help, whether or not he actually was. As viewed from this setting, the Inspired Version is more a look at the mind of Joseph Smith than a revelation of the mind of God, and hence it is not a binding document of truth.

The impact of this redefinition and its reverberating effects on RLDS evaluation and use of the Inspired Version can hardly be overstated. The published record shows that there is definitive movement towards eliminating altogether a belief in the Inspired Version's plenary revelation. William D. Russell (1983), a sociologist at RLDS-sponsored Graceland College, gives his opinion: "I came to the conclusion that the New Translation is simply . . . based on the personal hunches of Joseph Smith [and] while the King James Version has serious problems, the New Translation fails to correct these problems and simply adds additional problems" (p. 56).[6]

2. *Changes made in the revision represent what Joseph Smith believed to be inspired commentary, and grew out of his effort to clarify and correct the Bible text according to his nineteenth-century understanding and resources. Such changes probably do not represent actual restorations of ancient text:*

> The Inspired Version is not to be regarded as an accurate textual revision, restoring the "pure" text of the original (RLDS Department of Religious Education, *Position Papers*, 1967).

> Ancient copies [of original texts] do not support the traditional view of Joseph's work as being a restoration of the original texts. The Inspired Version is a valuable resource for understanding the thoughts of Joseph Smith, Jr., regarding certain scriptural passages. . . . But Saints do both Joseph and themselves a serious injustice if they view his work as a restoration of the original texts of the Bible. . . . It seems clear that Joseph's changes, regardless of whether they are theologically preferable, reflect his own theology and not that of the original biblical author. (Mesle, *Restoration Studies III*, 1986.)

Uniform RLDS support of Joseph Smith's revision as a restored and corrected biblical text is found up through the 1950s. After that period a gradual movement to identify problems in the Inspired Version culminates in the opinion that Joseph's revisions do not seem to be a restoration of ancient text or a correction of problems extant in the King James Version.

3. *The Inspired Version should not be considered categorically better than other Bible versions, particularly those produced by modern Bible scholarship:*

> Modern versions such as the Revised Standard and Jerusalem Bible represent the best available knowledge of the original biblical texts and their meanings. They should be used also by any who wish to fully honor Joseph's deep passion to understand the scriptures. (Mesle, *Restoration Studies III*, 1986.)

Christians today enjoy a great number of Bible translations and versions. . . . In the final analysis the Bible's authority (in any version) depends on its demonstrated values. . . . Ultimately, the version we use is not as important as our openness to the guidance of the Holy Spirit. (Foreword to the 1991 Edition of *The Holy Scriptures*.)

From a pre-1960s position of viewing the Inspired Version as the best version available, the general publication trend regresses to being "better" (particularly in cases of doctrine and morals), and finally to a posture that considers the Inspired Version as textually inferior to versions produced by modern scholarship.

4. *Members should not disparage the King James, or other versions, but should use the Inspired Version in preference to them, particularly where differences occur:*

Modern versions such as the Revised Standard and Jerusalem Bible represent the best available knowledge of the original biblical texts and their meaning (Mesle, *Restoration Studies III*, 1986).

Literature about the position that other versions should not be disparaged even though the Inspired Version is better has experienced considerable evolution. However, unlike the clear and consistent changes found in elements 1 through 3 of the RLDS position, varied and occasionally conflicting statements on this position are found at least through 1974 (see McDonnell, *Saints' Herald*, December). From the 1960s on, virtues of modern versions are frequently elaborated with the attendant encouragement to use the version that provides the best understanding. However, the 1980s witnessed considerable deterioration of this position to the point that the Inspired Version has largely become viewed as an interesting but unhelpful historical "relic" when understanding scriptural text is at issue (see Russell, 1983; Luffman, 1986; and Mesle, 1986).

5. *Note: The formerly held RLDS position which stated that "Divine commands to preserve, publish, and give to the world Joseph Smith's revision of the Bible were accomplished by the RLDS church and therefore mark it as the true church of the Restoration" is no longer expressed in current literature.*

In 1937 Bailey wrote the most pointed article detailing this position. The revelatory promises and commandments cited by Bailey as having been fulfilled through the RLDS church were: (1) that the scriptures would be preserved in safety; (2) that they should be taught to all men, to all nations, kindreds, tongues, and peoples; (3) that they should be a law to govern the church; and (4) that Joseph's revision of the New Testament would be published together with the Book of Mormon (accomplished in 1872 with the scripture publication, *The Two Records*).

Whether or not the feeling produced by such a posture has abated in the RLDS church since the mid-1900s is difficult to discern from published documents. No mention of this position was found after the 1966 history published by Gibson (*Emma Smith the Elect Lady*). However, the absence of published statements involving this position suggests a change of attitude, or at least discomfort with it as a public posture. Perhaps the lessened status of the divine nature of Joseph Smith's Bible translation in RLDS thought would naturally make them withdraw from this position.

Summary of RLDS Position to 1992

When compared to the pre-1960s "position" and attitudes of the RLDS church regarding the Inspired Version, a significant shift in attitudes and practices is evidenced in their publications from 1960–1992. In a narrow sense the Inspired Version may still be revered and used (although with less central focus) as a showpiece of the "restoration," particularly as a look into the mind of Joseph Smith and as an example of personal struggle to understand the revelations of God. At contrast are the more frequent publications which see little theological or practical use for the Inspired Version when compared to other versions produced from modern biblical scholarship. William Russell criticized Robert Matthews's studies on the Inspired Version, stating that Matthews had erred in seeing it as a restoration of original biblical text. "To perpetuate this idea seriously retards Biblical understanding among Latter Day Saints" (*Courage*, 1970). RLDS historian Richard Howard felt similarly. He saw in Matthews a fault typical of Latter-day Saints who ought to take more "seriously the fruit of centuries of Christian scholarship and reflection" (*Courage*, 1971). Russell again typified this latter position in a 1983 address: "The New Translation is the work of a supremely confident young man. . . . But [when methods of historical analysis were applied to the JST] the evidence as to the accuracy of the New Translation was hardly impressive." (*Journal of Mormon History*, p. 56.)

The call to reevaluate traditional understandings of Joseph Smith's Bible revision generally found in RLDS publications since the 1960s has not resulted in a newly defined appreciation for the Inspired Version, or for the Prophet through whom it came. Rather, the trend seems to have presaged a declining practice of acceptance and use of the revision and a tempered view of the divinity of Joseph Smith's prophetic role.

LDS Position, 1960–1992

In LDS literature before the 1960s there were comparatively few publications dealing with the JST. In 1965 Robert J. Matthews published the first extensive treatment of the JST in LDS literature since Sperry and Van Wagoner's 1940 exploration. By 1968, master's and doctoral dissertations on the JST by Reed C. Durham (BYU, 1965), and Robert J. Matthews (BYU, 1960, 1968) had been completed, and Matthews had begun his study of the original manuscripts in Missouri. As those studies were disseminated, the number of LDS publications began to rise significantly.

Regarding the pre-1960s position of the LDS church toward the JST, Elements 1 and 3 have since been significantly modified; 2 has found extensive support, particularly since 1965; and while Element 4 has essentially stayed the same, the introduction of the 1979 LDS edition of the Bible calls for an expanded meaning.

A 1992 statement of position on the JST, as reflected in official publications, would likely convey the following attitudes and positions: 1) The work of revision was divinely commanded, guided, and completed sufficiently to be used; 2) The revision clarified and corrected many difficult or erroneous aspects present in other versions, and "restored many plain and precious" lost parts of the Bible record; 3) Since the accuracy of the RLDS Inspired Version has been verified (by comparison with original manuscripts), changes found therein may authoritatively be used; 4) The LDS edition of the Bible, containing King James Version text and employing numerous references from the JST, is the standard Bible of The Church of Jesus Christ of Latter-day Saints until the Lord directs otherwise.

Progression to each of these four elements of the position will now be viewed through the publication history:

1. *The work of revision was divinely commanded, guided, and completed sufficiently to be used:*

> There has been an assumption that the JST was deliberately not published because it was grossly unfinished. That assumption is not based on all of the facts. . . . During the eleven years of his life after [1833] the Prophet apparently did much of what he desired to do with the JST. . . . The basic conclusion [from historical records] seems to be that the work of translation was acceptable as far as the Lord required of the Prophet at that time, but the manuscript was not fully prepared for the press. (Matthews, *Ensign*, 1983.)

> The added truths [Joseph] placed in the Bible and the corrections he made raise the resultant work to the same high status as the Book of Mormon and the Doctrine and Covenants. It is true that he did not complete the work, but it was far enough along that he intended to publish it in its present form in his lifetime. (McConkie, *Ensign*, 1985.)

Modification of point 1 might be summarized by the following progression: Pre-1900—the revision was incomplete; early 1900s—the revision was as complete as the Lord required at the time; mid to late 1900s—while it was not fully printer ready, Joseph (as directed by the Lord) intended to publish the revision, and hence we can accept the changes that were made and were faithfully reproduced in the Inspired Version. Studies of the original manuscripts by Matthews made the progression to this position possible. The evolution to this latter position was also a critical link in the decision to include changes from the Inspired Version in the 1979 LDS edition of the Bible. The most vocal proponent on this point was Elder Bruce R. McConkie. In an address on the JST's role in "The Doctrinal Restoration" of the latter days, Elder McConkie stated: "Since when do any of us have the right to place bounds on the Almighty and say we will believe these revelations but not those? . . . True, the Joseph Smith Translation . . . has not been completed in the full and true sense. But for that matter neither has the Book of Mormon. . . . Does anyone think we have all of the words [of] . . . prophets and apostles without number?" (Symposium on the JST, BYU, November 1984.)

While this attitude represents a historic change (as applied to the JST), it is only a brief step from the concept of revelation as always unfinished in a technical sense to that of deeming that which has been received to be acceptable and useable. Beyond that, to consider revealed (yet "incomplete") inspiration binding while allowing the possibility of yet further changes is, I think, a posture unique to LDS thought.[7]

2. *The revision clarified and corrected many difficult or erroneous aspects present in other versions, and restored many plain and precious lost parts of the Bible record:*

> We learn from the Book of Mormon that many plain and precious things were taken from the Bible. . . . However, 1 Nephi 13:39 says that "other books" would make known again many of the plain and precious things that had been removed. The JST would be one of these other books. (Matthews, *Ensign*, 1980.)

> We are deeply indebted to the Prophet Joseph Smith . . . [for] making available to the Saints plain and precious principles once had by earlier peoples (Millet, *Ensign*, 1986).

There are no LDS publications that demur in any way at the concept of the JST being a "restoration of plain and precious" truths once had in ancient times and records. The belief that Joseph's revision would be an act of restoration has become strengthened with the passage of time. Particularly after 1970, publications have dealt more consistently with JST content than history, the primary theme being that of restoration. There has been, however, clarification that not all JST changes are explained solely from a restoration perspective. In his book, *A Plainer Translation*, Matthews suggests that in addition to its restorative nature, the JST may also represent "inspired commentary" and "harmonization of doctrinal concepts" revealed to the Prophet Joseph Smith (1985, p. 253).[8]

3. *The accuracy of the RLDS Inspired Version having been verified (by comparison with original manuscripts), changes found therein may authoritatively be used:*

> When the Book of Mormon, Doctrine and Covenants, and Pearl of Great Price . . . do not provide significant information which is available in the Inspired Version, then this version may be used (Editorial opinion, *Church News*, 1974).

> If the [original] manuscript is correct then the Inspired Version is correct, for they [the RLDS church . . .] have followed the manuscript very, very closely (Gardner, *Ensign*, 1985, quoting Robert J. Matthews).

The early posture which held the RLDS published Inspired Version as "unauthorized" (and by implication not to be used) found little attention in the post-1960s era, with the exception of two articles from the 1970s. This element was significantly modified as a result of scholarly studies done on the original manuscripts by Robert J. Matthews and others. Matthews's work in particular confirmed the theretofore questioned accuracy of the Inspired Version as a faithful representation of revisions made by the Prophet Joseph and further evidenced the Prophet's determination to publish the translation despite his continued revisions through the years.

With the accuracy of the RLDS publication of the Inspired Version largely confirmed, the LDS church seems to have been freed to evaluate JST changes on their own merit, which eventually led to their inclusion in the historic 1979 publication of the LDS edition of the KJV Bible. So profound was the impact of this historic progression on official attitudes toward the JST that in 1992 we find Elder Neal A. Maxwell stating: "I do not know of any of the present First Presidency or Quorum of the Twelve who question in any way the use of quotations from the Joseph Smith Translation. . . . I believe they would be disappointed if you did not use the Joseph Smith Translation extensively."[9]

4. The LDS edition of the Bible, containing King James Version text
and employing numerous references from the JST, is the standard Bible of
The Church of Jesus Christ of Latter-day Saints until otherwise directed by
the Lord:

> "On the basis of [established] guidelines, almost every JST passage of
> doctrinal significance was selected" for inclusion in the LDS edition of
> the King James Version of the Bible (Matthews, Ensign, 1992).

> Since the days of the Prophet Joseph Smith, The Church of Jesus Christ
> of Latter-day Saints has used the King James Version of the Bible for
> English-speaking members. . . . While other Bible versions may be easier
> to read than the King James Version, in doctrinal matters latter-day
> revelation supports the King James Version in preference to other
> English translations. All of the Presidents of the Church, beginning with
> the Prophet Joseph Smith, have supported the King James Version by
> encouraging its continued use in the Church. In light of all the above, it
> is the English language Bible used by The Church of Jesus Christ of
> Latter-day Saints. (First Presidency Statement, Ensign, 1992, p. 80.)

There is no mention or intimation in LDS publications that the
King James Version has ceased or will cease to be the officially accepted LDS Bible. The latter portion of the pre-1960s position, that
there might be divine direction to LDS leaders to complete the revision, has not been specifically mentioned in officially published literature since Joseph F. Smith's 1914 article in the Improvement Era.
The publication of the 1979 LDS edition of the Bible, however, may
have permanently harmonized the two elements of the former position. By the inclusion of hundreds of key changes from the JST in this
edition of the King James Version, the Church preserved the long-
held reverential position of that version while sanctioning additional
information provided through Joseph's revision. Perhaps in doing this,
there is the implicit message that in part the Lord had empowered and
directed modern leaders to prepare an acceptable publication of
changes made by Joseph Smith.

Summary of LDS Publications Through 1992

LDS publications since the 1960s evidence modification in most elements of the position held for a century prior to those years. Conceptual reformation on the issue of "completion" as it applies to Joseph Smith's work of revision and its accurate transmission to the RLDS Inspired Version, was largely made possible by the studies of Robert J. Matthews. His research eliminated much of the "haunting uncertainty" surrounding the JST and intimated in the first and third elements of the past LDS position. Element 2, the belief that the JST represents a restoration of ancient content and meaning, occupies center stage in LDS publications since 1979 and finds continued support.

In the resolution of Element 4, accomplished by welding the King James Version with the JST in the new LDS edition of the Bible, there may be witnessed one of the most significant developments in LDS scripture and history. The joining of these two sacred texts signals to members that past negative attitudes and reticence toward use of the JST have given way to a new and supportive era.

Summary of Changing Attitudes in the RLDS and LDS Churches

Prior to the death of Joseph Smith, early publications dealing with "the new translation" evidence broadly held beliefs that the revision represented the following: 1) Joseph Smith's divinely directed and guided work of scripture revision was an integral part of his role as Prophet of the latter-day restoration of the gospel of Jesus Christ; 2) the revision was "made by the power of God"; 3) Joseph Smith's revision was, in part, a restoration of lost meaning and material; and 4) the revision was intended to be received and understood as part of the revealed word for the salvation of mankind (see Supplement B). Publications examined in this paper suggest that in general the RLDS church is progressively moving away from those foundational beliefs while the LDS church has become progressively more committed to them.

For the RLDS church, movement away from a belief in the essential nature of the Inspired Version may remove one of the features that has made it distinctive in the world of religion. Distinction is frequently a two-edged sword. On the one hand, it draws attention to a peculiar message and provides a rallying point around which members can congregate. On the other hand, it becomes a focal point of criticism for those highlighting differences. RLDS members who grew up under the century-long tradition of counting the Inspired Version as a distinct blessing and "evidence of the restoration" may become dissatisfied as a result of this trend away from the formerly accepted divinity and centrality of belief in Joseph Smith's revision. However, a collision course with modern biblical scholarship, which has tended to demean the JST, has perhaps largely been avoided by the gradual move to acknowledge the Inspired Version as a historical fact but not a revelatory reality in the propositional sense of the term.

The LDS church is moving in nearly an opposite course. Members who grew up under a century of traditional non-use and suspicion towards the JST now find themselves "back in school" regarding its place and use. Strong views on the divinity of the changes made by Joseph Smith evidenced in LDS publications have laid the foundation for conflict with some biblical scholarship which has tended to view the translation as neither accurate in its restoration nor divine in its origin.

Question Three: What attitudes are evidenced in other publications not officially sponsored by the two churches?

While the main focus of this study was to examine changing attitudes and positions of the LDS and RLDS churches toward the JST, the research process included non-affiliated publications as well. The resulting bibliography of publications covering the period of 1847–1992 was divided into six categories: 1) Bible editions; 2) Books, dissertations, theses; 3) RLDS publications; 4) LDS publications; 5) Miscellaneous publications such as tracts, symposia, periodicals, and so on; and 6) Books on Mormon history. The body of this paper has dealt primarily with categories three and four. However, some observations from the other categories also seem in order. Publications in those categories reflected literature in official church publications as well as gave shape and response to others.

Bible Editions: Through 1970, there were five Bible editions employing the Prophet Joseph Smith's revisions, all of which were produced by the RLDS church. Correlated to the studies of Howard and
Matthews is a marked increase both in official Bible publications and
in those reflecting private concerns. Since their studies in the 1960s,
nine JST-related scripture publications have appeared. In 1979 the
LDS church published its edition of the King James Version with JST
changes reflected in footnotes and in a lengthy appendix. In 1991 the
RLDS church published a new edition of the Holy Scriptures and also
the Inspired Version of the New Testament and the book of Psalms
bound together. The remaining six private publications creatively em-
ploy the JST in various harmonies of scripture text.

Books, Dissertations, Theses: Prior to the 1960s five titles appear in
this category, three of which were master's theses. Since that time
twenty additional titles have appeared, five of which have been doctoral dissertations and three master's theses. The two most prominent
books were the 1969 publication of RLDS historian Richard P.
Howard (*Restoration Scriptures*), and the 1975 work of Robert J.
Matthews (*A Plainer Translation*). In general, most of the works in this
category have been cautiously or wholly supportive of the divine nature of Joseph Smith's revision.

Philip Barlow's 1991 book, *Mormons and the Bible* (based on his
1988 Harvard dissertation), has drawn and will continue to draw significant attention, in part because of its unique bridge-building capa-
bility between lay believers and the scholarly world of historical and
biblical criticism (though probably neither camp will find total satisfaction with his presentation). In somewhat of a summary opinion,
Barlow states: "Joseph Smith, like many of the biblical writers, felt he
had received revelation and inspiration from God. With his broad
sense of authorship and his strong sense of prophetic license, he felt
the authority—indeed, the calling—to inculcate his insights into his
revision of scripture, much as prophetic writers in ancient times had
done. . . . His dominating concern, however, was not with textual pre-
cision but with enlightening the world through revealed truth. He
thus did not feel bound by what he took to be the original writings in
the Bible, and yet he continued to revere the Bible. The results of his
practices are sharply distinctive in antebellum America." (P. 61.)

A marked departure from other supportive studies was the 1988 thesis of Kornelis Compier (of RLDS affiliation). Compier's study compares ancient Greek texts with Joseph Smith's revisions in the Gospel of Mark. He concludes that such changes are not confirmed by ancient texts and in some cases do harm to the literary beauty of Mark. His recommendations include: "For the RLDS Church, this means that they consider as scripture a Bible translation that is very outdated. . . . Both the RLDS Church and other churches using Joseph's New Translation should consider this document as representing a certain phase of their church history and move on to and recommend the use of newer and better translations of the Bible." (P. 96.)

Miscellaneous Publications: Of the 130 entries in this category, all but 18 have been published since the 1960s, when the first sophisticated and scholarly examinations began to appear. Many of these works center around some response to the earlier mentioned landmark studies of Howard (1969), and Matthews (1975). Both Howard and Matthews continue to write for both official and private publishing outlets and remain singular voices in this field. Howard has come to represent the measured "pulling back" of the RLDS church, while Matthews champions the LDS revelatory view.[10]

While early works related to the JST frequently dealt with historical issues surrounding the creation and preservation of Joseph Smith's new translation, entries in the miscellaneous category have increasingly dealt with textual content and doctrinal implications. Responses to those two central issues are sharply divided. Those conducting ancient text comparative studies are generally condemnatory of the restorationist concept and that of seeing divine guidance in Joseph's revision.[11] Few critical studies have had an interest in doctrinal implications of changes made by Joseph Smith. However, LDS writers reflective of the fundamentalist view have concentrated a great deal on matters of doctrine and generally conclude that this represents a central contribution of the Joseph Smith Translation of the Bible.

Books on Mormon History: Probably the most significant comment to be made about the role of the Joseph Smith Translation in book treatments on the history of the Restoration churches is its sheer lack of any detailed attention. While historian Thomas Alexander (1980) cites Joseph's work on the inspired revision as "one of the three most influential roots of doctrinal reconstruction which developed during the 1832–1844 period," most historical works devote only a few lines or paragraphs to its role. Its skimpy command of space suggests that some historians are either lacking education regarding the JST or are quite unconvinced by evaluations such as Alexander's (and those of other writers), who sees Joseph's revision as a major "branch of his calling" as prophet of the Restoration and therefore exerting a significant force on the history of the Latter-day Saints.[12]

Final Comments

It is interesting to note that in the last five years of this study (1988–1992) fifty publications were found to deal with JST-related issues. This high level of interest, however, seems not to have been prominent in official publications of either church. RLDS periodicals carried only one article on the Inspired Version, and it was primarily uncomplimentary (Jones, 1988). LDS periodicals also published just one (positive) article, by Robert J. Matthews (1992).

This study has noted that "battle lines" between fundamentalist and revisionist views of the JST have been drawn quite sharply. For the LDS church to foster a fundamentalist point of view regarding the divinity and centrality of the JST, it would seem wise to periodically give in official publications continued attention to various aspects of this work. However, while attention in periodicals has fallen off somewhat, the LDS church continues to give consistent and strong support to the JST through its Church Educational System. Each year, nearly half a million students (high school and college) regularly engage in Church-sponsored religious education. Their curriculum materials give frequent supportive attention to the JST, and thousands of teachers are regularly exposed to its importance as well as trained to teach from the revision. A feel for the intensity given the role of Church Education in propagating positive exposure to the JST can be seen in the following two passionate statements directed to those involved:

As teachers and students in the Church Educational System, we are not merely "invited" to become acquainted with the JST, but I think we are expected to do so. . . . If you do not already have a testimony, by the Spirit, of the worth of the JST, then there is waiting for you one of the fruitful experiences in your career. . . . I have tasted of its spirit, and I know it is a great aid in teaching the gospel and in serving as a tangible witness for the divine ministry of the Prophet Joseph Smith and for the mission of Jesus Christ. (Matthews, 1979, p. 212.)

Use and rely on the Joseph Smith Translation of the Bible. This counsel can scarcely be stated with too great an emphasis. The [JST] is a thousand times over the best Bible now existing on earth. . . . It is one of the great evidences of [Joseph Smith's] prophetic calling. (McConkie, 1984, p. 5.)

Such encouragement continues to find solid support with two of the three LDS official publications of the last five years being directed to the Church Educational System, which seems to have become the hope of continuing propagation of fundamental beliefs in Joseph Smith's translation of the Bible. As a Church educator myself, I have felt some of the spirit Robert J. Matthews spoke of, and have been touched by the significance of the Bible revision work of Joseph Smith both in understanding the gospel of Jesus Christ and in confirming the divinity of the Lord's guidance through modern prophets. For both, I am deeply grateful.

The Prophet Joseph Smith once said of the Bible that "as we hold the record of truth in our hands [we can] see God's own handwriting in the sacred volume: and he who reads it oftenest will like it best."[13] My experience has led me to the same conclusion regarding the JST. It is a work of divine origin, and "he who reads it oftenest will like it best."

Notes

1. For a detailed look at Joseph's efforts to publish the new trans-lation, see chapter 10 of *A Bible! A Bible!* by Robert J. Matthews (Salt Lake City: Bookcraft, 1990), pp. 133–43.

2. In the 1878 semi-annual conference of the RLDS church, two resolutions were passed: (1) that the Inspired Version was made by divine inspiration; and (2) that the Inspired Version be the accepted standard from which to decide relevant matters of doctrine and counsel (see *Saints' Herald*, October 1, 1878, pp. 295–96).

3. In a letter to the RLDS church in 1898, President Wilford Woodruff directed his secretary to convey that "The Church of Jesus Christ of Latter-day Saints does not use the revision of the scriptures made by the Prophet Joseph Smith, for the reason that he never completed the work." (Letter to C. J. Hunt, cited in A. H. Parsons, *Parson's Text Book* [Lamoni, IA: Herald House Publishing, 1902], p. 315.)

4. For a brief summary of the guidelines used to determine which JST changes made their way into the 1979 LDS edition KJV Bible, see Robert J. Matthews in the June 1992 *Ensign*, p. 29.

5. A recent publication dealing with this issue during the period of this study is RLDS church historian Richard P. Howard's article in *The Word of God* (edited by Dan Vogel, 1990). Howard defines propositional revelation as "the divine revealing of certain knowledge or information about God and the church, usually in the form of propositions or doctrines." The article questions the reception of such revelation by any figure past or present.

6. William D. Russell, "History and the Mormon Scriptures," *Journal of Mormon History*, vol. 10, 1983, pp. 53–63.

7. Latter-day Saints seem to be comfortable in noting the Book of Mormon and Doctrine and Covenants reminders of the imperfect human medium through which the sacred record comes, without considering the revelations that come through them to be so fraught with human error as to destroy faith and confidence in their divine applicability (2 Nephi 33; Mormon 9:31–37; Ether 12:23–26, 40; D&C 1:24–28; 68:1–4).

8. Though individuals have sought to explain the nature of JST changes in various ways, it is generally recognized by careful scholars that the Prophet himself never explained exactly how he understood his "translation." In the most thorough exploration outside LDS and RLDS publications, Philip Barlow suggests six basic types of changes which characterize the nature of JST emendations: (1) long revealed

additions that have little or no biblical parallel; (2) logical corrections (or, as Barlow implicates the Prophet's mind, "common sense made uncommon by inspiration"); (3) interpretive additions and expansions; (4) harmonization; (5) grammatical improvements, technical clarifications, and modernization of terms; and (6) other idiosyncratic changes not easily classified (*Mormons and the Bible*, pp. 51–56).

9. Cited in Daniel H. Ludlow's 1991 (August 13–15) LDS Church Educational System Religious Educators Symposium address entitled "The Old Testament: A Witness for Christ."

10. See the author's dissertation (pp. 216–17), and the five-year update study (p. viii) for references to the nine significant publications of Richard P. Howard and the forty-four entries of Robert J. Matthews. The influence of these two authors on the changing attitudes of their respective churches can hardly be overstated.

11. For recent examples of critical articles, see Voros (1987), Compier (1988), Hutchinson (1988), Mesle (1989), Barney (1990), Howard (1990), and Groat (1991). For contrary conclusions, see Millet (1985), Sandberg (1989), Matthews (1990), Christensen (1991), and Miles (1991).

12. Some notable exceptions are found in Backman (1983), Bushman (1984), Matthews (1988), Millet (1989), and Barlow (1991).

13. Joseph Smith, *Teachings of the Prophet Joseph Smith*, comp. Joseph Fielding Smith (Salt Lake City: Deseret Book Co., 1969), p. 56.

Supplement A
Chronological Summary of Publications

The table and graphs that follow tracked JST publication history in ten-year blocks of time through 1987. Beginning in 1988, the first five-year update was completed.

Summary of All Publications

Ten-Year Block	Bible Editions	Books, Diss., Theses	RLDS Pubs.	LDS Pubs.	Misc. Pubs.	Books on Mormon History	Totals
1847–1857	0	0	0	0	1	1	2
1858–1867	1	0	17	0	0	0	18
1868–1877	1	0	4	1	0	1	7
1878–1887	0	0	9	1	0	1	11
1888–1897	0	0	7	1	1	2	11
1898–1907	0	0	5	4	1	3	13
1908–1917	0	0	5	2	1	1	9
1918–1927	0	0	7	1	0	3	11
1928–1937	1	0	6	2	1	3	13
1938–1947	1	1	18	13	2	5	40
1948–1957	0	3	19	3	8	5	38
1958–1967	0	4	33	4	10	7	58
1968–1977	1	6	11	8	28	8	62
1978–1987	3	5	10	16	56	6	96
1988–1992 5-Yr. update	6	6	2	3	22	11	50
Totals	14	25	153	59	131	57	439

Supplement B
The JST: A Fundamental Standard of Belief

The following "standard of belief" is a harmony of statements about the New Translation attributed to Joseph Smith, Jr., or as found in books of holy scripture accepted by both the LDS and RLDS churches. In essence, they represent what the Prophet Joseph himself said about the "new translation," or what he said the Lord said about it. In either case, both churches accept the sources of these statements as legitimate records of history, given to latter-day saints of the "restoration."

1. *Joseph Smith's divinely directed and guided work of scripture revision was an integral part of his role as prophet of the latter-day restoration of the gospel of Jesus Christ.*

I resumed the translation of the Scriptures, and continued to labor in this branch of my calling (Joseph Smith, HC 1:238).

Thou shalt ask, and my scriptures shall be given as I have appointed . . . and I give unto you a commandment that then ye shall teach them unto all men (D&C 42:56–58; RD&C 42:15–16).

Wherefore I give unto you that ye may now translate [the New Testament] (D&C 45:60–61; RD&C 45:11a, b).

Publish the new translation of my holy word unto the inhabitants of the earth (D&C 124:89; RD&C 107:28b).

2. *The revision was made "by the power of God."*

A translation of the New Testament translated by the power of God (written on the title page of the original ms. for the Gospel of Matthew).

And the scriptures shall be given, even as they are in mine own bosom (D&C 35:20; RD&C 34:5b).

In connection with the translation of the scriptures, I received the following explanation of the Revelation of St. John (D&C 77, heading; HC 1:253).

For while we were doing the work of translation, which the Lord had appointed unto us, we came to the twenty-ninth verse of the fifth chapter of John, which was given unto us as follows. . . . Now this caused us to marvel, for it was given unto us of the Spirit. (D&C 76:15, 18; RD&C 76:3c–e.)

3. *Joseph Smith's revision was, in part, a restoration of lost meaning and material.*

To the joy of the little flock . . . did the Lord reveal the following doings of olden times, from the prophecy of Enoch (HC 1:132–33).

From sundry revelations which had been received, it was apparent that many important points touching the salvation of man, had been taken from the Bible, or lost before it was compiled. . . . Accordingly, on the 16th of February, 1832, while translating St. John's Gospel, myself and Elder Rigdon saw the following vision. (HC 1:245.)

Thou seest—because of the many plain and precious things which have been taken out of the book . . . an exceedingly great many do stumble. . . . And after the Gentiles do stumble exceedingly, because of the most plain and precious parts of the gospel of the Lamb which have been kept back . . . I will bring forth unto them, in mine own power, much of the gospel. (1 Nephi 13:29, 34.)

And in a day when the children of men shall esteem my words as naught and take many of them from the book which thou shalt write, behold I will raise up another like unto thee; and they shall be had again among the children of men—among as many as shall believe (Moses 1:41; IV preface.)

4. *The revision was intended to be received and understood as part of the revealed word for the salvation of mankind.*

And the scriptures shall be given, even as they are in mine own bosom, to the salvation of mine own elect (D&C 35:20; RD&C 35:5b).

Supplement C
Positions Toward Joseph Smith's Translation of the Bible

LDS Position to 1960	*LDS Position, 1992*
1. The work of revision was divinely commanded and guided, but not completed.	1. The work of revision was divinely commanded, guided, and sufficiently completed to be used.
2. The revision clarified and corrected many difficult or erroneous aspects present in other versions, and restored many plain and precious lost parts of the biblical record.	2. (Same)
3. Since Joseph Smith did not complete his revision, the RLDS Inspired Version is an unauthorized publication.	3. The accuracy of the RLDS Inspired Version having been verified (by comparison with original manuscripts), changes found therein may be authoritatively used.
4. The King James Version is the standard Bible of the Church until such time as the Lord directs otherwise. Presumably, this would be the preparation of Joseph Smith's revision for an officially authorized publication.	4. The LDS edition of the Bible, containing King James Version text and employing numerous references from the JST, is the standard Bible of The Church of Jesus Christ of Latter-day Saints until the Lord directs otherwise.

RLDS Position to 1960	*RLDS Position, 1992*
1. The work of revision was divinely commanded, guided, and completed.	1. Joseph Smith perceived his work of Bible revision as being divinely commanded, guided, and sufficiently

complete to warrant publication plans.

2. The revision clarified and corrected many difficult or erroneous aspects present in other versions, and restored many plain and precious lost parts.

2. Changes made in the revision represent what Joseph Smith believed to be inspired commentary, and grew out of his effort to clarify and correct the Bible text according to his nineteenth-century understanding and resources. Such changes probably do not represent actual restorations of ancient text.

3. Having been divinely initiated, guided, and approved, the revision was a better product than those Bible versions limited to human scholarship.

3. The Inspired Version should not be considered categorically better than other Bible versions, particularly those produced by modern Bible scholars.

4. Members should not disparage the King James, or other versions, but should use the Inspired Version in preference to them, particularly where differences occur.

4. Members are encouraged to use the version of the Bible which best meets their particular needs.

5. Divine commands to preserve, publish, and give to the world Joseph Smith's revision were accomplished by the RLDS church and hence mark it as the true church of the Restoration.

5. (Modification of elements 1–4 have resulted in no comparable position being taken since 1966.)

Parallel Column Comparisons

RLDS Position to 1960	*LDS Position to 1960*
1. The work of revision was divinely commanded, guided, and completed.	1. The work of revision was divinely commanded and guided, but not completed.
2. The revision clarified and corrected many difficult or erroneous aspects present in other versions, and restored many plain and precious lost parts.	2. The revision clarified and corrected many difficult or erroneous aspects present in other versions, and restored many plain and precious lost parts of the biblical record.
3. Having been divinely initiated, guided, and approved, the revision was a better product than those Bible versions limited to human scholarship.	3. Since Joseph Smith did not complete his revision, the RLDS Inspired Version is an unauthorized publication.
4. Members should not disparage the King James, or other versions, but should use the Inspired Version in preference to them, particularly where differences occur.	4. The King James Version is the standard Bible of the Church until such time as the Lord directs otherwise. Presumably, this would be the preparation of Joseph Smith's revision for an officially authorized publication.
5. Divine commands to preserve, publish, and give to the world Joseph Smith's revision were accomplished by the RLDS church and hence mark it as the true church of the Restoration.	

Parallel Column Comparisons

RLDS Position, 1992	LDS Position, 1992
1. Joseph Smith perceived his work of Bible revision as being divinely commanded, guided, and sufficiently complete to warrant publication plans.	1. The work of revision was divinely commanded, guided, and completed sufficiently to be used.
2. Changes made in the revision represent what Joseph Smith believed to be inspired commentary, and grew out of his effort to clarify and correct the Bible text according to his nineteenth-century understanding and resources. Such changes probably do not represent actual restorations of ancient texts.	2. The revision clarified and corrected many difficult or erroneous aspects present in other versions, and restored many plain and precious lost parts of the biblical record.
3. The Inspired Version should not be considered categorically better than other Bible versions, particularly those produced by modern Bible scholars.	3. The accuracy of the RLDS Inspired Version having been verified (by comparison with original manuscripts), changes found therein may be authoritatively used.
4. Members are encouraged to use the version of the Bible which best meets their particular needs.	4. The LDS edition of the Bible, containing King James Version text and employing numerous references from the JST, is the standard Bible of The Church of Jesus Christ of Latter-day Saints until the Lord directs otherwise.
5. (Modification of elements 1–4 have resulted in no comparable position being taken since 1966.)	

Supplement D
Selected References

Alexander, Thomas G. (1980, July/August). "The Reconstruction of Mormon Doctrine: From Joseph Smith to Progressive Theology." *Sunstone*, 5(4), 24–33.

Backman, Milton V. (1983). *The Heavens Resound: A History of the Latter-day Saints in Ohio, 1830–1838*. Salt Lake City: Deseret Book Company, pp. 82–89, 212, 222–23.

Bailey, J. W. (1937, February 6). "The Inspired Version of the Holy Scriptures Identifies the Reorganized Church of Jesus Christ of Latter Day Saints as Being the True Church in Succession." *Saints' Herald*, 84(6), 171–74, 191.

Barlow, Philip (1991). *Mormons and the Bible*. New York, NY: Oxford University Press.

Barney, Kevin L. (1990). "The Joseph Smith Translation and Ancient Texts of the Bible." In Vogel, Dan, (ed.) *The Word of God: Essays on Mormon Scripture*. Salt Lake City: Signature Books, pp. 143–60.

Blair, William W. (1884, August). "Penrose, on the Inspired Translation." *Saints' Advocate*, 7(2), 466–67.

Blair, William W. (1881, July). "The Inspired Translation." *Saints' Advocate*, 4(1), 105.

Blair, William W. (1867, February 15). "The New Translation of the Bible." *Saints' Herald*, 11(4), 53–56.

Bushman, Richard L. (1984). *Joseph Smith and the Beginning of Mormonism*. Chicago, IL: The University of Illinois Press, pp. 184–88.

Chase, A. M. (1938, August-September, five-part series). "Notes on the Inspired Version of the Bible." *Saints' Herald*, 85, 1005–6, 1035, 1075–76, 1110–11, 1173–74.

Chase, A. M. (1939, January 14). "The Inspired Version of the Bible v. Popular Theology." *Saints' Herald*, 86(2), 53.

Chase, A. M. (1938, January 22). "The Use of the Inspired Translation of the Bible." *Saints' Herald*, 85(4), 110–11.

Christensen, Kevin (1991, Fall). "New Wine and New Bottles: Scriptural Scholarship as Sacrament." *Dialogue*, 24(3), 121–29.

Church Educational System (1976, December). *The Joseph Smith Translation*. Salt Lake City, UT: The Church of Jesus Christ of Latter-day Saints. Unit 4, Booklet 2.

Clark, J. Reuben, Jr. (1954, June). "Our Bible." *Improvement Era*, 57(6), 395–99.

Compier, Kornelis (1988). "Joseph Smith's 'New Translation' and Its Effect upon the Interpretation of the Text in the Gospel of Mark." Unpublished thesis project. Iliff School of Theology, Denver, CO.

Davies, Charles (1961, September 4). "Is there any explanation for the discrepancy of dates given in different chapters of Genesis concerning the age of Noah at the time of the flood?" *Saints' Herald*, 108(36), 856.

Davies, Charles (1962, March 15). "What is the opinion of the church on the "New English Bible?" *Saints' Herald*, 109(6), 216.

Davies, Charles A. (1965). Problems in the Inspired Version. Unpublished paper.

Durham, Reed D. (1965). A History of Joseph Smith's Revision of the Bible. Unpublished doctoral dissertation, Brigham Young University, Provo, UT.

Edwards, F. Henry (1967, November 15). "The Bible in the Early Restoration." *Saints' Herald*, 114(22), 762–64, 778.

Ferris, Joseph A. (1950, April 24). "The Inspired Version." *Saints' Herald*, 97(17), 406.

First Presidency Statement on the King James Version of the Bible. (1992, August) *Ensign*, p. 80.

Gardner, Marvin K. (1985, January). "BYU Hosts Symposium on JST." *Ensign*, 15(1), 76–78.

Gibson, Margaret W. (1966). *Emma Smith the Elect Lady*. Independence, MO: Herald Publishing, pp. 188–89, 221–22, 224, 226, 300–1.

Groat, Joel B. (1991). "Joseph Smith's Inspired Translation in Light of the Greek New Testament." Grand Rapids, MI: Gospel Truth Ministries.

Harris, James R. (1958). *A Study of the Changes in the Contents of the Book of Moses from the Earliest Available Sources to the Current Edition.* Unpublished master's thesis, Brigham Young University, Provo, UT.

Howard, Richard P. (1969). *Restoration Scriptures: A Study of Their Textual Development.* Independence, MO: Herald Publishing House.

Howard, Richard P. (1971, June). "Latter-day Saint Scripture and the Doctrine of Propositional Revelation." *Courage,* 1(4), 209–25.

Howard, Richard P. (1976, Winter). (Review of) *"A Plainer Translation": Joseph Smith's Translation of the Bible: A History and Commentary,* by Robert J. Matthews. *Brigham Young University Studies,* 16(2), 297–301.

Howard, Richard P. (1990). "Latter Day Saint Scriptures and the Doctrine of Propositional Revelation." In Vogel, Dan (ed.) *The Word of God.* Salt Lake City, UT: Signature Books, pp. 1–18.

Hunt, C. J. (1944, January 8). "The Inspired Version." *Saints' Herald,* 91(2), 52–53.

Hutchinson, Anthony A. (1988, Winter). "A Mormon Midrash? LDS Creation Narratives Reconsidered." *Dialogue,* 21(4), 11–74.

Jones, Bruce (1988). "The Significance of His Conception of the Biblical Zion as a Source for Joseph Smith's Self-Understanding." In Troeh, Marjorie B. and Terril, Eileen M. (eds.) *Restoration Studies IV: A Collection of Essays About the History, Beliefs, and Practices of the Reorganized Church of Jesus Christ of Latter Day Saints.* Temple School, Independence, MO: Herald Publishing House.

Koury, Aleah G. (1961, October 23). "The Inspired Version." *Saints' Herald,* 108(43), 1016–17.

Ludlow, Daniel H. (1992). "The Old Testament: A Witness for Christ." In *Old Testament Symposium Speeches, 1991, The Fifteenth Annual Church Educational System Religious Educators' Symposium.* Salt Lake City, UT: The Church of Jesus Christ of Latter-day Saints, pp. 15–25.

Luffman, Dale E. (1986). "The Roman Letter: An Occasion to Reflect on Joseph Smith's New Translation of the Bible." *Restoration*

Studies III. Independence, MO: Herald Publishing House, pp. 197–203.

Madsen, Truman G. (1970, March). "A Study of the Text of the Inspired Version of the Bible." *Improvement Era*, 73(3), 70–71.

Matthews, Robert J. (1965, February-May). "The Inspired Revision of the Bible." 4-part series. *Improvement Era*, 68, 104–5, 156–58, 216–19, 236–37, 302–5, 352, 404–5, 431–35.

Matthews, Robert J. (1968). "A Study of the Text of the Inspired Revision of the Bible." Unpublished doctoral dissertation, Brigham Young University, Provo, UT.

Matthews, Robert J. (1975). *"A Plainer Translation": Joseph Smith's Translation of the Bible, A History and Commentary*. Provo, UT: Brigham Young University Press.

Matthews, Robert J. (1979, August). "How the Joseph Smith Translation Will Help Us to Be Better Teachers." *LDS Church Educational System Religious Educators Symposium on the Old Testament*. Provo, UT: Brigham Young University, pp. 204–12.

Matthews, Robert J. (1980, September). "What Is Joseph Smith's Translation of the Bible, and How Can It Help Me to Understand the Old Testament?" *Ensign*, 10(9), 63–64.

Matthews, Robert J. (1983, January). "Joseph Smith's Efforts to Publish His Bible Translation." *Ensign*, 13(1), 57–64.

Matthews, Robert J. (1988). "The Prophet Translates the Bible by the Spirit of Revelation." In Porter and Black (eds.) *The Prophet Joseph: Essays on the Life and Mission of Joseph Smith*. Salt Lake City, UT: Deseret Book Company, pp. 175–91.

Matthews, Robert J. (1990). "Beyond the Biblical Account: Adam, Enoch, Noah, Melchizedek, Abraham, and Moses in Latter-day Revelation." In Draper, Richard D. (ed.) *A Witness of Jesus Christ*. Salt Lake City, UT: Deseret Book Company, pp. 134–54.

Matthews, Robert J. (1990). *A Bible! A Bible! How Latter-day Revelation Helps Us Understand the Scriptures and the Savior*. Salt Lake City, UT: Bookcraft.

Matthews, Robert J. (1992, June). "Why Does the LDS Edition of the Bible Not Contain All of the Corrections and Additions Made by Joseph Smith?" *Ensign*, 22(6), 29.

McConkie, Bruce R. (1984). "The Bible, a Sealed Book." *LDS Church Educational System Symposium on the New Testament*. Provo, UT: Brigham Young University.

McConkie, Bruce R. (1985). "The Doctrinal Restoration." In Nyman and Millet (eds.), *The Joseph Smith Translation*. Provo, UT: Brigham Young University, Religious Studies Center, pp. 1–21.

McConkie, Bruce R. (1985, December). "Come: Hear the Voice of the Lord." *Ensign*, 15(7), 54–59.

McDonnell, John (1974, December). "Two Versions." *Saints' Herald*, 121(12), 757.

Meservy, Keith H. (1976, April). "A Plainer Translation." *Ensign*, 6(4), 71–72.

Mesle, C. Robert (1986). "Reinterpreting the Inspired Version." *Restoration Studies III*. Independence, MO: Herald Publishing House, pp. 254–58.

Mesle, C. Robert (1989). *The Bible as Story and Struggle*. Independence, MO: Herald Publishing House, pp. 41–50.

Miles, Donald J. (1991). "Preservation of the Writing Approaches of the Four Gospel Writers in the Joseph Smith Translation of the Bible." Unpublished master's thesis. Provo, UT: Brigham Young University.

Millet, Robert L. (1985). "Joseph Smith's Translation of the Bible and the Synoptic Problem." *The John Whitmer Historical Association Journal*, 5, 41–46.

Millet, Robert L. (1986, December). "Joseph Smith and the New Testament." *Ensign*, 16(12), 28–34.

Millet, Robert L. (1987, January). "Joseph Smith's Translation of the Bible: Impact on Mormon Theology." *Religious Studies and Theology*, 7(1), 43–53.

Millet, Robert L. (ed.) (1989). *Joseph Smith: Selected Sermons and Writings*. New York, NY: Paulist Press, pp. 24–26, 160, 185, 218, 222, 236–37, 240–41.

Millet, Robert L. (1992). "From Translations to Revelations: Joseph Smith's Translation of the Bible and the Doctrine and Covenants." In Porter, Backman, Black, (eds.) *Regional Studies in Latter-day Saint Church History—New York*. Provo, UT:

Department of Church History and Doctrine, Brigham Young University, pp. 215–34.

Millet, Robert L., and Nyman, Monte S. (eds.) (1985). *The Joseph Smith Translation: The Restoration of Plain and Precious Things*. Provo, UT: Brigham Young University Religious Studies Center.

Moler, H. E. (1903, February 18). The Book of Mormon and the Inspired Translation—Do They Agree? *Saints' Herald*, 50(7), 152–53.

Penrose, Charles (1881, April 22). "The Revised Scriptures." *Deseret Evening News*, p. 4.

Penrose, Charles (1900, February 21). *Deseret Evening News*, p. 8.

Petersen, Mark E. (1953). *Your Faith and You*. Salt Lake City, UT: Bookcraft, pp. 19–20.

Petersen, Mark E. (1958, July 8). "The Publications of the Church." Address to LDS Religious Educators, Provo, UT: Brigham Young University.

Petersen, Mark E. (1966). *As Translated Correctly*. Salt Lake City, UT: Deseret Book Company, pp. 29–31.

Peterson, Vernon L. (1983, December). "Joseph Smith's Translation (Lord's Prayer) Revisited." *Saints' Herald*, 130, 550–51.

Position Papers. Department of Religious Education of the Reorganized Church of Jesus Christ of Latter Day Saints (1967). "The Nature of Scripture and Its Use in the Life of the Church." Independence, MO: Cumorah Books, Inc., pp. 20–29.

Pratt, Orson (1872, December 15). Pre-existence of our spirits. *Journal of Discourses*, 15, 247–49.

Question/Answer (1890, August 23). "Did Joseph have any of the original manuscripts in his compilation of the Holy Scriptures? If not, why call it the 'Inspired Translation?' " *Saints' Herald*, 37(34), 546.

Question/Answer (1907, May 1). "What necessitated the Inspired Translation of the Bible? Is it universally used in the "Mormon" pulpit?" *The Liahona*, 1(5), 56.

"Resolved" (1873). "Motion to declare that the Inspired Version was translated by divine inspiration." *Saints' Herald*, 20, 300.

Russell, William D. (1983). "History and the Mormon Scriptures." *Journal of Mormon History*, 10, 53–63.

Sandberg, Karl C. (1989, Winter). "Knowing Brother Joseph Again:

The Book of Abraham, and Joseph Smith as Translator." *Dialogue*, 22(4), 17–37.

Selden, Eric (1968, January 15). "Calls for I.V. evaluation." *Saints' Herald*, 115(2), 90.

Sherry, Thomas E. (1988). "Attitudes, Practices, and Positions Toward Joseph Smith's Translation of the Bible: A Historical Analysis of Publications, 1847–1987." Unpublished doctoral dissertation, Brigham Young University, Provo, UT.

Skinner, C. A. (1946, April 6). "Report of Herald Publishing House." *Saints' Herald*, 93(14), 51–52.

Smith, Heman C. (1879, December 1). "Superiority of the Inspired Translation of the Bible." *Saints' Herald*, 16(23), 353–64.

Smith, Israel A. (1949, August 1). "Two prophecies concerning the 'elect lady' fulfilled." *Saints' Herald*, 96(31), 723.

Smith, Israel A. (1955, November 14). "The Inspired Version." *Saints' Herald*, 102(46), 1089–91, 1105.

Smith, Joseph Jr. (1831). *History of the Church* 1:238.

Smith, Joseph Jr. (1832). *History of the Church* 1:245.

Smith, Joseph III (1895, April 3). "The Holy Scriptures." *Saints' Herald*, 42(14), 209.

Smith, Joseph F. and Anderson, Edward H. (1900, March). "The Inspired Translation." *Improvement Era*, 3(5), 388–89.

Smith, Joseph F. (1914, April). "Joseph Smith's Translation of the Scriptures." *Improvement Era*, 17(6), 590–96.

Smith, Joseph Fielding (comp.) (1969). *Teachings of the Prophet Joseph Smith*. Salt Lake City, UT: Deseret Book Company, p. 10 (footnote).

Sperry, Sidney B. and Van Wagoner, Merrill Y. (1940, April–September, six-part series). "The Inspired Revision of the Bible." *Improvement Era*, 43, 206, 270, 336, 408, 472, 536.

Stevens, Thelona D. (1945, June 16). "Why We Need the Inspired Version." *Saints' Herald*, 92(24), 556–57.

The Two Records (1892). Lamoni, IA: The Reorganized Church of Jesus Christ of Latter Day Saints.

Voros, Frederic J. Jr. (1987, August 27). "Another Look at Joseph's Revision of Romans." *Sunstone Symposium IX*. Salt Lake City, UT.

Yale, Alfred H. (1956, July 23). "How do we account for all the errors in the Inspired Version if the Lord corrected it?" *Saints' Herald*, 103(30), 726.

Contributors

Elder Dallin H. Oaks
A member of the Quorum of the
Twelve Apostles,
The Church of Jesus Christ of
Latter-day Saints

Larry E. Dahl
Associate Dean of Religious Education and
Professor of Church History and Doctrine,
Brigham Young University

Robert J. Matthews
Professor Emeritus of Ancient Scripture,
Brigham Young University

Joseph Fielding McConkie
Professor of Ancient Scripture,
Brigham Young University

Robert L. Millet
Dean of Religious Education and
Professor of Ancient Scripture,
Brigham Young University

Monte S. Nyman
Professor of Ancient Scripture,
Brigham Young University

Thomas E. Sherry
Institute of Religion Director,
Oregon State University, Corvallis, Oregon

Andrew C. Skinner
Assistant Professor of Ancient Scripture,
Brigham Young University

Scripture Index

BOOK OF MORMON

PEARL OF GREAT PRICE

Subject Index